HUMAN RESOURCE MANAGEMENT

A Diagnostic Approach

Dr. Kenneth Kovach

UNIVERSITY
PRESS OF
AMERICA

Lanham • New York • London

Copyright © 1992 by
University Press of America®, Inc.
4720 Boston Way
Lanham, Maryland 20706

3 Henrietta Street
London WC2E 8LU England

Library of Congress Cataloging-in-Publication Data

Kovach, Kenneth A.
Human resource management : a diagnostic approach /
Dr. Kenneth A. Kovach.
p.   cm.
1. Personnel management.   I. Title.
HF5549.K6655   1992   658.3—dc20   91–42217 CIP

ISBN 0–8191–8551–5 (pbk. : alk. paper)

 The paper used in this publication meets the minimum requirements of
American National Standard for Information Sciences—Permanence
of Paper for Printed Library Materials, ANSI Z39.48–1984.

Table of Contents

Readings

Cases

Compensation

Separation

Improving Employee Motivation in Today's Business Environment

A wide gap exists between what workers want and what management thinks they want from their jobs.

In today's complex business world with rapidly changing technology, crumbling traditions, and growing pressures from labor unions, stockholders, consumer groups, and militant minority groups (both within and outside the organization), employee motivation has become both more difficult and more important than ever before.

People today are subjected to a more varied and less stable set of influences than in the past. Local traditions and conventional wisdom are no longer the chief determinants of most people's ideas. Although human basic nature has not changed, the information available to us for shaping our ideas about ourselves and our jobs has increased explosively. As our ideas have become less predictable, so has our behavior.

Ever since 1972 when workers at the General Motors plant in Lordstown, Ohio, walked off their jobs for 22 days to protest the monotony of their work, American concern with worker discontent has grown.

Evidence of this discontent was found by Studs Terkel while developing material for his book, *Working*. When asked to condense into a few words the meaning of these interviews, his response was "loneliness and boredom." "The price our nation is paying from manifestations of worker alienation is staggering: under production, poor quality, sabotage, turnover, absenteeism, and alcoholism are but a few of them."[1]

Keeping employees motivated so as to accomplish company objectives in the face of growing obstacles is one of the major keys to business success. Consequently, over the past several years a great deal of research has been conducted by both managerial and behavioral scientists on the subject of motivation. A wide range of theories and differing viewpoints have evolved. The purpose of this article is to compare some of the more significant theories and viewpoints on motivation and to suggest some practical steps which, if followed, should improve motivation in any organization today.

Definitions and Theories of Motivation

Disagreements and conflicting definitions frequently appear in the literature on the subject of motivation. Many writers, however, conclude that the various theories on motivation are not really incompatible, but deal with different aspects of the entire motivation process.

1

Motivation theories can generally be classified as either process theories or content theories.[2]

Process Theories

Motivation in the more traditional sense refers to the process of stimulating people to act and to accomplish desired goals. In other words, motivation is a function that a manager performs to get subordinates to achieve job objectives. Process theories of motivation generally are based on the assumption that behavior which leads to rewards tends to be repeated, while behavior which does not lead to rewards will not be repeated. These theories consider pay as the major motivating factor. Expectancy Theory and equity theory are among the significant types of process theories.

Expectancy theory assumes that people have certain built-in beliefs (reinforced by management attitudes) regarding their expected roles within an organization and that their behavior must conform to these roles if they are to be rewarded.

Equity Theory assumes that each individual is most concerned with personal contribution and expected outcome (for example, income) compared to peers, and that an employee will tend to limit production to the level of fellow employees.

Content Theories

Instead of viewing motivation as a management process, it can also be looked at from the standpoint of the individual being motivated. People act differently because of different personal experiences. These differences, in turn, cause each person to view the work situation in a manner not quite identical to fellow employees. Content theories of motivation focus on individual motives that relate to job performance.

The achievement motivation theory hypothesizes that individuals who derive satisfaction from resolving difficult problems, influencing others, making decisions, and achieving results possess achievement motivation. This theory tends to explain the motivation of higher-level executives.

Need hierarchy and self-actualization theories assume that employees have a hierarchy of needs, and that as more basic needs – such as food, shelter, and security – are fulfilled, they become more concerned with higher-level needs such as self-actualization.

The two-factor theory divides motivation into *intrinsic* or job content factors and *extrinsic* or hygienic factors.[3] Under this theory the hygienic factors like wages and working conditions do not actually motivate; they merely minimize dissatisfaction. On the other hand, intrinsic factors such as "full appreciation for work performed" contribute to real job satisfaction and serve as real motivators.

Process versus Content Theories: Two Sides of the Same Coin

Dwight Eisenhower is credited with saying that "leadership is the ability to get a person to do what you want him to do, when you want it done, in a way you want it done, because he wants to do it,"[4] representing the process approach to motivation. Rensis Likert termed motivation the core of management and concluded that "the nature of human motivation shows that every human being earnestly seeks a secure, friendly, and supportive relationship which gives him a sense of worth in face-to-face groups which are most important to him. . .a superior should strive to treat individuals with dignity and a recognition for their personal worth,"[5] representing the content approach to motivation.

What People Want from Their Work

To some people, their jobs—while pleasant, and at least not distasteful —are, nevertheless, merely a means to secure sufficient funds to purchase necessities or luxuries for themselves and their families. To others, work—while not an end in itself—is, in a very real sense, a way of life. To those latter persons, the complex relationships of the job situation—social as well as economic—are quite as satisfying as the outside social contacts of the person who engages in work solely as a means of earning a living.

Numerous surveys have been conducted to determine what employees want from their jobs. One of the most widely known surveys was published in *Foreman Facts* by the Labor Relations Institute of New York in 1946.

Table 1
What People Want from Their Work

Employee Ranking		Supervisor Ranking
1	Full appreciation of work done	8
2	Feeling of being in on things	10
3	Sympathetic help on personal problems	9
4	Job security	2
5	Good wages	1
6	Interesting work	5
7	Promotion and growth in the organization	3
8	Personal loyalty to employees	6
9	Good working conditions	4
10	Tactful disciplining	7

The ranking of items is not necessarily the important thing to observe, since conditions have changed since 1946 when the survey was taken. The significant point is the wide variance between what workers consider to be important in their jobs and what their supervisors think workers *believe* to be important. Research indicates that a wide gap still exists between what workers want from their jobs and what management thinks they want.

Wages and Motivation

Traditionally, wages have been considered to be the primary motivating force behind employee action. Wages, however, operate like a price mechanism to distribute the labor supply among employers, but do not affect job performance in any lasting or significant way.

Money can motivate or influence action only when the increment is large enough relative to existing income.[6] Most salary increases, bonuses, profit sharing plans, and many commission and incentive pay plans, do not provide an increment that is large enough to motivate any action other than the purely passive action of remaining in the organization.

Employees tend to expect pay increases as something they are entitled to, rather than something they must earn. When the time at which the increase is expected is still remote, the prospect of the increase serves to motivate continued membership in the organization, provided the expected increase is considered to be equitable.

If the increase does not occur on schedule, that fact will generate disappointment and feelings that the system is unjust. If the delay is prolonged, the employee may search for another job or be motivated to complain, not necessarily about money alone, but about all the petty annoyances ordinarily tolerated. Work performance will probably be reduced.

When the size of the increase becomes known and it is less than expected, the worker may feel deceived. Although expectations may have been unrealistic, it is likely that the individual will become cynical and mistrustful of the organization.

If the increase is about equal to what was expected, an employee will simply see the company as having purchased continued membership at a fair price. The person will also be reassured that the system is fair; however, *such reassurances only satisfy, they do not motivate.*

If the increase exceeds expectations, productivity may increase somewhat or the feeling may exist that compensation is being given for work already performed.[7]

There can be serious problems associated with the rapid growth of income, e.g., when the job is not sufficiently satisfying to the individual. There is a tendency for some workers in repetitive, unchallenging jobs to demand wage increases that bear little relationship to the contribution of their work, either to profits or to the growth of their productivity. They tend to demand whatever the traffic will bear and support militant union leaders who press management for the largest possible wage settlement. These workers can hardly be said to be motivated by their incomes, in the sense of deliberately producing at a higher-than-usual rate.

Such situations suggest that the monetary drives of some may really have psychological origins, that is, money may be a sort of "revenge" against management, a way of hitting back at an adversary where it presumably will hurt most. The tendency of these individuals to see management as an adversary has less to do with feelings of inadequate pay, than with feelings of alienation. Present day management has done little to change this situation.

Human Goals

People are diversely motivated. Each individual's heredity, environment and experience shape attitudes, motives, behavior, and goals in life. The basic needs of people are classified as: physiological needs, safety needs, social needs and egoistic needs.[8] Although these needs are found in all people, each person places a differently prioritized hierarchy on them, and this hierarchy is constantly changing. This explains why each employee acts differently and views the work situation in a manner not quite identical to all other employees.

Although psychologists are not in complete agreement, there are several generalizations regarding human behavior that sustain the most agreement.[9]

1. Individuals strive to satisfy needs on the job. The twelve most important factors affecting job satisfaction are: security, interesting work, opportunity for advancement, recognition, working conditions, wages, supervision, social aspects, opportunities to learn or use ideas, hours, ease of job, and fringe benefits.
2. Individuals differ greatly in the importance they attach to the satisfaction of various needs. Their attitudes also change with time and circumstances, and are heavily influenced by the attitudes of their colleagues and superiors.
3. Needs may be unconscious and unspoken or they may be expressed as aspirations or goals. Motivation is weakest when the individual perceives a goal as either unattainable or too easily attainable. Motivation is strongest when the goal is perceived as both a challenge and attainable.

4. Individuals are receptive to changing their ways of doing things only when they personally recognize the inadequacies of the present method, or when they are given an opportunity to participate in the development of the new method.
5. Individuals resist change when they perceive it as a threat to any of the twelve motivation factors listed in #1.
6. Individuals tend to accept evidence of their performance more willingly and use it more constructively when it is presented in a manner that they regard as objective, i.e., without personal bias, and when the information is perceived as coming from a valid source.
7. Beyond a certain point, pressure for improved performance accomplishes nothing, and may, if continued, reduce performance.

Organizational Goals

Organizations were created as a device used to satisfy needs that individuals working alone could not satisfy. Organizations were designed to serve people, and not vice versa. Once established, however, they tend to become entities with goals of their own. Their goals consist of growth, efficiency, productivity, profits and survival. As organizations grow, there is usually a separation between their ownership (stockholders) and control. The stewardship for operating business organizations is usually entrusted to a group of "professional managers." Because of the interdependency of individuals both within and outside the organization, these managers are in a position of great power and influence.

Managers today, as never before, have to maintain the balance between satisfaction of human needs and the accomplishment of organizational goals. The following are a few of the changing conditions that management must adapt to, while trying to maintain this delicate balance: everchanging human needs, changing organizational goals, the population increase, rapid transportation, improved communications, mass education, automation, development of more bureaucracies, urbanization, more government controls, increases in non-skilled workers, technological unemployment, higher wages, more leisure time, standardization, and increases in the number of administrative personnel.

To the extent that an individual accepts organizational objectives as being desirable, fulfilling them becomes a need. Understanding and accepting objectives, both organizational and job are necessary to work productively.[10]

A Current Trend: Job Enrichment

Job enrichment permits workers' planning and controling more of their work, even to the point of encroaching on management decision making. More and more companies think it may be a way to overcome absenteeism, high turnover, and lagging worker productivity, as well as a way to challenge workers, especially the restless younger ones.

As a case in point, American Telephone and Telegraph encourages subsidiaries to grant technicians greater autonomy and make each of them responsible for maintaining the telephones in entire neighborhoods. Chrysler Corporation involves workers in departmental decisions. In some cases workmen are allowed to run their own departments when supervisors are on vacation. General Electric gives machine operators at its Lynn, Massachusetts, plant a greater role in scheduling work and devising work rules.[11]

Job enrichment is, however, a controversial concept. Even though it seems to be working in some locations, it has collapsed at others. Among urban blue-collar workers it has fallen into disrepte.

Frederick Herzberg, who is widely regarded as the originator of job enrichment, believes that workers become motivated when their jobs are seasoned with motivators like recognition, a sense of achievement, and personal growth. Once these conditions are met, this **motivation-hygiene theory** implies that employees will become far more industrious.

Support for this concept considers typical rewards offered today by companies: higher wages, medical benefits, vacations, pensions, profit sharing, bowling and baseball teams. But not one can be enjoyed *on the job.*

Critics argue that enrichment efforts are based on a faulty view of human nature. Charles L. Hulin observed that "the assumption behind job enrichment is that everyone can be made to think that his job is his life. That simply isn't always the case."[12]

Motivation Under Different Political/Economic Systems

Motivation appears to be a worldwide problem. A.S. Tannenbaum conducted a study of in Italy, Israel, Yugoslavia, Austria, and the United States to compare worker attitudes under various political/economic systems.[13]

Although under Communism the alienated worker is supposed to become the "happy producer," Tannenbaum found that workers in Marxist Yugoslavia were no happier or more motivated than their American counterparts.

An analysis of American participation indicated that worker participation in plants does make a difference, "but not entirely," as Marxists would expect. Yugoslav workers participate in more decision making than do American *workers, but their attitudes toward the plant were no more favorable, and* communication was no more open.

Supervisors are not necessarily more interested in and responsive to ideas of their subordinates in plants where there is a formal worker-participation plan, than where there is no such plan. Tannenbaum found that attitudes were worse in Italy, under the "autocratic version of the way to run a business."

Steps Toward Improving Motivation

What management needs most is not so much a revolutionary *technique* for motivating employees, but a new *perspective*. Once managers realize that the rules for motivating have changed, they can begin making progress toward discovering new and better ways of motivating workers.

Although each work situation is different, steps that managers could and should implement to improve motivation are the following:

1. *Grant individual freedom, but maintain control.* Authority and responsibility should be delegated to the level closest to the problem situation. Allowing subordinates to make decisions (particularly those decisions where they are more qualified) fosters a feeling of confidence.[14] It gives the subordinate a feeling of independence and individual expression. It gives an employee a chance to learn and an opportunity to make a personal contribution. Controls can be set up which will enable the manager to take corrective action, in case things go astray. Individual freedom is basic to any motivational strategy.

2. *Create an atmosphere conducive to growth.* Management should not be expected to play the role of mother, father, minister, and psychiatrist to its workers. It should, however, create an atmosphere that affords each employee the opportunity to develop and utilize voluntarily any capacities, knowledge, skill, and ingenuity to contribute to the success of the enterprise.[15] It is in this type of atmosphere that management can derive the greatest benefits from its human resources.

Employees should feel comfortable when making suggestions. All new ideas begin in a nonconforming mind that questions conventional ideas. All improvements originate in a critical mind that mistrusts the popular image.

Robert N. McMurray stated that great progress can be made if top management can be led to see that (1) their points of view are not the only ones, (2) most issues are not absolutely black or white, but do have some gray areas, (3) they personally do not enjoy a monopoly on the truth, and (4) because someone espouses a system of values which differs from theirs, that person is not necessarily ignorant, stupid, or disloyal.[16]

Most people can learn to accept and to seek responsibility. The average person has the capacity to exercise a high degree of imagination, ingenuity and creativity in proper conditions that encourage them, thus increasing their contribution and level of responsibility.

The intellectual potential of the average individual is only partially used. The authoritarian leader, by inhibiting the intellectual growth of subordinates, denies their contribution. Management should create situations where employees' intelligence can create group goals to coincide with their individual needs. As a result, the individual, organization, customers and society will experience the benefits.

3. *Foster good communication within the organization.* Most individuals work for a business that provides their sole source of income, security, social status, and self respect. Through feedback, they want to know what their supervisors think of them.[17]

Sometimes, the supervisor may say one thing, but convey another through gesture, intonation, and expression – hence subordinates may complain that they do not really know where they stand. This is precisely where the impact of motivation can be realized. The employee is eager to have the organization confirm an internal estimate of expressed capabilities, and where the supervisor can be regarded as a valid source of feedback on performance, good communication of information is vitally important.[18]

4. *Preserve competence.* Competence, after all, is a relative, rather than an absolute quality. It is a matter of being able to do what is expected of one. Until recently, most employees were never really free of the fundamental pressures of job security and income, keep up their skills.

Today, income is a less crucial problem and people tend to become concerned with such esoteric motivators as dignity, recognition, and a sense of fulfillment in their work. David McClelland stated that money is no longer the incentive it used to be, but is now the measure of its success.[19] The tendency is to demand more of one's job and less of one's self, and the typical result is a gradual decline in output. Most jobs should not be designed in ways that minimize or deny the exercise of intelligence.[20] With the exception of relatively few people, it is much wiser to incorporate difficulty, variety, and challenge into most jobs. If employees become less competent, an attempt can be made to restore competence with refresher courses, retraining and encouragement. Management must try to keep the problem of competence in perspective and avoid overly pessimistic conclusions about human capabilities.

5. *Change the organization's structure.* In a large organization, a position could be created for a fulltime analyst of, or worrier about, motivation. This

person should be a member of every planning committee and every major decision-making conference. This analyst should know as much as possible about what is going on in the organization. However, the only responsibility, or at least the chief responsibility, should be to assure that the motivational impact of all management decisions is weighed before actions are implemented.[21]

An organization that is left to its own devices will seek to run smoothly, and this is all too easily accomplished by stressing what is superficial, by ignoring what is difficult and discouraging dissent. The organization whose members accept its ways passively is likely to conclude that its ways are right. But the main purpose of an organization is to achieve results, not to exist merely to create harmony.[22]

Conclusion

To fully capitalize upon our existing knowledge and insights into the nature of motivation and its effect upon human performance, the manager's attitudes must be changed radically. The basic motivational deficiency in many businesses today is the lack of sufficient decision-making authority and responsibility in jobs held by people who are best qualified to make decisions.

There is no actual shortage of decision-making power; it is simply and unnecessarily monopolized by management, and especially by higher organizational levels. This is due to the traditional concept that relatively few people are capable of making effective decisions or willing to accept responsibility. Such attitudes cause managers to limit their principal task to deciding what should other people do, and then making sure they do it. This type of thinking is already antiquated and will become increasingly distant from reality in the future.

To effectively motivate the people whose work they direct, managers will need to learn to be a "bit of a behavioral scientist" themselves. At the very least, they will need to know how to use the findings of behavioral scientists in practical, discriminating ways.

It is doubtful whether scientists will ever learn enough about people to reduce the practical problems of management to a simple system that can be applied without a great deal of judgment. However, we already know enough to improve substantially both the individual's contributions to the organization and personal satisfaction in belonging to it.

Robert Townsend, past president of Avis-Rent-A-Car, put it this way:

Get to know your people. What they do well, what they enjoy doing, what their weaknesses and strengths are, and what they want and need from their job. And then try to create an organization around your people, not jam your people into those organization-chart rectangles. The only excuse for organization is to maximize the chance that each one, working with others, will get for growth in his job.[23]

You cannot motivate people. That door is locked from the inside. You can create a climate in which most of your people will motivate themselves to help the company to reach its objectives. Like it or not, the only practical act is to adopt Theory Y assumptions and get going.

Footnotes

[1]"No 'heigh-ho' it's off to work we go," *Business Week,* 13 April 1974, pp. 10–13.

[2]John B. Miner, *The Management Process-Theory, Research and Practice* (New York: The MacMillan Company, 1973), pp. 297–322.

[3]Frederick W. Herzberg *et al., The Motivation to Work,* 2nd ed. (New York: John Wiley & Sons, 1959), pp. 12–35.

[4]Bradford B. Boyd, *Management-Minded Supervision* (New York: McGraw-Hill Book Co., 1968), p. 113.

[5]Rensis Likert, "Motivation: The Core of Management," *American Management Association Personnel Series, 155,* 1953, p. 21.

[6]Edmund Faltermayer, "Who Will Do the Dirty Work Tomorrow?" *Fortune,* January 1974, pp. 132–38. Faltermayer believes that in the case of "menial jobs," the only way to motivate people is "more money."

[7]Saul W. Gellerman, *Management by Motivation* (New York: Vail-Ballou Press, Inc., 1968), pp. 187–196.

[8]A.H. Maslow, *Motivation and Personality* (New York: Harper & Brothers, 1954), pp. 20–35.

[9]William G. Scott, *Human Relations in Management* (Homewood, IL: Richard D. Irwin, Inc., 1962), pp. 43–68.

[10]William H. Newman, Charles F. Summer, and E. Kirby Warren, *The Process of Management.* 2nd ed. (Englewood Cliffs, NJ: Prentice-Hall, Inc., 1967), p. 197.

[11]"Job Enrichment: Sometimes It Works," *Wall Street Journal,* 13 December 1971, p. 3.

[12]Charles L. Hulin, *New Perspectives in Job Enrichment* (New York: Van Nostrand Reingold, 1971), p. 4.

[13]Arnold S. Tannenbaum, "Rank, Clout and Worker Satisfaction: Pecking Order-Capitalist and Communist Style," *Psychology Today,* September 1975, pp. 40–51.

[14]Gerald C. Davidson and G. Terence Wilson, "Behavior Therapy: A Road to Self-Control," *Psychology Today,* October 1975, pp. 54–60. The authors suggest that workers should be allowed to choose their own goals: "As long as the boss sets the goals, workers will feel manipulated."

[15]Robert Kreitner, "PM—A New Method of Behavior Change," *Business Horizons,* December 1975, pp. 79–85. Positive Management (PM) stresses learning, instead of motivation. Kreitner's thesis is that managers should be trained in "proper attitudes" and that productivity increases will follow.

[16]Robert N. McMurray, "Conflicts in Human Values," *Harvard Business Review,* May-June 1963, pp. 130–45.

[17]Rick Minicucci, "Motivating Employees in a Down Economy," *Administrative Management,* June 1975, p. 20. Minicucci believes that the key to motivation is "rapport between management and employees."

[18]"Personal Problem Roundtable: Motivating the Worker," *Administrative Management,* December 1975, pp. 26–30. This article stresses the importance of communication in motivating workers.

[19]David McClelland, *The Achieving Society,* (Princeton, NJ: Van Nostrand Co., Inc., 1961), p. 62.

[20]"Those Boring Jobs—Not All That Dull," *U.S. News & World Report,* 1 December 1975, pp. 64–65.

[21]Joan Zaffarano, "Management's Leading Edge: Future Trends—Human Resources Matrixing—Motivation Control," *Administrative Management,* January 1976, pp. 31–42.

[22]George A. Steiner, *Business and Society,* (New York: Random House, Inc., 1971), p. 225.

[23]Robert Townsend, *Up the Organization,* (London, England: Coronet Books, Hodder-Fawcett, Ltd., 1971), p. 130.

Improving Employee Motivation:
Theories Galore, But How Do You Get Results?

When motivators change, who listens?
How can we meet the challenge?

Despite voluminous writing on the subject, today's manager who supervises others is no closer to understanding employee motivation than a counterpart of fifty years ago. If anything, employee motivation today is *more* of a problem than it was in the early 1900's.

This is not to say that the work of behavioral scientists has gone unnoticed, for their efforts have actually given today's manager better insight into motivation. Rather, this is to imply that the advances made in understanding what motivates workers have not kept pace with the rapid changes in employee attitudes and, hence, changes in those things that do *in fact* motivate them. In other words, by the time employee attitudes (which should provide an insight into motivation) are studied through a number of individual research efforts, and the results digested, disseminated, and perhaps implemented, it is usually too late. Rapidly changing technology, crumbling traditions, media influence, etc., have all conspired against the manager by changing worker's attitudes, desires, and motivations. I am not implying that drastic changes take place everyday, but the change is rapid enough to make most theories of motivation outdated by the time they are implemented.

An additional problem encountered when dealing with employee motivation is that the theories for improving motivation are just that – *theories* – until implemented. Unlike physical science theories that can be tested before implemented, social science theories can only be tested through implementation with human subjects. Managers, being human, have the human tendency to shy away from implementing theories that are not in accordance with their own preconceived notions. They are, like all of us, subject to what I would call a "self-reference criteria," whereby they practice those suggested behavioral patterns that are most closely aligned with their own intuition. The manager will offer rewards or exhibit behaviors toward workers that would motivate him as a manager, but this is not necessarily what may motivate the employees. When dealing with certain interpersonal relationships this does not present a problem, but when dealing with worker motivation, it is one of the biggest stumbling blocks, since a supervisor receives a different level of monetary and psychological reward – often resulting in a different lifestyle – than those people the manager is attempting to motivate. Thus, one of the biggest mistakes made by today's manager is the use of a self-reference criteria when deciding what rewards, behavioral patterns, etc., will and will not motivate employees.

It has been my experience that while many practitioners feel that self reference used to be a problem, but they do not view it as a major obstacle to employee motivation today. This situation is usually attributable to the fact that the earnings gap between nonsupervisory employees and first-line supervision has been drastically narrowed by labor organizations, thus creating a wage-earning middle class who hold similar values and motivations as their supervisors. The logical conclusion to this line of reasoning is that self reference is not a problem since those practicing it hold the same motivational values as their target. I disagree, because this argument's face validity does not support the negative evidence against it.

Numerous surveys have been conducted to determine what employees want from their jobs, i.e., what can be offered to motivate them. The following survey, published in *Foreman Facts* by the Labor Relations Institute of New York in 1946 is reproduced here because it was one of the most widely known and representative of that time period. Subjects were first line supervisors and employees who worked directly for them. After the employees had ranked the items in order of importance their supervisors were asked to rank them as they thought their employees would.

What People Want From Their Work (1946)

Employee Ranking		Supervisor Ranking
1	Full appreciation of work done	8
2	Feeling of being in on things	9
3	Sympathetic help on personal problems	10
4	Job security	2
5	Good wages	1
6	Interesting work	5
7	Promotion and growth in the organization	3
8	Personal loyalty to employees	6
9	Good working conditions	4
10	Tactful discipline	7

The absolute ranking of particular items is not the most important issue, but rather the significance of the above survey lies in the wide variance between what employees considered to be important in their jobs and what their supervisors *thought* was important to their employees. Since, as stated previously, of many surveys during the immediate post War era, and the use of self-reference was undoubtedly a problem. I contend that the variance found is clear evidence of the use of self reference by supervisors.

The more relevant question today, however, is this: does this gap still exist between workers' "wants" and supervisor's perceptions of these wants? If it does, then the logical explanation is that despite all the theories, self reference is still a major stumbling block to improving employee motivation. To address this issue, I administered the 1946 questionnaire to a sample of over 200 employees and their immediate supervisors, to see if the results bore any resemblance to those of 35 years ago. (See Table 2).

While a comparison of the results shows an improvement in the differences between the two groups (1946 sum of differences across items = 42, present sum of differences = 34) 7 of the 8 improvement points are attributable to the change in the ranking of 'sympathetic help with personal problems', 6 of those coming from its devaluation by employees. With the exception of this one factor, the gap between supervisors and their employees has not closed significantly since 1946.

Perhaps the most revealing comparisons appear in the two rankings of security/wages and appreciation/being in on things. In 1946, wages and security were ranked as having middle importance by employees and as having top importance to employees by supervisors, while appreciation of work and feeling in on things were of top importance for employees, yet perceived as least important to employees by supervisors. This is exactly the situation uncovered by the present survey. There has been no improvement in these discrepancies since at least 1946! Hence any argument that self reference is not still a major problem is not supported by the evidence. One of the most important things for today's manager to do, when trying to improve employee motivation, is to first find out what it is that employees want from their work, i.e., what will motivate them. As shown by the table below and on page 3, any reliance on a manager's own judgment about what will motivate employees, will likely only aggravate the problem.

Table 2
What People Want From Their Work (Present)

Employee Ranking		Supervisor Ranking
1	Interesting work	5
2	Full appreciation of work done	8
3	Feeling of being in on things	10
4	Job security	2
5	Good wages	1
6	Promotion and growth in the organization	3
7	Good working conditions	4
8	Personal loyalty to employees	7
9	Sympathetic help on personal problems	9
10	Tactful discipline	6

The use of attitude surveys is the cheapest, most direct approach to gathering such information. Surveys can employ ranking, Likert scales, or other techniques to quantify, tabulate, and understand. For very little time and monetary investment the organization, and particularly its supervisors, are likely to get very insightful feedback that can go a long way toward improving employee motivation.

A word of caution is necessary here. We must learn from our earlier mistakes and make sure that the results are transmitted to those supervisors who most directly interact with the employees involved. Many times the results are made available only to managers at levels above those having direct daily employee contact, and, as a result, the individuals who could make best use of the findings are never aware of what they are, or, at best, get a biased verbal summation (recall the human tendency to remember data we agree with during verbal transmission).

While allowing for variance due to the length and cost of administering the instrument, a good rule of thumb is to administer the attitude survey approximately once a year. Such frequency is necessary to avoid the problem discussed earlier, that of attempting to improve employee motivation using outdated, and often inaccurate, information.

Additionally, it is important to analyze the responses not only collectively, but in subsamples based on task groups and earning levels, if there is a variance within the respondent group. According to Maslow's theory, we are motivated by our desire to fulfill certain hierarchial needs. After fulfilling a lower-order need, motivation arises from a desire to satisfy the next level need. Individuals at different organizational levels or different task groups, with different levels of earning power, may well be at different levels in Maslows hierarchy. Hence, what motivates individuals at one level of the organization very likely will not be the same as what motivates those at another level. Thus, the necessity exists to differentiate *by level* when analyzing attitudes for motivational purposes.

The results of the present ranking by employees indicate that when analyzed collectively, nonsupervisory employees in this sample have progressed beyond the basic needs which can be satisfied by economic rewards. Yet it is important to remember that the results presented in the tables are averages for all employees and are intended only to show discrepancies between the two groups. They should not be interpreted to mean that **all** employees see money as having middle, relative importance, or that all employees see interesting work and appreciation of work, as what they want most from their jobs.[1] Within a given organization, and certainly across individuals, results will vary. This emphasizes why it is so important that each organization conduct its own attitude survey. Reward structures can then be established to observe any motivational impact on the organization. If, for instance, interesting work is the major desire of the particular respondents, then perhaps job enlargement or enrichment can be tried on a limited basis; if higher wages are what will motivate employees then the introduction of an incentive-pay system might be a wise move.

Robert Townsend, past president of Avis-Rent-a-Car, put it this way:

> Get to know your people. What they do well, what they enjoy doing, what their weaknesses and strengths are, and what they want and need from their job. And then try to create an organization around your people, not jam your people into those organization-chart rectangles.[2]

The key is to remember that you cannot motivate people. That door is locked from the inside. What todays manager can do however, is create a climate in which most of the employees will find it personally rewarding to motivate themselves, and in the process contribute to the company's attainment of its objectives. If a manager can achieve this state of mind among a reasonable number of his employees many of his other problems will take care of themselves.

---

[1]If such were the case, and interesting work was the number-one desire of every employee, then programs of job enlargement/enrichment would be a cure-all and would not have been such a major disappointment, despite self-serving articles to the contrary.

[2]Robert Townsend, *Up the Organization* (London, England: Coronet Books, Hodder-Fawcett, Ltd., 1971), p. 130.

Employee Motivation: A Blue-Collar Perspective

Introduction

Since the rise of the field of study known as 'behavioral science' over a decade ago, as much has been written by management theorists about employee motivation, as any other single subject. It has been studied, probed and diagnosed from every conceivable direction: the impact of various monetary compensation systems, the effect of assorted intrinsic rewards, to name a few.

I am convinced, however, that a thorough review of the literature reveals one area in which motivation theory has an exceptionally dismal track record. When one looks objectively at the results of applying various motivation theories to blue-collar workers in general, and those located in a large metropolitan area in particular, it is obvious that the operationalization of the theories leave much to be desired. It is understandable that this sector should cause the most trouble, since the jobs are more mundane, unchallenging, etc., than those of higher organizational levels. By the same token, however, this is the very reason that the success of motivation theories is more important at this level, than at any other. If the theories are ineffective in the sector where the problem is most acute, then one must question the value of the theories. I find this to be the case.

It is one thing to apply a theory to individuals at an organizational level where intrinsic rewards are meaningful and the organization is flexible enough to allow various reward systems to function simultaneously, and then to find that these individuals have become motivated. The jobs must have been such that they allowed for the easy introduction of motivating factors. It is here that motivational theorists have realized their greatest success. It is quite another matter to work with jobs where the job description, formal or otherwise, does not permit such flexibility, i.e., the blue-collar sector. This is not to say that there is any shortage of *theories* concerning motivation in this sector, but rather the success when actually applying these theories has been minimal.

Reviewing the published literature, one would probably come away with the opposite impression, but I would caution the reader to keep in mind that theorists in the behavioral sciences are more inclined to report instances where their theories have proven successful that when the opposite is true. No academician ever satisfied the "publish or perish" demand by consistently writing about failures, and no consultant ever made a name by publishing the fact that results could not be produced. Once in a while, such an article is acceptable, but it must be more than compensated for by numerous articles detailing instances where the theory held true. Should the reader doubt this, I urge you to look at a sample of research results published by any particular motivation theorist. If these people really realized the success-versus-failure ratio indicated by their articles, there would be no reason for any manager to ever tolerate unmotivated employees. All that would be necessary would be to contact one of these individuals, or easier still, apply the theory. This is obviously not the case, the reason being that failures to motivate do not get the publicity that successes do.

Take management by objectives for example, one of the most written-about theories. While it has worked for a limited time at higher organizational levels, it has been a dismal failure among most blue-collar employees. (Even among upper-level employees, the impact fades drastically after a short period.) Yet it is clear from a study of the literature that these failures have been skimmed over, and undue emphasis given to the original successes at higher levels.

The Cause of the Problem

As mentioned previously, the problem is particularly acute at the blue-collar level. I believe this is so, because many employees at this level have been conditioned by years of unstimulating, repetitive, unchallenging work to simply accept things as they are. They have come to expect nothing more than a paycheck from their job, and have been taught by labor organizations, peers, and company policies to view management as the enemy. To many the relationship of employees to management is an "us and them" type of relationship, and employees seek their satisfaction, enjoyment, etc., not on the job, but through more time *away* from the job—longer vacations, more holidays, earlier retirement, etc. American businesses have no one but themselves to blame for this attitude, for they fostered it through their own company policies for generations. Rather than follow the examples of Japan, Sweden, etc., and make the blue-collar worker feel *part* of the organization, they have made the worker feel like a tool of the organization: a replaceable, interchangeable serf.

It is only in the last decade that we have seen any large-scale attempt to depart from this position. Here we run into the management theorists concerned with motivation. Through programs such as job enlargement and job enrichment, they have tried to motivate today's employee. While, as stated earlier, they have worked on a limited scale where such programs could be practically implemented (white collar, lower and middle management, skilled laborers, etc.) they cannot, do not, and will not work to any degree among blue-collar employees, the majority of whom have internalized the attitude toward their job discussed above. In such a situation the introduction of one program of job enlargement/enrichment will not overcome the barrier of years of conditioning. Job enlargement and enrichment programs have as an implicit assumption that the job can be made an important part of the employee's life. While this may be true among upper-level jobs where there is room for the introduction of meaningful job alterations, it is not necessarily true of blue-collar jobs where such flexibility is not available. In such instances, a facade is introduced with no real, substantive changes. This is why motivation interventions fail more often than not among blue-collar environments.

Numerous times I have heard the argument from company executives that the reason programs such as MBO (Management by Objectives) or enlargement fail among blue-collar employees in their organization, is that the employees at that level just are "not ready for it" or "are incapable of handling it." Nonsense! That is the exact type of thinking that *caused* the present situation. "People can't handle it, therefore, I will not allow them to try." While there are obviously differences between individuals in terms of intellectual capabilities, it cannot be seriously entertained that blue-collar employees are mentally and emotionally incapable of handling anything more than the robot-like jobs that many of them now perform. If they had been challenged originally, their attitude might be far different now. At this point however, it is natural for them to be skeptical of attempts to enrich their jobs.

I must summarize, therefore, that not all the blame for unsuccessful implementation of motivation strategies at the blue-collar level lies with the theory itself. Part of the problem is management's conditioning process the employees have experienced for most of their working lives, *before* the theory was introduced.

This is not to excuse the theorists entirely, however, for the rest of the blame is clearly theirs. An intelligent practitioner or other outsider reading a cookbook of motivational theories will find that the theories fall into one of two categories: either they are so abstract and theoretical that nobody with any sense would actually attempt to operationalize them in an actual organization, or they are simply commonsense approaches cloaked in academic jargon. Ninety-nine percent of motivation theories, and 75% of all management theories, originating from academicians fall into one of these two categories.

An additional problem occurs when the researchers study a small, select group of subjects; a look at even the most respected journals reveals that most research studies are based on less than 200 subjects. These subjects are usually chosen because they are all in one location, or, at best, one occupation, and thus easily accessible to the researcher. When this is not the case, they are most often chosen at random. In neither instance are they chosen to represent an adequate cross-section of an industry, occupation, etc.—how much can be expected from a sample of less than 200? The point is that the findings, based as they are on such a nonrepresentative sample, cannot be generalized beyond the environment being studied. At best they may give an indication for the particular organization in which the subjects worked. An attempt to attribute universality to such findings must be seriously questioned. Yet this is exactly what has happened in the motivation area over the last ten years! Today there are particular journals where the entire publication is composed of researchers talking to other researchers through the medium of such studies. No astute supervisor with responsibility for blue-collar employees should take any of this writing seriously. Yet it is those academicians who engage in such a rhetoric to the greatest degree, that are awarded the highest scholarly honors. When honors are based on the published results of questionable methodology, it denigrates any prestige the award could convey. Should such a trend continue, the gap between practitioners and academicians can only widen and, speaking as a practitioner turned academician, I must side with the former.

Conclusion

In conclusion, I contend that operationalizations of today's theories of motivation are useful only in select environments, and that their biggest failure comes in the blue-collar sector, owing to the attitudes forced on employees at that level by employer practices, and to the inadequate, limited research methods used to operationalize the same theories.

The best applications of motivation theory cannot be found by studying academic pontifications, but by watching the day-to-day routine of first-line supervisors in a particular organization. There are no universal theories of motivation. Each organization and each subunit has its own peculiar set of values and rewards. The best way for supervisor to decide what is appropriate as far as motivation of the blue-collar workers is to watch successful, motivating supervisors in the organization unit closest to, or most similar to, their own. In other words, learn from the available successful practitioners everything you can observe; many of whom, while not formally educated, have enough common sense to tell academicians that, while their applications of motivation theory may satisfy "publish or perish" requirements, they do not have a chance of large-scale success in the real world.

The Privacy and Freedom of Information Acts

A retrospective analysis reveals
interepretation as the key issue
until a body of case law develops
to provide clarity.

A new issue of national concern, based on fears about the centralized use of personal information, has emerged in recent years. The issue involves the right to privacy, a poorly defined and vague concept that recently has been given new meaning by the Congress.

Congressional interest in privacy, reflecting a broad national concern, arose out of the fear that a dictatorship of dossiers and data banks was developing. The misuse, and even the ordinary use, of government record systems threatened to invade our privacy.

In passing the Privacy Act of 1974, Congress specified that the privacy of an individual is directly affected by the collection, maintenance, use, and dissemination of personal information by federal agencies. The Privacy Act was the first general attempt by Congress to define individual rights of privacy by restricting government handling of personal information.

The balance of this discussion will consist of a broad examination of the growth of interest in privacy, a sketch of recent events that led up to the Privacy Act of 1974, an outline of the act, a statement of the goals implicit in the act, a discussion of the act and the private sector, a detailed presentation of the Freedom of Information Act, and a discussion of the effects of the act on the National Labor Relations Board.

The growth of privacy as a personal and national issue reflects, to a significant degree, the growth of technology that can collect, store, interrelate, and disseminate information. This technological ability was very limited in the early years of the United States, and interest in personal liberties was directed elsewhere. The word "privacy" does not appear in the Constitution, although the Bill of Rights does contain restrictions on governmental actions in areas related to privacy, such as speech, association, religion, and intrusion into homes, possessions, and lives of citizens.

The concept of legal protection of personal privacy developed toward the end of the nineteenth century, generated in part by an article written in 1890 by Samuel D. Warren and Louis D. Brandeis, entitled "The Right to Privacy." The article was inspired by what the authors viewed as misuse of a new method of collecting and disseminating information.

"Recent inventions and business methods call attention to the next step which must be taken for the protection of the person, and for securing to the individual . . . the right 'to be let alone.' Instantaneous photographs and newspaper enterprise have invaded the sacred precincts of private and domestic life; and numerous mechanical devices threaten to make good the prediction that what is whispered in the closet shall be proclaimed from the house-tops."[1]

Other technological developments of the nineteenth and twentieth centuries had far-reaching consequences for privacy, although concern over these consequences did not surface until much later. The telegraph was invented in the mid-nineteenth century, along with the telegraph wiretap. Photographic equipment became cheaper, smaller, more mobile, and easier to use, a development that continues today. Telephones and telephone wiretaps followed, along with other sound-transmitting, recording, and intercepting devices. Developments in personality assessment produced personality and intelligence tests, polygraphs, and other psychological and psychoanalytic measurements. More advanced technology brought faster communications—automobiles, improved printing processes, radio, airplanes, television, and satellites.

Negative Consequences

Many of these inventions were so useful, so capable of bringing measurable improvements to people's lives, that the negative privacy consequences did not immediately become a matter of public notice or anxiety. The use of these devices for surveillance was (and still is) tangled with issues such as law enforcement and national security—problems remote from everyday experience, especially earlier in this century. In 1958, the Supreme Court weighed some of these issues and, by a vote of 5–4 in *Olmstead v. United States,* came down on the side of law enforcement. The Court held that the difficulties in bringing offenders to justice permitted the admission of illegally obtained wiretap evidence.

In a famous dissent, Mr. Justice Brandeis discussed the importance of privacy: "The makers of our Constitution undertook to secure conditions favorable to the pursuit of happiness. They recognized the significance of man's spiritual nature, of his feelings and of his interest. They knew that only a part of the pain, pleasure and satisfactions of life are to be found in material things. They sought to protect Americans in their beliefs, their thoughts, their emotions and their sensations. They conferred, as against the Government, the right to be let alone—the most comprehensive of rights and the right most valued by civilized men."[2]

The holding of Olmstead—that illegally obtained wiretap evidence is admissible—was reversed by statute, and later by a Supreme Court decision, as well.

As the fruits of technology improved, multiplied, and came into common use, other changes in American society began to make individuals aware of privacy-invading developments that could affect their daily lives. The tremendous growth of government, beginning with the New Deal of the 1930's, resulted in greater demands for personal information. Social service responsibilities accepted by the federal government at that time required that individuals be identified, measured against economic and social yardsticks, and then categorized for purposes of determining eligibility for personal or regional assistance.

As a result of these and other programs, Americans interacted with their governments in an increasing number of ways, and each new contact forced individuals to reveal additional personal data. Expanding government intervention in the economy necessitated increasingly detailed social and economic information as an input to developing planning and budgeting efforts. The widening scope of government activity in these areas is still apparent today.

With the rapid growth of business, most notably in the period following World War II, the need for the collection of commercial information grew also. Management techniques to extract and employ this information were developed. Business planning became more important and more scientific. Industry was not only interested in its markets, products, and consumers, but also in its personnel. Large corporations found the need and capability for improving the methods of employee selection and control, by means of personality testing and other screening procedures. The polygraph also became a tool of some importance to business.

The postwar period has been marked by an explosion of consumer credit. In the 25 years after the end of World War II, consumer borrowing increased by more than 2000 percent. Because of the nature of the risks involved, lending is an information-intensive industry, and extensive facilities have evolved to meet the need. Changes in banking technology have enabled banks to provide checking accounts at a price that many consumers can afford. One less visible cost of this convenience is the increasing centralization individuals' financial transactions recorded at banks. The success of the credit-card industry has also contributed to the concentration of financial records that previously had been scattered. The next step in this development may be the so-called "cashless society," where individual central accounts will be used for all personal financial dealings.

While all of these structural changes were taking place, and while people relinquished more and more personal information to governmental and private organizations, widespread concern over loss of personal privacy was slow to appear. Although many factors have contributed to the recent surge of interest in privacy, it is the ever-increasing ability of computers to store, analyze, recall, and exchange information that has focused the attention of the public on the dangers that began to develop many years ago.

The computer is viewed as the quintessential threat, despite not being used to extract new types of information from individuals; it is able to bring together, to coordinate, and to manage all of the information that has been collected by others. Thus, the computer could, if permitted, collect and analyze financial information from a bank or credit bureau, medical records from a hospital, tax returns from the Internal Revenue Service, employment history from an employer, educational records from schools, etc.

Virtually everything that a computer is able to do can also be done manually. Conversely, the manual collection and analysis of diverse records is not only time consuming and expensive the first time it is collected, but is equally time consuming and expensive *each* time it is done. Because of the difficulties involved, such investigations are not usually done for casual purposes. Programming a computer to collect information from other computers and to analyze the information is a complex task, but once completed, the use of the program to prepare reports on individuals may be a simple and cheap operation. It is the automatic, mindless fashion in which computers can operate that is perceived as threatening, perhaps generating more fear than is warranted by actual computer use. Gerald Ford, who as Vice President chaired a Domestic Council Committee on the Right of Privacy, said on this subject:

> "In dealing with troublesome privacy problems, let us not, however, scapegoat the computer itself as a Frankenstein's monster. But let us be aware of the implications posed to freedom and privacy emerging from the ways we use computers to collect and disseminate personal information. A concerned involvement by all who use computers is the only way to produce standards and policies that will do the job. It is up to us to assure that information is not fed into the computer unless it is relevant."[3]

Recent Events

Many events of the past ten years have highlighted privacy as an issue of continuing concern. While the effect of these events has not been uniform—some have increased privacy protections and others have established or threatened new invasions—the open discussion of privacy in the courts, in Congress, and in the press has raised public consciousness in this area and contributed to the passage of the Privacy Act of 1974.

—In 1965, the Supreme Court in *Griswold v. Connecticut* struck down a state law prohibiting the use of contraceptives, because the law violated the right of marital privacy, a protected freedom. The Court found that "the First Amendment has a *penumbra* where privacy is protected from governmental intrusion."[4] The case reactivated interest in privacy rights under the Bill of Rights.

—In 1966, Congress passed the Freedom of Information Act, an act designed to make available to the public as much information possessed by the government as is consistent with legitimate needs for secrecy. Since federal agencies have tremendous amounts of personal data, the act raises the possibility of disclosure of this data.

—In 1967, after hearings conducted the previous year, the Senate passed a bill designed to protect the privacy and the rights of federal employees. Similar legislation was considered by subsequent Congresses and was approved by the Senate several times, but the failure of the House to concur prevented the proposal from becoming law. Among other things, the bill would have generally prevented asking federal employees any questions on race, religion, or national origin, severely limited any interference with the exercise of first amendment freedoms by employees, prohibited serious invasions of privacy in interviews, interrogations, and personality testing, narrowed the use of polygraphs, and set standards for disclosure by employees of financial information.

—The Fair Credit Reporting Act was passed by Congress in 1970 to insure fairness, impartiality, and respect for consumer privacy in the reporting of credit information. The act contains rules for treatment of obsolete credit information, disclosure provisions for credit bureau records, and a disputes procedure. However, at the same time that Congress took these steps to aid privacy rights, it also required banks to keep copies of all checks written by customers, and to report currency and foreign transactions of customers. These latter requirements increase the numbers and types of required disclosures of personal financial information.

—There have been a series of disclosures in the press and in Congressional hearings of secret activities by government agencies involving invasions of privacy of citizens. The U.S. Army conducted surveillance of civilians and maintained computerized dossiers on suspicious persons. President Nixon ordered "national security" wiretaps of newsmen and government officials. The Federal Bureau of Investigation has been accused of illegal counter-intelligence and undercover operations. The Central Intelligence Agency has admitted to various domestic intelligence projects, as well as to monitoring and opening mail of United States citizens.

FEDNET

—The concept of a Federal Information Network (FEDNET) as a Government-wide system of data processing and communication equipment designed to serve the entire federal community was developed in 1972 by the General Services Administration's Automated Data and Telecommunications Service. When the General Services Administration and the Department of Agriculture began to take the first steps to implement FEDNET, a wave of Congressional opposition forced a drastic reduction in the scope of the project and an elimination of interconnection features that would have permitted computer-to-computer communications. Realization of its great potential of such a system to violate the privacy of individuals was a factor in the drafting and passage of the Privacy Act of 1974.

—In 1973, President Nixon signed Executive Order 11697, permitting the Department of Agriculture's inspection of farmers' tax return to prepare statistical information about farming operations. When the order's existence became known, there were strong protests from Congress and, as a result, the order was modified and later revoked. The opposition was based largely on the invasion of privacy issue; information collected on tax returns for one purpose was to be used for another purpose, without the permission of the taxpayers and without any controls on the actual use of the data.

—The Crime Control Act of 1973 restricts the use of criminal history information. This act requires that, to the maximum extent feasible, records of dispositions be kept with records of arrest, that procedures for collection, storage, and dissemination be reasonably designed to insure that all information is kept current, that the security and privacy of all information be adequately maintained and that information be used only for law enforcement, criminal justice, or other lawful purposes. Also, individuals are granted a right of access to records about themselves contained in automated systems so that they may check the accuracy of the information.

—Two 1974 laws limit the use of educational records by educational institutions receiving federal funds. The effect of these laws is to make records of students available to students' parents, to provide for procedures whereby the contents of the records can be challenged, to limit generally the disclosure of student records without the consent of the parents, and to require that schools account for all disclosures that are made.

—In 1974, Congress established the National Commission on Electronic Fund Transfers to conduct a study and to recommend legislation in connection with the development of public or private electronic fund transfer systems. One of the factors that the commission considers is the need to afford maximum rights to privacy and confidentiality for the user and consumer.

—Those events that have come to be known collectively as "Watergate" have probably had the greatest public impact. One witness before the Senate hearings on privacy described the effect:

"Watergate has thus been the symbolic catalyst of a tremendous upsurge of interest in securing the right of privacy: wire-tapping and bugging political opponents, breaking and entering, enemies lists, the Huston plan, national security justifications for wiretapping and burglary, misuse of information compiled by government agencies for political purposes, access to hotel, telephone and bank records; all of these show what government can do if its actions are shrouded in secrecy and its vast information resources are applied and manipulated in a punitive, selective, or political fashion."[5]

Watergate focused attention on the potential abuses of government collection and use of information, but all of the events listed (and others not included) helped educate the public and the Congress about privacy. The identification and discussion of abuses also served to highlight those areas appropriate for legislative action. In response, Congress translated concern over secret surveillance records of questionable purpose into publication provisions and relevance standards for record-keeping. Evidence about misuse of records led to limitations on uses. Access provisions were prompted by widespread use of erroneous information to make adverse determinations about individuals. The Privacy Act of 1974 is the product of these and other influences, and its major provisions are outlined below.

Because the Privacy Act is the first law of its kind, future developments in this area will probably depend largely on the effectiveness of the act. As with the Freedom of Information Act originally passed in 1966 and not substantively amended until 1974, it is probable that Congress will not make any major changes in the law in the near future. Private-sector activities and legislation by the states are likely to be delayed as well, or else based on the Privacy Act. As the act's shortcomings become apparent, alterations and new proposals will become ripe for adoption. Therefore, the most significant privacy issue for the next several years will be the implementation of the Privacy Act and the evaluation of its solutions.

The Privacy Act

The Privacy Act of 1974, which became law on the last day of 1974, is the first attempt by Congress to legislate general government-wide standards for the protection of individual privacy. The act was enacted to "safeguard individual privacy from the misuse of federal records, provide that individuals be granted access to records concerning them which are maintained by Federal agencies, establish a Privacy Protection Study Commission, and for other purposes."[6] The outline of the Act that follows indicates the issues that Congress viewed as important and how Congress chose to deal with them.

The Act's restrictions on the maintenance, collection, use, and dissemination of systems of records apply only to federal agencies, except for certain minor limitations imposed on government contractors and state and local governments. A system of records subject to the act's provisions is a group of records from which information about an individual is retrieved by name, Social Security number, fingerprint, photograph or other individual identifier. The act applies only to records about individuals and does not cover records about corporations.

A basic premise of the law is that information about individuals should not be maintained in secret files. Agencies are required to publish at least an annual notice of the existence and character of a system of records. The notice must include a description of the categories of individuals on whom records are maintained, the categories of records maintained, the types of sources for the information, and the routine uses of the records.

Upon request, an agency must permit the subject of a record to gain access to the record and to copy it. An individual disagreeing with the contents of the record may request an amendment and the request must be acted on within ten days. If dissatisfied with the result, an individual may appeal the decision within the agency and then, if still dissatisfied, may appeal the matter to a district court or place a statement about the disagreement in the record. The agency is obliged to distribute the statement of disagreement with all disclosures of the record.

Records contained in a system of records may not be disclosed without the consent of the subject of the record, unless the disclosure is specifically permitted by the act. There are eleven categories of permissible disclosures, including disclosure to employees of the agency that maintains the record with a need for the record in the performance of their duties, disclosures to Congress or to the General Accounting Office, and disclosures for a "routine use."

"Routine use" is a term of art in the act, meaning a disclosure defined by the agency maintaining the system that is compatible with the purpose for which the record was collected. Since routine uses must be included in the published descriptions of systems, individuals theoretically will have notice of all uses that will be made of information supplied to the government.

Agencies are also required to keep an accounting of the date, nature, and the purpose of most disclosures, as well as the names and addresses of the persons to whom the record was disclosed. These persons must be notified of all subsequent corrections of the record and of any disputes about the contents.

Other provisions of the act require that agencies:

— maintain only such information as is relevant and necessary to accomplish a legal purpose of the agency;
— collect information to the greatest extent practicable directly from the subject when the use of the information may result in an adverse determination;
— inform each individual asked to supply information of the authority for the request, the principal purpose for which the information will be used, any routine uses that may be made, the consequences of failing to provide the requested information, and whether the disclosure is mandatory or voluntary;
— maintain records with such accuracy, relevance, timeliness, and completeness as is reasonably necessary to assure fairness;
— prior to the dissemination of a record, make a reasonable effort to assure that the records are accurate, complete, timely, and relevant;
— maintain no records describing how any individual exercises rights guaranteed by the first amendment, unless expressly authorized by statute or unless the records are pertinent to authorized law enforcement activities;
— establish appropriate administrative, technical, and physical safeguards to insure the security and confidentiality of records;
— sell or rent mailing lists only when specifically authorized by law; and
— promulgate rules establishing necessary procedures.

Agencies planning to establish or to alter any systems of records must provide adequate advance notice to Congress and to the Office of Management and Budget to permit an evaluation of the impact of the proposal on privacy and other personal rights.

The act permits systems of records maintained by the Central Intelligence Agency or other agencies involved with law enforcement to be exempted from many of the provisions of the act. More limited exemptions are permitted for systems of records that contain classified information, statistical data, or information from confidential sources. The exemption provisions are permissive and not mandatory, i.e., they apply to a system of records only when specifically invoked by the head of an agency.

Federal, state, and local agencies are restricted by the act in asking individuals to disclose their Social Security numbers. Unless the disclosure is required by law or by a regulation that predates the Privacy Act, no rights, benefits, or privileges can be denied an individual who refuses to reveal a Social Security number. Requests for the number must indicate whether the disclosure is voluntary or mandatory, the request, and what use will be made of the number.

The act also created a Privacy Protection Study Commission composed of members appointed by the President of the United States, the President of the Senate, and the Speaker of the House. The commission is directed to carry out studies of data banks, automated data processing programs, and governmental and regional information systems in order to determine the standards and procedures in force for the protection of personal information.

Even for a new law, the Privacy Act presents many difficult questions of interpretation. The law introduces several new concepts—record, system of records, routine use—but does not define them as fully as might be desired. In practice, some requirements appear to be pointless, unduly burdensome, or both. Until the courts set clear standards for the interpretation of the act, wide variations are likely.

One major area of difficulty will be the coordination between the Freedom of Information Act and the Privacy Act.

Privacy Policy Goals

Because privacy is a subject that has recently undergone thorough legislative scrutiny, and because full implementation of the legislative directives is still to come, it is both easier and harder to define the goals of privacy policy than it might be in the case of a subject with more of a history. It is easier, because the congressional description of goals, as revealed in the statute and accompanying materials, is recent, and because policy choices have been made and conflicts resolved in a reasonably clear and consistent fashion.

However, the task of goal definition is also harder because the lack of experience makes it more difficult to identify all the consequences, conflicts, and constraints that follow from a given policy choice. With experience, the possible can more easily be separated from the impossible and the unlikely, so that the definition of goals can be more realistic and more useful. Subject to these caveats, five privacy goals can tentatively identified. The discussion includes a brief description of the goal, the reasons for its selection, and an indication of conflicts that are likely to arise with other desirable ends.

— **Limiting Systems of Records.** The limitations envisioned by this goal include not only restrictions on numbers of systems, but on the contents of the systems as well. The maintenance of unnecessary records or information is unwise for at least three reasons: (a) it is expensive, (b) the information may be misused and thereby violate someone's privacy, and (c) the mere compilation of personal information is an invasion of privacy that can only be justified by some legitimate governmental need. Defining what information is "relevant and necessary" (the statutory standard) will present substantial problems in many cases. For example, how "dangerous" must a person be before it is appropriate to be included on the list of those who may threaten the President? What financial or other information is sufficiently reliable and useful to justify its collection from potential welfare recipients to determine eligibility?

— **Eliminating Secret Record Keeping.** The abuses resulting from the maintenance and use of secret records were a strong factor contributing to the passage of the Privacy Act. Without any notice of the existence or use of a record containing personal information, individuals may be and have been denied a right, benefit, or privilege for unstated reasons. Unaware of the reasons for the denials because of the secret nature of the records, it is virtually impossible for an individual to react.

Openness of record keeping also provides a check on the substantive activities of government agencies. It may be more difficult for agencies to engage in activities of questionable legality, because the existence of the underlying records (although not the contents) is public information. However, this goal is not absolute, and some law enforcement and national security record systems should be kept secret. Identifying those systems whose existence is properly hidden will present a major line-drawing problem.

— **Protecting Records from Misuse.** In the context of this goal, "misuse" must be very broadly defined. It includes such things as unauthorized access to records, use of records for purposes other than those for which the records were collected, improper sharing of data, etc. This goal is important, because if successfully met, it will alleviate many of the fears engendered by the existence of large and numerous record systems. Individuals will have more control over personal data because they will know how and when the information is to be used. The constraints in this area are the cost and difficulty of proper physical security of records, the cost of administrative controls over users of records, and the possible interference with substantive functions because of restrictions on the use of records.

— **Permitting Individuals' Access to Their Records.** The advantages of this goal benefit both the keeper and the subject of the record. Accessibility not only contributes to an individual's control over personal data in the possession of others, but also to the accuracy of the record-keeping process. In many cases, the subject of the record will be able to correct errors resulting from clerical mistakes, mechanical errors, and other shortcomings inherent in the collection of data. Even when disputes cannot be resolved, both sides of the issue can be presented to users of the record.

The sense of fairness that follows from compliance with this goal is not without costs, both financial and administrative. To the extent that those who compile records are inhibited from including material that legitimately belongs in the record, then the right of access imposes a limitation on the usefulness of the records. Maintaining the facilities of access will obviously require revisions of existing record-handling procedures.

—**Assuring the Accuracy of Records.** This goal is very similar in many respects to the previous one, differing primarily because the burden of assuring accuracy is on the record keeper and not the subject. The setting of standards for accuracy, timeliness, and completeness of records should not only improve the quality of the records but should also help to create and maintain the appearance of fairness. Because the affirmative responsibility on record keepers and compilers is much greater than for the fourth goal, the costs of compliance will necessarily be greater.

The Privacy Act and the Private Sector

It is well to remember that the Privacy Act of 1974 was not enacted in response to actions taken by members of the private sector, but rather out of concern over the misuse of information about private citizens during the activities of the Nixon Administration. The expressed intent of the law does not have as its focus the private sector.

Members of the private sector began to anticipate and formulate responses in 1973 and 1974 to the then pending legislation which is now the Privacy Act. In June of 1973 and again in November of 1974, *Business Week* dealt with several probable impacts of the privacy legislation. The thrust of their concern developed out of a recognition that much of the act or acts was concerned with controlling record-keeping functions; specifically, automated data-retrieval systems designed to provide access to numerous data concerning specific individuals.

It was well recognized in the private sector that the issues of the intended bills did more than give slight attention to the invasion of privacy implications inherent in massive and rapid input and output data-retrieval systems. It was also well recognized that such systems were being used extensively throughout the private sector. These systems housed massive amounts of information pertaining to the financial, medical and personal activities of individuals and their interactions with the business community. It was also of no small concern to many within the private sector that vast income streams were being provided by developers of the technology for such data bases, utilizing these data bases as products themselves or providing some service or marketing capability for some group of products.

The intended legislation represented an economic threat to the private sector. Concern over the economic implications of the act, after anticipated implementation, had already been expressed within the government itself. The Office of Management and Budget estimated that it would cost some $200 million a year in operational expenses for the various agencies within the government to maintain compliance with the proposed provisions of the act. It requires little speculation to imagine the concern which developed within the private sector for the possible implications of this bill.

Notwithstanding long established precedence, including all that has passed before us in the arena of government regulation of business activity, it is my position that much of the anticipated impact on the private sector will never be forthcoming, or, at best, will develop only over an extended period of time. This position is developed out of an examination of several key elements associated with the socio-political environment, within which the bill was made law, the political mechanisms operating among the United States Senate, United States House of Representatives and the Executive Branch during the formulation of the legislation, and the expressed omission of several early provisions of the act from that act which was made law.

Separate privacy bills were passed by the United States Senate and the United States House of Representatives on November 21, 1974. A major provision of the Senate bill would have established an independent privacy protection commission empowered to develop guidelines and assist agencies in implementing the law, and to receive and investigate charges of violations. House members opposed the creation of a commission and the Ford Administration opposed the commission idea. The Senate, House, and the Administration finally agreed to establish a two–year, seven-member Privacy Protection Study Commission whose duties are specified in the act itself to give much of its attention to problems in State and local governments and the private sector. One senatorial staff member commented that the failure to establish an overall enforcement agency significantly weakened the bill.

It is also important to note that the appointed commission membership was composed of five people appointed by the House and the President. This insured the blunting of this commission's activities, as both House and Executive Branches were opposed to its creation.

It was the concern over the purported mission of the Privacy Commission that sent shock waves through local governments and businesses. However, a thorough examination of the *Congressional Quarterly* and the *National Journal* reveals no comments or articles pertaining to the activities of the commission, whose term ended early in 1977. It is apparent from the immediate political activity surrounding the enactment of the bill, as well as subsequent impotence on the part of the commission, that a thrust into the private sector is highly unlikely, at least with any immediacy.

The final agreement on the act between the House and Senate deleted two Senate provisions governing the collection of records by business. The first would have permitted citizens to remove their name and address from a business' mailing list. The second would have prevented a business from discriminating against people for refusal to disclose their Social Security numbers.

Although a great deal of legal and historical precedent has been provided to enable the provision of this act to be brought to bear in the private sector, the political process, as well as expressed deletions from the act itself, and the weakening of the primary vehicle for implementation outside of government, i.e., the Privacy Commission, has served to blunt considerably the act's possible impact on the private sector.

The Freedom of Information Act

The Freedom of Information Act is the base legislation for the Privacy Act. In fact, the Freedom of Information Act is Section 552 of Title V of the United States Code and the Privacy Act is Section 552 a. of the same title. The Freedom of Information Act was signed into law on July 4, 1966, to become effective on July 4, 1967. The act is an amendment to Section 3 of the Administrative Procedures Act, which first attempted to legislatively address the "right to know" of the public.

There were problems with Section 3, however. The wording of the section allowed withholding of information if, in the judgment of the agency concerned, the information was such "requiring secrecy in the public interest," or "required for good cause to be held confidential." In addition, Section 3 allowed for no appeal or judicial review of the agency's decision. Section 3 was being used to *increase* secrecy instead of opening up the records of government. The problem was that Section 3 was written in broad terms and attempted to provide a guideline for release of information to the public. The text of section 3 is short and is produced here in its entirety.

"SECTION 3 Except to the extent that there is involved (1) any function of the United States requiring secrecy in the public interest, or (2) any matter relating solely to the internal management of an agency—

"(a) RULES—Every agency shall separately state and currently publish in the Federal Register (1) a description of its central and field organization including delegations by the agency of final authority and the established places at which, and methods whereby, the public may secure information or make submittals or requests; (2) statements of the general course and method by which its functions are channeled and determined, including the nature and requirements of all formal or informal procedures available, as well as forms and instructions as to the scope and contents of all papers, reports, or examinations; and (3) substantive rules adopted as authorized by law, and statements of general policy or interpretations formulated and adopted by the agency for the guidance of the public, but not rules addressed to and served upon named persons in accordance with law. No person will in any manner be required to resort to organization or procedure not so published.

"(b) OPINIONS AND ORDERS—Every agency shall publish or, in accordance with published rule, make available to public inspection all final opinions or orders in the adjudication of cases (except those required for good cause to be held confidential and not cited as precedents) and all rules.

"(c) PUBLIC RECORDS—Save as otherwise required by statute, matters of official record shall in accordance with published rule be made available to persons properly and directly concerned, except information held confidential for good cause found."[7]

There were many abuses of Section 3. The ambiguity of the two general exemptions "secrecy in the public interest," or "matter relating solely to the internal management of an agency," allowed for wide interpretation. Some of the information kept secret under these exemptions were telephone books, the names and salaries of government employees, and the amount of the bids for bidders who were not awarded government contracts.

If all else failed, there was the catchall exemption of Subsection C stating that the information could be withheld "for good cause." This was just too much to beat. Rather than opening government records, Section 3 was cited as reason to *withhold* information. A direct turnaround from the intent of the law! The Freedom of Information Act attempted to remedy this by the use of very specific language and by specifying exemptions to the act.

The Freedom of Information Act breaks down into several subsections. The first subsection restates Section 3(a) pertaining to publishing in the *Federal Register.* This was not a problem under the original Section 3, except for complaints about the volume of information required to be published. The act allowed information to be published by reference, if the source data was ". . . reasonably available to the class of persons affected thereby."

The act also changed the sanction for not publishing from ". . . no person shall in any manner be required to resort to organization or procedures not so published," to "Except to the extent that a person has actual and timely notice of the terms thereof, a person may not in any manner be required to resort to, or be adversely affected by, a matter required to be published in the *Federal Register* and not so published," for it is possible for a person to be "adversely affected" without having to "resort to" the agency.[8] This implies that the agency cannot use the lack of publication as a defense against someone favorably affected by unpublished material, another incentive for publication.

The next subsection of the act stipulates that the information must be made available for "public inspection and copying," for in most cases, unless the data can be copied for future reference, its value is severely diminished. This subsection states certain classifications of information which must be made available:

(a) final opinions, including concurring and dissenting opinions, as well as orders, made in the adjudication of cases;

(b) those statements of policy and interpretations which have been adopted by the agency and are not published in the *Federal Register;* and,

(c) administrative staff manuals and instructions to staff that affect a member of the public.

It does allow an agency to delete identifying details from the information ". . . to the extent required to prevent a clearly unwarranted invasion of personal privacy." Although the Freedom of Information Act is specific in other areas, this area was left largely undefined until the passage of the Privacy Act.

This subsection also requires that agencies index information ". . . as to any matter issued, adopted, or promulgated after July 4, 1967." This index requirement meant that agencies could not withhold information simply by preventing anyone from having knowledge of its existence, and thus being unable to ask for it.

Subsection 3 establishes judicial review of agency decisions to withhold information under the Freedom of Information Act and places the burden of proof on the agency to prove that the information should not be realized. It also specifies that the case should be considered *de novo,* i.e., from the beginning, with no reference to past cases. This section also enlarged on the old Section

3(c) by specifying that the material must be made available to "any person" and not just to "persons properly and directly concerned."

The fourth subsection requires that agencies composed of more than one member shall keep a record, and make it available to the public, ". . . of the final votes of each member in every agency proceeding."

Exemptions

There are nine exemptions provided in the law for withholding data.[9] It is important to note that the wording of the Freedom of Information Act permits, rather than requires, withholding data within these categories.

—Exemption 1 pertains to matters ". . . specifically required by Executive Order to be kept secret in the interest of the national defense or foreign policy." There is a conflicting interpretation here, however. If it is interpreted that only material relating to the national defense or foreign policy and covered by Executive Order to be kept secret can be withheld, then there are some documents covered by Executive Order to be kept secret which must be released under this law. This could be construed as an attempt to limit the powers of the President and violating the constitutional provision of separation of powers. If it is intended to exempt all Executive Orders, then the agencies could cite some vaguely worded executive order as authority to withhold information. Since the courts have shown great reluctance to enter into disputes between the executive and legislative branches, they will probably allow the agencies great latitude in this area.

—Exemption 2 concerns matters ". . . related solely to the internal personnel rules and practices of an agency." Basically this refers to information intended to guide agency personnel which, if disclosed, would impede the function of the agency.

—Exemption 3 is for matters ". . . specifically exempted from disclosure by statute." This exemption is important, because the ability to obtain judicial review under the Freedom of Information Act allows a person to challenge situations where sovereign immunity was previously cited as a defense. The Freedom of Information Act also shifts the burden of proof to the agency claiming exemption by statute.

—Exemption 4 involves ". . . trade secrets and commercial or financial information obtained from a person and privileged or confidential." The problem here comes from the logical connectives *and* and *or.* Must the trade-secrets-plus-the-commercial-or-financial-information both be privileged or confidential, or all trade-secrets-plus-commercial-or-financial-information that is privileged or confidential, or all trade-secrets-plus-all-commercial-

or-financial-information-plus-any-other-information that is privileged or confidential? So far, there is no clearcut case law defining this section, although the Attorney General has opted for the last interpretation.

—Exemption 5 is for ". . . interagency or intraagency memoranda or letters which would not be available by law to a party other than an agency in litigation with the agency." This exemption was included so that agencies could have a free flow of information and exchange of views without being subject to scrutiny during the decisionmaking process. It is only after a policy or decision is made that it (the policy or decision) must be made public. There are some problems with interpretation of this exemption. Items like legal memoranda, staff analysis prepared for internal use, and recommendations of experts or consultants are clearly covered, but what about a purely factual report with no opinions expressed? The latter would probably not be protected. One interesting sidelight is the problem of interagency involving Congress. If Congress is not considered an agency (and it is expressly excluded from the definition of an agency by the Administrative Procedures Act), then transmittals between Congress and an agency of government would not be protected by the act. It is doubtful that Congress meant to exclude itself from protection under this exemption.

—Exemption 6 concerns personal privacy, specifically ". . . personnel and medical files and similar files, the disclosure of which would constitute a clearly unwarranted invasion of personal privacy." This exemption is self-explanatory. It was intended to prevent personal information, which a person was required by law to provide, from being available to anyone. It was not intended, and has not been interpreted, to prevent someone from seeing his own personnel or medical files.

—Exemption 7 concerns ". . . investigatory files compiled for law enforcement purposes, except to the extent available by law to a party other than an agency." The intent of this exemption was to prevent any earlier or greater access to government investigatory files than would have been previously available. This exemption includes investigations leading to administrative action, as well as to criminal action.

—Exemption 8 concerns matters that are ". . . contained in or related to examination, operating, or condition reports prepared by, on behalf of, or for the use of an agency responsible for the regulation or supervision of financial institutions." This is somewhat a restatement of Exemption 4, since that exemption protects "commercial or financial information" from disclosure. The restatement was primarily to emphasize the importance Congress placed on protecting this type of data from disclosure. This has had its major effect on the Federal Home Loan Bank Board, the Comptroller of the Currency, and the Federal Reserve System.

—Exemption 9 covers ". . . geological and geophysical information and data, including maps, concerning wells." This exemption also is somewhat superfluous, since the information could be considered covered under the "trade secrets" and "commercial or financial" language of Exemption 4.

The Effect of the Act on the NLRB

The National Labor Relations Board must certainly be included among those organizations upon which the Freedom of Information Act has had a profound effect. The board's involvement with the administration of the National Labor Relations Act has caused it to be concerned with many of the issues addressed by the Freedom of Information Act. Basically, the board's concern is with the use of the act for purposes of discovery when litigation is, or may be involved. The board can invoke the act for discovery of information known to private employers, and at the same time these private employers can---and do---invoke the act to discover information known to the board. At any given time, there are anywhere from twenty to forty cases in District Courts involving the board, in which the Freedom of Information Act is invoked. Thus, much time and money (an estimated $500,000 in 1975) is spent by the board to assure its compliance with the act.

Yet more important than the monetary investment necessary for compliance, are the psychological implications of the act's interpretation on the parties involved. For instance, if individuals' names are to be disclosed as part of the pretrial publicity, what are the implications of this policy on the willingness of these individuals to testify? Is the opportunity for intimidation of witnesses not enhanced by such disclosure? I think it a reasonable expectation that testimony will be affected by such a policy. Most personnel managers will assert that, since the mandatory disclosure to employees of the content of personal and work reference checks by prospective employers, an increasing number of sources have either (1) refused to give any reference, positive or negative, or (2) taken to giving all very positive references.

We can expect the same two reactions from those individuals asked to testify before the NLRB, should mandatory early disclosure of witnesses' names become the norm. I hope that this will not happen is based on the rulings in *Title Guarantee v. NLRB*[10] and *Goodfriend Western Corporation v. Fuchs*,

---

[10](CA–2, 1976) 78 LC ¶ 11,363.

et al.,[11] in which it was held that affidavits obtained by the board in connection with an unfair labor practice proceeding were protected from disclosure under Exemption 7(A).

Another major concern of the board is the tendency of certain parties at NLRB proceedings to view the act as a vehicle for obtaining information that is not otherwise available. In the already famous case of *NLRB v. Sears Roebuck and Company*,[12] the Court ruled exempt from discovery documents not otherwise available in such proceedings, i.e., under Section 5, ". . . inter-agency or intra-agency memorandums or letters which would be available by law to a party other than the agency in litigation with the agency."

Also under the Sears ruling, the board was required to provide memorandums in cases where the ultimate decision was to not issue an unfair labor practice complaint, but was not required under the act to provide similar information where the decision was to issue such a complaint. This holds even though Sears contended that their status as a charged party gave them an interest greater than an average member of the public. This ruling will hopefully remove some of the problem of intimidation of witnesses, since mandatory early disclosure will not occur in cases where it is known that a complaint will be, or has been, issued.

The Act has also necessitated administrative changes at the board. For example, responsibility for answering information requests under the act has been decentralized to the regional offices, to comply with the ten-day response time limit as called for in the February 1, 1975, amendment to the act. A set of guidelines has since been issued to the regional offices, instructing them in procedures for responding to requests made of the board under the act.

It can be seen then, that the Freedom of Information Act has had an impact on the National Labor Relations Board in a number of ways. The General Counsel of the NLRB has said that, for the board to use the act to better enforce the NLRA, the coming years must ". . . produce a final resolution of the question of whether some form of discovery should be permitted in board proceedings. To answer this question, consideration must be given to the feasibility of meeting four conditions which are essential prerequisites of establishing a workable system of pretrial disclosure."[13] The four conditions are:

(1) "disclosure must speed, rather than delay board proceedings,

---

[11](CA-1, 1976) 78 ¶ 11,409.
[12]421. US 132 (US 1975) 76 LC ¶ 10,803.
[13]John S. Irving, General Counsel, NLRB, speech at the 29th annual New York University Conference on Labor Law in New York City, entitled "The Right to Privacy and Freedom of Information: the NLRB and Issues Under the Privacy Act and the Freedom of Information Act."

(2) disclosure must result in more actual settlements,

(3) such disclosure must insure against the intimidation of witnesses, and

(4) such disclosure must be available to the General Counsel, as well as private parties."[14]

I could not agree more.

Conclusion

The Freedom of Information Act is a substantial improvement over the old section 3, but there are still problems. The approach of making all information presumptively available is laudable. To withhold information, the agency concerned must show that the information falls under one of the exemptions. But the exemptions can cover too many situations. Exemption 4 is especially vague and lends itself to many interpretations. Until a body of case law is developed, the exact meaning and coverage of the act will remain unclear.

This fact, coupled with the still-emerging interpretation of the Privacy Act, means that those individuals in the public and private sectors concerned with the collection, use, and dissemination of information and/or records will continue to be forced to rely on their own best judgment as to what is acceptable and what is not. I find this an unacceptable, and hopefully temporary, state of affairs.

---

[14]*Op Cit.*

Canada Moves Comparable Worth into the Private Sector

Pay equity has been an issue of considerable discussion in the United States for decades. This discussion has led to such legislative and judicial initiatives as the Equal Pay Act of 1963, the Bennett Amendment to Title VII of the 1964 Civil Rights Act, and the Gunther and State of Washington court cases. Comparable worth is the most current area of pay equity to be addressed, yet major concerns have been expressed over the practicality of implementing this concept. The validity of such concerns is now being tested in the province of Ontario, Canada. For the first time in this hemisphere, an aggressive comparable worth law has been enacted that is applicable to both the public and private sectors. All Ontario employers are now attempting to achieve compliance. To say that proponents and opponents of comparable worth are watching the unfolding drama with intense interest would be a drastic understatement. The implications of the success or failure of this pioneering legislation are self-evident and enormous. Practical support for the validity of proponent or opponent arguments will emerge, and such support may well prove crucial in determining the future course of comparable worth in the U.S. and elsewhere.

Overview

Simple economic justice dictates that wages in the workplace should be the same for both men and women. Legislation in pursuit of this idea was first content to strive for equal pay for equal, or substantially similar, work as it took form in the United States. In recent years, however, strong advocates have urged that wage equity between the sexes should not be confined just to similar jobs performed by both, but expanded to include jobs that are dissimilar but of comparable value. This extension of the pay equity concept has gathered a considerable following over the last 15 years in this country, and become widely identified as the theory of *comparable worth.*

An imposing literature has evolved over the years addressing the subject of comparable worth/pay equity from diverse perspectives. Although there have been applications of comparable worth theory through legislation in the United States, these have been confined to state and local jurisdictions and applicable to only the government-public-sector workplaces. There have been no instances where a political jurisdiction has imposed the application of comparable worth policies on its private-sector employers. Canada had likewise exhibited the same reluctance to move comparable worth dictates into the private sector, until the Province of Ontario stunned many observers by breaking ranks this year.

This article will explore the implications of this Canadian initiative by first sketching the evolution and application of comparable worth policy in the United States. The pioneering Canadian law will then be carefully examined from its origins in a broader setting, to its final configuration and requirements. In conclusion, I will explore the broader implications of this type of legislation and offer some observations on its applicability in the current U.S. setting.

I. Comparable Worth Policy: The United States Perspective

The importance society is attaching to pay equity and to gender corresponds with the emergence of women in the labor force. The rise of the feminist movement and the increasing percentage of working women have been the two major factors driving the concern for wage comparability. Demographic changes reflected in the modern American workforce in particular, are instructive.

A. Demographic Underpinnings

The stereotypical family unit of a generation ago, with the male breadwinner, the female housewife and one or more children, applies to only 15% of U.S. families today.[1] While the vast majority of unmarried women have traditionally worked outside the home, today in the U.S. nearly 50% of married women with children under two-years-old are working, with 62% of all mothers working outside the home. These figures have doubled since 1973, and there is every indication that the trend will continue. It is projected that by 1995, over 80% of all mothers with children at home will be employed outside the home.[2]

Part of this increase comes from women seeking self-fulfillment through careers—the feminist influence mentioned earlier. The rest is the result of economic necessity. From 1960 to 1973, family income increased every year, but the level achieved in 1973 has not been matched since, despite the rapid increase in dual-income families resulting from women entering the labor force.[3] One reason for this can be found by looking at sex-segregated labor markets that confine women to a limited number of low-paying jobs. For example, according to the last U.S. Census, women constitute 44% of all workers but fill 81% of clerical, 97% of private household and 61% of other service occupations.[4] Other reasons include the average number of years of professional preparation (male = 4.2, female = 0.4) and average years of job seniority (male = 12.6, female = 2.4), both of which depress the wages of women and confine them to lower-paying jobs.

The earnings from jobs such as these, which are typically filled by an increasing percentage of married women, are not enough to offset the decrease in their husband's real wages caused by inflation and the technologically forced shift from manufacturing jobs to lower paying service jobs. Thus, the decrease in real family income.

Proponents of comparable worth argue that one of the reasons these and other jobs like elementary- and high-school teacher, nurse, librarian, etc., are paid at their present low level, is because most of the positions are held by women. The same proponents contend that a fairly applied standard of comparable worth would raise the wages associated with these jobs and drastically alter many of the demographic patterns evident in today's workplace.

B. Legislative History

Congress first addressed the problem of gender pay equity through an amendment to the 1938 Fair Labor Standards Act (FLSA). In 1962 a bill was introduced to amend FLSA requiring equal pay for "comparable work." First the House and subsequently the Senate, voted to narrow the concept to "equal work." This resulted in the passage of the Equal Pay Act (EPA) of 1963. Its provisions applied to those workers performing closely related jobs, not different jobs, even though they demanded the same degree of skill, effort and responsibility, and had the same working conditions. Exceptions were recognized to allow for merit and seniority systems, along with the quality of the work product.

The following year Congress passed the Civil Rights Act. Under the language of Title VII, discrimination in employment decisions based on sex was outlawed. When concerns were raised about potential conflicts between the sex discrimination provisions of Title VII and the wage equality guarantees of the Equal Pay Act, Senator Wallace Bennett advanced an amendment designed to eliminate the perceived problem. Ultimately enacted, this amendment stated that an employer may differentiate on the basis of sex in determining pay under Title VII, if the differentiation is authorized by a fair reading of the Equal Pay Act of 1963. By limiting gender-based wage discrimination under Title VII to EPA standards (equal work, not comparable), the Bennett Amendment seemed to eliminate the statutory authority necessary to advance wage discrimination claims based on the theory of comparable worth.[5]

This question was later settled by the U.S. Supreme Court holding in *Gunther v. County of Washington*,[6] which ruled that claims of sex discrimination in compensation under Title VII were not necessarily limited to equal work situations. A claim of discriminatory pay, the High Court instructed, is not barred under Title VII, simply because the type of work associated with the jobs being compared is not identical.

Judicial sentiment for comparable worth as a viable legal doctrine was further tested in the celebrated case of *AFSCME v. State of Washington*.[7]

Responding to a comparable-worth pay-discrimination complaint, the State of Washington ordered a study to identify female-dominated job classifications that had salaries falling below male-dominated classifications of comparable skill and responsibility. This study, the first of its kind in the United States, found numerous such classifications. Breaking new ground, the District Court recognized the plaintiff's comparable-worth arguments and ruled in their favor. This decision was subsequently reversed by the Ninth Circuit Court of Appeals. A settlement between the parties prevented an opportunity for Supreme Court review, but this widely followed litigation symbolized the substantial moral sentiment, public opinion and pressure-group interest in promoting the comparable-worth approach to pay equity.[8]

In 1984 Congress enacted the Pay Equity and Management Act, reflecting the federal government's interest in the comparable-worth theory applied to the government workforce. The law requires that outside experts conduct a study of pay and job classifications of federal employees to determine if gender-based wage discrimination is present. In 1987 the U.S. Federal Employee Compensation Equity Study Commission Act appeared, which also examined and attempted to promote equitable-pay practices within the federal workforce. In search of ever-greater levels of sophistication, the Congress recently enacted the Federal Equitable Pay Practices Act of 1988, which has directed a study to determine the extent wages are affected by gender alone across the board, and the role this may play in the formation of wage differentials between male- and female-dominated occupations.

This flurry of federal activity has been matched by numerous state government actions as well. A recent survey indicated that some 31 states were formally examining their workforces for gender-based pay equity. Twenty states had specifically enacted legislation or adopted policies aggressively implementing comparable-worth standards in the state and civil service. Ten states simply enacted a legal prohibition against unequal compensation rates for comparable jobs within their civil service ranks.[9]

Alongside the federal and state government activity must be placed that of the thousands of local government units throughout the country. Despite a lack of data as to the precise extent, it is clear that comparable-worth pay policies are deeply penetrating the personnel systems of cities, counties and school districts around the nation today.[10] The comparable-worth approach to combat gender-based wage discrimination is clearly gaining acceptance in the public sector.

Despite considerable public-sector acceptance and experience to date, the merits of comparable worth as a matter of broad public policy remain highly controversial in the United States. While proponents argue for the concept based on its inherit fairness, its moral underpinnings, and its impact on wage-based discrimination against women, opponents cite its lack of consideration of market forces, its impact on labor supply and demand, and the seemingly impossible task of consistent, objective, and fair enforcement. These opponents contend that market forces such as inflation rates dictating higher real wage rates for those most recently hired in a particular job, the hazardous or unpleasant nature of certain tasks within a job or group of jobs, geographic location, location-specific inflation rates, and the level of competition for labor within a particular area, all make implementation of comparable worth on a wide scale impractical.

Opponents further argue that even if implementation could surmount these problems, it would cause major labor-force movements that have no relation to supply and demand of labor. How then are employers to entice applicants to those jobs not favored in a comparable-worth system? By paying more, and thus upsetting the balance again? Finally, who is to administer and enforce such a system on a nationwide scale? Few in the private sector doubt what the answer will be, but even fewer look forward to government intervention to the degree seemingly required.

Although those opposed fiercely disagree, the proponents of a comparable-worth approach to pay equity contend that it is equally as necessary and appropriate in the private sector, as it is in the public sector. For this and many other reasons, the recently enacted Ontario private-sector comparable-worth law will be followed closely by opponents and advocates of greater pay equity. Its implications for eventually moving an aggressive comparable-worth policy into the private sector in the United States need to be carefully examined.

II. The Canadian Comparable-Worth Initiative

Canadian public policy concerning gender-based wage discrimination has undergone the same evolution as that experienced in the United States. Initially requiring comparisons between substantially similar jobs, the working definition of "equal pay" is gradually being expanded to jobs which may be dissimilar, but of comparable value. Unlike the United States, Canadian pay-equity legislation has not been confined just to the public sector.

A. Equal-Pay Laws: Legislative Background

Equal-pay legislation in Canada first began to appear in the provinces and territories some four decades ago. Following the lead of Ontario in 1951,[11] legislation subsequently enacted in all provincial jurisdictions generally mandates that women be paid the same as men for equal or "substantially similar" work.[12]

At the national level, the principle of equal pay is addressed in careful detail in the Canadian Human Rights Act. Enacted in the mid–70's, evidence of the Canadian evolution toward a comparable-worth view of pay equity appears in the language of this statute. Under the title of "Equal Wages," the legislation clearly states that wage differentials between male and female employees are illegally discriminatory if both are performing "work of equal value". This law and the provincial pay-equity laws throughout Canada are enforced by the Canadian Human Rights Commission, provincial departments of labor, or human rights agencies, separately or in combination.

Despite long-standing pay-equity provisions such as these in Canadian law, survey data in the 1980's suggested that a substantial wage gap between men and women persisted. For example, female average earnings by occupation, as a percentage of male average earnings, was 59.4 percent, a full seven years after the Human Rights Act was passed, with a range across occupations of 46 to 68 percent.[13] Even comparisons between the same occupations within the same firm reflected wage disparities between 10 to 20 percent.[14] Reasons advanced to explain the lack of sufficient progress under existing pay-equity law included the prevailing narrow interpretation of the laws, and the extent of their enforcement. Despite the support for a comparable-worth approach to attaining pay equity on the part of a growing number of lawmakers and public-policy advocates, existing laws were interpreted as only applying to the same or similar jobs within the same firm. Enforcement was found to be lacking, because most laws were passive or essentially reactive in posture—merely declaring a general prohibition against gender-based wage discrimination. Cited also were impediments to meaningful litigation in the courts, such as the unavailability of class actions and a specific intent burden-of-proof associated with enforcing some of the prevailing statutes.[15] It is largely the disappointing results experienced under the old regime that are fueling support for a new generation of aggressive, proactive pay-equity legislation utilizing comparable-worth standards in Canada today.

B. The Ontario Experiment: Proactive Comparable-Worth Pay Equity

Before its daring new comparable-worth law took effect, Ontario's long-standing pay-equity statute carried the title "Equal Pay for Equal Work" and predictably set up a standard prohibition against gender-based wage discrimination between ". . . substantially the same kind of work in the same establishment, the performance of which requires substantially the same skill, effort, and responsibility and which is performed under similar working conditions. . ."[16] Impatient with the marginal results this traditional approach had produced over the years, the government began work on pay-equity legislative reform in the Fall of 1985.

Drawing on legislative ideas already emerging in Manitoba, Ontario first proceeded on the notion that two separate statues would be necessary—one for the public sector, and the other for the private sector. Through a lengthy two-year process that enlisted the participation of the province's citizenry and organized interest groups, the legislative provisions applicable to both sectors were ultimately combined into a single law.

Secure in its determination and expertise at writing legislation for its own employees, the provincial government concentrated on an approach best suited to private-sector regulation. To stimulate public discussion on the proposition of extending an aggressive comparable-worth law to cover the provinces' private economy, the Ontario government issued a document entitled "Green Paper on Pay Equity."[17] A panel of distinguished citizens was then appointed to conduct public hearings on the proposition all across the province, gathering ideas and gauging public sentiment. At the same time, one advisory group from business and another from organized labor were appointed to advise the Premier and senior government officials regularly as the legislation was developed.

The result was the ultimate enactment of the Pay Equity Act of 1987 by the Ontario Legislative Assembly in June of that year, with its provisions enforced as of January 1, 1988. This precedent-setting law defines male and female job classes, establishes the criteria by which they are to be valued, mandates equality of pay between classes of comparable worth in both the public and private sectors, and creates two permanent government agencies to insure its enforcement. A close look at each of the law's five major parts is instructive.

(1) Part I: Definitions and Purpose

The act's singular purpose is ". . . to redress systematic gender discrimination in compensation for work performed by employees in female jobs" (Sec. 4(1)). Discrimination in this form is identified by comparing each male and female job class in an organization in terms of compensation for the work performed and its value. Female job classes are defined as those comprising 60-percent-or-more female members, while male job classes are considered to be those with 70-percent-or-more male members (Sec. 1(1)).

The formulation employed to place a value on each designated job class specifies the criterion to be applied. The criterion is described as ". . . a composite of the skill, effort and responsibility normally required in the performance of the work and the conditions under which it is normally performed" (Sec. 5(1)). Nowhere in the law is it specified how the skill, effort and responsibility are to be evaluated. Thus far, most firms are using the point system of job evaluation to assess the level of each factor.

Once job-class valuation has been completed and if the employer's workforce contains a trade union, only job classes contained within the bargaining unit may be compared. The same rule holds for comparisons of job classes established within that segment of the workforce falling outside a bargaining unit (Sec. 6 (4)).

The act specifically prohibits employers from reducing the compensation of any employee or position in order to meet the new pay-equity requirements (Sec. 9(1)).

(2) Part II: Implementation by Public-Sector and Large Private-Sector Employers

Where wage discrepancies appear, employers are required to prepare and post pay-equity plans in the workplace. The employer with a segment of employees within a bargaining unit and the remainder without, must prepare a separate plan for each (Sec. 14(1)). Employees not part of a bargaining unit have 90 days from posting to suggest changes in the employers' proposed plan. Whether these are incorporated or not, is left to the discretion of the employer (Sec. 15(4)(5)).

The pay-equity plan and wage adjustment posting deadlines under the new law are summarized in the table below.

Table 1
Pay-Equity Plan Requirements[18]

No. of Employees	Mandatory Posting	Wage Adjustment
Public Sector	January 1, 1990	January 1, 1990
Private Sector		
500 or more	January 1, 1990	January 1, 1991
100–499	January 1, 1991	January 1, 1992
50–99*	January 1, 1992	January 1, 1993
10–49*	January 1, 1993	January 1, 1994

*(Employers with 10 to 99 percent *may elect* to post a pay-equity plan.)

If an employer and the employees cannot agree on a plan, the Pay Equity Commission is to be notified (Sec. 15(7)). A review officer is then assigned to investigate and affect a settlement. Failing a settlement, the review officer is empowered to decide on a plan and order it placed into effect. Objection to the review officer's disposition may be filed from either party with the Commission within 30 days, in which case a "Hearings Tribunal" (discussed below) shall make a final resolution of the matter (Secs. 16, 17).

(3) Part III: Implementation by Small Private-Sector Employers

Formal pay-equity plans for employers of more than nine, but less than 100 employees, are optional (Sec. 19). Should the employer choose to establish a plan, however, it would then be subjected to the same posting, amending and formal objection requirements for mandatory plans (Sec. 20).

(4) Part IV: Enforcement

The creation of a formal Hearings Tribunal and a discussion of its powers are found in this section. Among the powers allocated to the Hearings Tribunal is the authority, when necessary, to order a review officer to prepare a pay-equity plan for an establishment (at the employer's and the bargaining agent's expense), to order reinstatement of an employee to his or her job and previous pay level, to order back pay and wage adjustments, and to order revisions in an employer's pay-equity plan (Sec. 25 (2)). Failure to comply with any provision of the act or any order issued by the Hearings Tribunal can result in fines of up to $2,000 in the case of individuals, and up to $25,000 in the case of firms or bargaining units.

(5) Part V: Administration

This section describes the various institutional arrangements referred to briefly in the preceding parts of the statute. For example, the creation and establishment of a "Pay Equity Commission of Ontario" is called for first. This agency is to consist of two subagencies, the "Pay Equity Hearings Tribunal" mentioned above and the "Pay Equity Office" (Sec. 27 (1)(2)).

The Hearings Tribunal is similar in concept to the Industrial Tribunals introduced into British industrial relations in the mid-1960's. A Pay Equity Hearings Tribunal is comprised of a presiding officer and deputy officer, and includes representatives from employers and employees in equal numbers (Sec. 28 (1)).

The Pay Equity Office is conceived as a permanent provincial agency responsible for the ongoing enforcement of the provisions of the act and the orders of the Hearings Tribunal (Sec. 33(1)).

Finally, the pay-equity review officer, as the foot-soldier of the statute's implementation and enforcement programs, is granted unsettling powers by current United States' standards. In pursuit of investigatory authority, the review officer is empowered to enter any premises at any time, request the production of relevant documents, remove those documents for purposes of making copies, and to interrogate persons (subject to their right to have counsel or another present) (Sec. 34(3)).

C. Employer Experience To Date

Since, as previously shown in Table 1, the first group to comply does not have to take any posting- or wage-adjustment actions until January 1, 1990, the best one can do presently is look at "early returns" from those companies preparing to meet the law's requirements.

The two large employers who are farther along the road to compliance than any others are Warner-Lambert, the Canadian arm of the Morris Plains, NJ, pharmaceutical company and T. Eaton Company, the Toronto-based retailer. At Warner-Lambert an eight-factor point system was used to determine comparable jobs. The plan was posted for employees to see in May and no negative feedback was reported. Donald Henley, Director of Employee Relations, attributes the ease with which the plan has advanced, to the lack of labor organizations within the company. The company is pleasantly surprised at the amount of positive employee feedback from those whose jobs were not directly affected.

T. Eaton Company has 15,000 employees in 580 jobs in Ontario, and in the past had used a different evaluation system at each of three organization levels. To comply with the new legislation, the company went to a computer-scored version of the Weighted Job Questionnaire, modified specifically for T. Eaton. According to William F. Robinson, Compensation Manager, completion of this task has required four full-time employees and the results will cost the company "quite a few million dollars annually" in equity adjustments. On the other hand, he notes benefits of increased internal communication, including a monthly bulletin devoted solely to company actions relative to the new law, and an awareness of compensation inequities that had gone undetected in the past.

In at least one heavily unionized sector, all major employers have come together in an attempt to achieve compliance. In the retail food industry where all employers deal with the United Food and Commercial Workers' Union, the industry has bargained as one with the union in an attempt to arrive at one overall plan. Here again the point system is being used but major problems have arisen over points assigned within each job factor for particular jobs. If this one situation is any indication of what lies ahead, large unionized firms or industries are going to have severe problems posting plans by the required January 1, 1990 date.

Wyatt Company, a Toronto-based consulting company is presently working with over fifty firms on compliance under the new law. Sizes range from 200 to 20,000 employees and include many U.S. subsidiaries. According to Marc Lattoni, compensation consultant for Wyatt, while most of the larger employers have now formulated their plan, the majority will not post until the absolute deadline of January 1, 1990, for fear of being singled out. Collective wisdom seems to be that, if your plan is posted at the same time as most others, less attention will be paid to yours, by either the general public or the Pay Equity Commission.

The major problem Wyatt clients are encountering is similar to that in the food industry—reaching agreement with bargaining agents over details of the plan. Those clients of Wyatt who are still struggling with formulation of their plan are those who have labor forces represented by automobile, steel and hotel workers' unions. To date the Pay Equity Commission has received over 80 formal complaints from unions under the Pay Equity Act, according to Nanette Weiner, the Commission Research Manager. Some employers are seriously considering letting the deadline for posting pass without complying. The rationale here is obvious, when one considers that the maximum fine is $25,000, while the difference between the plans proposed by the employer and the union is often several hundred thousand dollars. The lesson here for the U.S. is that if such legislation is enacted in this country, economic sanctions may not be enough, and if they are all that is available, the size of the fine should be such that it serves as a deterrent to even the largest employers.

III. A Canadian Model For The American Workplace?

As the Ontario Pay Equity Pay Act phases into effect over the next four years (1990–1994), attempts will be undertaken to gauge its success. With accumulated experience, the statute's impact on the political, social and economic life of the province will become more clear. In turn, this outcome will bear heavily on the influence this legislation will exert on lawmakers in the United States. For the present, there are certain features of the legislation that should be particularly noted and monitored.

A. Perspectives on the Ontario Law

The salient feature of this law distinguishing it from all those preceeding it in both the United States and Canada, is its proactive imposition of comparable-worth wage scales on the private sector. Less obvious, but of equal importance is its focus on jobs, as opposed to individual employees. The valuations and comparisons called for by the statute pertain to job classes, not the workers themselves. Because the law represents a crusade against discriminatory wages paid to female-dominated job classes, it is only these jobs which can be affected. Therefore, the workers who stand to benefit are confined to those employed in female-dominated job classes found to be underpaid in comparison to a comparable male-dominated class within the same establishment.

It is an intriguing irony that the structure of this approach to pay equity inevitably boosts the male worker minority, as well as female workers in those female-dominated classes where wage adjustments will be required under the law. Disappointedly, the same structural limitations prevent the law from reaching those female employees who suffer from gender-based wage discrimination, but fall outside a female-dominated job class. Because of these design limitations the Ontario legislation, as presently written, can never be said to ensure fair compensation for all female employees, let alone employees of both genders.

Another obscure but important feature of the law pertains to the mechanics of valuating job classes. Beyond the statutory requirement to take the criteria of skill, effort, responsibility and working conditions into consideration, the precise type of job evaluation scheme is left to the employer's discretion. This represents an area with potential for ongoing conflict between the Pay Equity Commission and the provincial employers it must regulate. Its' implementation could be extremely thorny and will bear watching.

Of far-reaching consequence is the statutory role envisioned for labor unions. In essence, implementation of the act for union members is largely a subject and function of collective bargaining. Presumably this allows critical aspects of how the law is to be applied to this segment of the workforce, to be negotiated between unions and employers. Permitting such key determinations, e.g., as what constitutes a single "establishment" or "gender dominance," to be made through negotiation seems to put the employee who is a union member on a footing different from that of a nonunion counterpart. In many respects, this feature of the new law would appear to benefit the unionized employee, by virtue of the leverage that collective bargaining affords. One can argue that organized labor lobbying may have come into play here. Were glaring discrepancies in the statute's application to appear between the unionized and nonunionized employee, the creditability and full acceptance of the new law could be seriously impaired.

The final feature of this legislation which should not be overlooked pertains to the surprisingly broad categories of wage discrepancies that have been exempted. Until some experience is gained, it is difficult to estimate the size of the hole which the exemption of wage differentials based on seniority, merit, temporary training, and the like, will put in the overall legislative scheme. It is unlikely that employers will seek wholesale refuge in these exclusions, but the incentive to move in this direction is certainly present. Whether or not the exceptions ultimately overrun the rule, the swath they cut is certain to be wide.

B. Adaptability to the United States

The adaptability of the Ontario Pay Equity legislative scheme to federal or local jurisdictions in the United States seems highly unlikely for the foreseeable future. Opposition to comparable-worth policies remains vocal and well-organized among business organizations and others. Surely the aggressive scheme adopted by the Ontario statute would be more palatable, if confined to the public sector where comparable-worth measures are gaining some degree of acceptability. Private-sector mandates such as these however, would predictably encounter stiff opposition in this country.

Private-sector commercial interests opposed the Ontario legislation in its initial form. This caused the lawmakers to accommodate a number of the business communities' concerns in the design and language of the legislation. Fully cognizant that moving comparable-worth dictates into the private sector raised problems not necessarily comparable to those in the public sector, the matter was studied intently.[19] The statutory accommodations to business interests that were adopted are particularly instructive to American policy analysts, since comparable-worth critics in the United States cite essentially the same objections.

The Ontario framers contemplated the concern that employers may be unable to afford the required wage adjustments, and that higher wages would lead to higher consumer prices and reduce much of the competitive advantage enjoyed by provincial employers. The lawmakers' response was to phase in pay-equity requirements starting with those sectors most easily able to make the adjustment, i.e., the public sector and large private-sector employers, followed by private firms of decreasing size. It was felt that the smaller firms could benefit from more time to adjust and the experience of the larger firms going before. Also, private-sector employers were not placed under a calendar date deadline for full compliance, as long as a minimum of 1 per cent of the previous year's payroll was devoted to wage adjustments annually.

To offset concerns that the law would intervene in labor markets to the extent it standardized wages across the entire province, the law limited wage comparisons geographically to single establishments, even though geographically dispersed establishments may share the same ownership. Wage comparisons were also limited to prohibit the matching of union with nonunion jobs, or the matching of job classes between different unions whenever possible. Wage control and standardization was further relaxed by allowing pay-equity plans and their implementation for unionized employees to be worked out through collective bargaining. Also, the statutory exemptions for established practices, e.g., seniority preferences and merit pay, can be viewed as an attempt to preserve certain wage-setting prerogatives important to the private sector.

IV. Observations and Conclusions

A private-sector experiment with mandatory comparable-worth standards has now been instituted in the Canadian Province of Ontario. The neighboring province of Manitoba is preparing similar legislation. Drawn with elaborate care in an attempt to accommodate private-sector interests, the Ontario legislation still carries liabilities considered unacceptable by contemporary U.S. standards. These shortcomings can be briefly summarized:

1. The problems which have long plagued the comparable-worth theory of pay equity have not been overcome through this legislation. A meaningful and practical definition of "job worth" remains elusive, as does the basis for job-class comparison with the requisite precision. The problems of applying these amorphous concepts in the private sector will only magnify as employer, employee and bargaining agent pursue advantage, while provincial review officers and hearings tribunals attempt to mediate and enforce.

2. The scale of intervention into labor markets and managerial operating prerogatives would be considered unnecessarily heavy-handed from a U.S. perspective. Only less-instrusive means could hope for acceptability.

3. The benefits sought are unlikely to outweigh the costs. The direct and indirect costs associated with employer compliance, sustaining an administrative provincial bureaucracy, and market intervention would not generally be viewed as appropriate, to achieve only marginal rate adjustments in a relatively small subsegment of the labor force.

It is certain that this controversial legislative experiment undertaken by our neighbors to the North will be closely followed by both the advocates of comparable-worth pay equity standards, and its detractors. The prospects of similar laws emerging in the United States will inevitably hinge, to a certain extent, on the success or failure of the Ontario initiative presently underway. With a case study in process, perhaps the debate concerning the efficacy of comparable-worth policy in the private sector can be joined once again. To be sure, the Canadian laboratory is, at best, a rough approximation of conditions in the United States. Much can be extra polated from the Canadian effort, however, that will inform our debate in the future. All serious followers of comparable worth would be well-advised to become familiar with, and to follow the progress of, this new piece of legislation. It may well be the most important development to date on the subject of comparable worth.

Footnotes

[1]"Job Protection Guarantees for Workers" *Congressional Quarterly*, June 14, 1986, p. 1361, and Samuelson, Robert J., "Uncle Sam in a Family Way" *Newsweek*, August 11, 1986, p. 40.

[2]Giraldo, Z.I., *Public Policy and the Family: Wives and Mothers in the Labor Force*, (Lexington Books, D.C.: Heath and Company, 1980), p. 31.

[3]Mann, Judy, "Families Need These Bills" *Washington Post*, July 3, 1987, p. B3.

[4]Patten, Thomas J., *Fair Pay*, (San Francisco: Jossey-Bass, 1988), p. 31.

[5]Patten, *op. cit.*, p. 40–41.

[6]452 U.S. 161 (1981).

[7]578 F. Supp. 846 (W.D. Wash. 1983), 770 F.2d 1401 (9th Cir. 1985).

[8]Hunter, F.C., *Equal Pay for Comparable Work: The Working Women's Issue of the Eighties* (New York: Praeger, 1986) p. 108.

[9]Patten, *op. cit.*, pp. 74–81.

[10]Patten, *op. cit.*, pp. 97–102.

[11]*Ontario Female Employees' Fair Remuneration Act*, 1951.

[12]Abella, R.S., "Employment Equity", 16 *Manitoba Law Journal* 187 (1987), p. 42.

[13]Statistics Canada, Unpublished data from the *Survey of Consumer Finances*, 1983, cited in Abella, *op. cit.*, note 12, p. 186.

[14]Gunderson & Morley, "Work Patterns" in *Opportunity For Choice: A Goal For Women in Canada*, ed., A. Cook (Ottawa: Statistics Canada, 1988) p. 120.

[15]Abella, *op. cit.*, p. 189. See generally L. Nieman, *Wage Discrimination and Women Workers: The Move Toward Equal Pay for Equal Value in Canada*, Bureau Series A: Equity in the Workplace, No. 5 (Ottawa: Labour Canada, Women's Bureau, 1984).

[16]*Ontario Employment Standards Act*, 1981, Part IX.

[17]Ontario, *Green Paper on Pay Equity*, (Toronto: Queen's Printer, 1985) p. 68.

[18]*Pay Equity Commission*, Pay Equity Implementation, Series 3:1, March, 1988.

[19]Discussed by the Assistant Deputy Minister of the Ontario Women's Directorate, in E.M. Todres, "With Deliberate Care: The Framing of Bill 154" 16 *Manitoba Law Journal* 202 (1987).

Is It Time To Amend The Overtime Provisions Of The FLSA?

Abstract

The Fair Labor Standards Act (FLSA) was passed in 1938 to boost a sagging economy by limiting working hours and establishing a minimum wage. Advocates contend that, if administered properly, it can serve the same function today. Views as to how the act should be amended/administered so as to bring rhetoric closer to reality are considered.

The Fair Labor Standards Act was enacted in 1938, during a period of economic crisis, to regulate employers in interstate commerce by establishing a minimum hourly wage, a standard work week's maximum number of hours (40 hours), and the rate of premium pay to be paid for those hours worked in excess of the fair work week (time-and-one-half). There were both humanitarian and economic reasons for passage of FLSA. The minimum wage is designed to maintain the health, efficiency, and general wellbeing of workers and their families, while economically the FLSA is designed to maintain the purchasing power of the public, hence promoting the free flow of goods in interstate commerce. This purchasing power (from the minimum-waged employee's disposable income) does, in itself, contribute to sustaining a higher-level of employment. Additionally, unfair competitive practices, gained from management's usage of substandard wages and long hours, are eliminated, hence enhancing fair trade practices. The premium pay-rates for overtime are designed as a penalty, to encourage management to hire additional employees, rather than have present employees work overtime. (There is a breakeven point, where it becomes less costly to hire additional employees at straight time, than to pay overtime pay to present employees.) Thus, the overtime provisions of the FLSA are designed to reduce unemployment.

Is the FLSA, as it exists today, helping the economy? Unemployment rates, during the past several years, have been exceedingly high: 6.5% and 6.7% in 1982 and 1983, and 6.6% in early 1984, with nearly ten million people underemployed or unemployed as of April 1984.[1] To make matters worse, the rate of inflation has also been exceedingly high, and the duration of unemployment has increased from an average of 8.8 weeks in 1980, to an average of 15.3 weeks in 1985. Given the hidden cost of such figures (it is estimated to cost $18,000 per year in social programs and lost revenue for every unemployed person in the United States), I question whether FLSA in its present form is helping the economy. Surely the entire blame for these economic problems cannot be placed at the doorstep of FLSA. But there are changes, to be discussed later, that would allow FLSA to have a more positive impact on these economic problems.

Is the FLSA, as it exists today, discouraging overtime employment? While the overall average weekly hours of work has decreased over the past decade, there is a marked difference between the work week in sectors of the economy covered by FLSA and sectors not covered. For the economy as a whole, 20% of all employees worked more than 40 hours a week in 1985, while in the uncovered sectors of service-producing industries and salaried employees, the number averaging more than 40 hours per week was 26% and 27.4%, respectively. Additionally, as of April 1985, only 11% of the workforce was receiving overtime pay, and over 90% of these were specifically covered by FLSA. The vast majority of workers who are working overtime and are not covered by FLSA are, therefore, not receiving overtime pay. This means that FLSA may be discouraging overtime for those it covers, but since so many are exempt (service, white collar, salaried, etc.), its overall effect is minimal.

Obviously, the original intent of FLSA, to promote full employment by discouraging overtime and to help the economy by establishing a minimum wage, has not been met. While, as stated earlier, it is too much to expect FLSA to achieve these goals in and of itself, there are changes to FLSA that if made, would increase its positive impact in those areas. One such amendment could establish new levels for the number of hours in a standard work week and for the overtime rate-of-pay.

During the past 15 years, several such amendments to the FLSA have been proposed. The Overtime Penalty Pay Act of 1964 (H.R. 9802) would have set an overtime pay rate of double the regular hourly rate in specific industries. The 1974 amendments to the FLSA (H.R. 12435) eliminated employees of hotels, motels, and restaurants from the overtime exemption and substituted a limited overtime exemption (by reducing the standard hours in a work week), to be phased in gradually. The Fair Labor Standards Amendments of 1975 (H.R. 10130) attempted to establish an overtime rate of two-and-one-half-times the regular hourly rate. In March 1978, Congressman Conyers introduced the Shorter Work Week Bill (H.R. 11784), which by 1982 would have shortened the work week to thirty-five hours, would have established an overtime rate of twice the regular hourly rate, and would have required employee consent for overtime work. (Although H.R. 11784 was defeated, Congressman Conyers introduced another such bill.)

In addition to the government's attempts to amend the FLSA, private organizations have also been interested in the hours and overtime standards. Leonard Woodcock and the UAW raised the issue of the FSLA's ineffectiveness about 12 years ago and expressed a desire to have it changed. Additionally, the AFLCIO has long been interested in a shorter work week and a higher overtime rate, and many union contracts already have an overtime rate of two- or two-and-a-half times the regular rate of pay, dependent upon the total number of hours worked, and whether the overtime is on a holiday or not. In 1984, about one-fourth of workers covered by a union contract were protected with graduated overtime provisions, i.e., the regular overtime rate was to be increased after a given number of overtime hours.[2]

The major argument against such amendments has been that such changes in overtime standards (a reduction in the work week or increase in overtime penalty) would only add to employer costs, inefficiencies, lost productivity, and disincentives to increase production. Employment may rise, but total hours worked would fall. Employers could either pay increased costs (due to either higher overtime pay or extra fringe benefits and training costs of hiring new employees), could cut back on production, or increase prices to maintain profit levels. Additionally, any amendments which would result in increased costs would have an inequitable impact on different industries, since the reasons for requiring overtime vary; many make the erroneous assumption that it is usually because of ineffective management. Overtime can be required for equipment breakdown, employee absenteeism, seasonal fluctuations, unpredictable demand for goods or services, strong pressures from current employees who want to work overtime, a lack of availability of skilled workers, or a lack of availability of workers willing to accept jobs of an uncertain duration. Hospitals experience both seasonal and unforeseeable demands for their services; rather than over-staff and add to the already high cost of medical care, it is more economical to pay overtime rates and have their regular staff work overtime or be on standby. Construction workers cannot easily change shifts in the middle of pouring concrete; a service technician on a repair call, located fifty miles away, cannot easily change shifts with another technician. Small business, with only one machine and one operator, cannot hire an additional tenth of a person to do the 10% surplus work, whereas big business could hire an extra person to perform the surplus work that its numerous workers could not complete in regular time. Cities, operating on fixed budgets, will not hire additional people to avoid overtime costs, rather, they will reduce services instead.[3] Thus, these industries would be exposed to increased costs, due to overtime pay and would cut down on production or service. Ultimately, the economy will be the loser.

In my opinion, each of these arguments against amending FLSA is legitimate in and of itself, but additionally, each is unique to a particular subset of the entire economy. While these problems will have to be worked out, they are nevertheless individualistic and should not overshadow the favorable effects of FLSA amendments on the economy as a whole.

Also to be remembered is that factors additional to the overtime penalty rate are considered by employers, when deciding whether to hire additional employees or to pay overtime premium pay. One such factor is the cost of fringe benefits. In 1938 fringe benefits amounted to five percent of the cost of total compensation, as compared to thirty-five percent today. These benefit payments (vacations; holidays; sick leave; life, accident, and health insurances; and retirement funds) are not considered when computing overtime pay; only the regular hourly rate is considered. Since fringe benefits are related only to the number of employees, and not to the number of hours the employees work, fringe benefits are fixed costs, regardless of the hours worked. Thus, overtime work actually decreases the costs-per-unit produced. As the cost of these benefits increases, the employer is no longer faced with a question of overtime pay for present employees versus new employees at straight time, but must also consider the additional cost of fringe benefits to these new employees. This factor, plus the increasing cost of hiring (advertising, interviewing, etc.) and training, has pushed the point higher where new employees will be hired, in terms of overtime hours.

Another consideration is that certain employers could substitute more equipment for employees, rather than pay the extra costs of overtime, or hiring and training new employees. Ultimately, this could lead to increased productivity and lower unit costs, but the immediate result would probably be increased unemployment and lower wages for those who are employed.

Thus, there are various arguments for retaining the present overtime provisions of the FLSA. As should be expected, there are equally numerous reasons in favor of changing the overtime provisions. Given the magnitude of the economic problem indicated by the unemployment statistics (discussed previously), *some* solution should be pursued.

One of the original purposes of the FLSA was to ". . .maintain the minimum standard of living necessary for the health, efficiency, and general well-being of workers." This is not being done today. The poverty guideline established by the U.S. Department of Labor in 1984 is almost 5% higher than the annual income of someone earning minimum wages, and the "lower budget necessary for decent living standard" set by the Labor Department is almost 80% higher.

Assuming the present provisions are not working, as seen by the data presented on unemployment, overtime hours, and minimum wages, I see no reason *not* to amend FLSA. There are several possibilities the author would suggest for such amendment(s). The standard work week could be reduced to 35 hours either immediately, or phased in over the next five years! This would create more jobs, including more full-tine, long-lasting jobs and would also satisfy a growing desire for more leisure time expressed by more and more workers. Another option is to establish a flexible work week, with automatic adjustments in the hours to reflect changes in the economy. That is, a shorter work week when the unemployment rate is up, and a longer work week when the unemployment rate is down. The "sliding" work week standard would become effective the first day of the second full month, following the date when the new unemployment rate is officially announced. Although there would be administrative problems with this changing work week (bookkeeping, etc.), experience could make these problems manageable.

Another amendment I would consider beneficial would increase the overtime penalty to double-time (or higher than the present time-and-a-half). This premium pay could be on a "straight" scale, i.e., be applied to all hours worked above the basic work week, or it could be on a "graduated" scale, i.e., becoming a higher penalty as the number of overtime hours increased. By increasing the overtime rate, new jobs would be created, as it would become more economical for employers to hire additional workers, at the regular rate, rather than to pay overtime premium pay. According to a Department of Labor study in late 1984, it was concluded after both theoretical and statistical work that an increase to doubletime would:

> "...cause employment to increase between 2 and 4 percent, or by 320,000 to 640,000 workers, depending on whether industry added to the workforce, substituted capital for labor, or reduced their workforce."[4]

Another study, based upon an average of 35.6 million overtime hours for 13.2 million production workers in a single manufacturing week in September 1984 projected an equivalency of almost 900,000 forty-hour week jobs.[5]

Another badly-needed amendment would repeal some (or all) of the overtime exemptions from the FLSA. No matter how strong the law is for those covered, it will continue to fall short of its goal if the large percentage of workers now exempt, are not brought under its coverage. If I were to pick the most-needed amendment among those I have recommended, I would choose this repeal of exemptions, since without it the rest is merely window-dressing.

In summary then, there are many ways the overtime provisions of FLSA could be amended. Considering the high levels of unemployment and the number of hours of regularly worked overtime, it appears to me that such amendments are in order. While it has been shown to be impossible to create a new law or amend an old one to be perfectly fair to all parties, this should not stop us from trying. Those who criticized to amending FLSA in this article, seem to expect the amendment(s) to deal equitably with every conceivable individual case that may arise. Such unrealistic thinking must not be allowed to impede progress. The U.S. economy needs help today, if not yesterday, and one way to help is to enact the FLSA amendments proposed herein.

Footnotes

[1]*Congressional Record – House of Representatives,* April 13, 1984, p. H2897.

[2]Statement of Abraham Weiss, Assistant Secretary of Labor for Policy, Evaluation, and Research, *et. al.,* Hearings before the *Subcommittee on Labor Standards of the Committee on Education and Labor, House of Representatives,* Ninety-fourth Congress, First Session, on H.R. 10130 (hereafter referred to as Hearings), November 6, 1984, p. 158.

[3]Prepared statement of Alan Beals, Executive Vice President, National League of Cities, *Hearings,* November 21, 1984, p. 211.

[4]*Congressional Record – House of Representatives,* p. cit., p. H2896. See also, Joyce Nussbaum and Donald Wise, *The Employment Impact of the Overtime Provisions of the FLSA,* submitted to USDL in response to RFP J-9-E-6-1015, December 14, 1984, pp. 8–9.

[5]Statement of Andrew J. Biemiller, on behalf of the AFLCIO, *Hearings,* November 6, 1984, p. 9.

A Systems Perspective on the Uniform Selection Guidelines

Introduction

The legal aspect of employment selection is becoming a dominant concern in personnel management today. Under Title VII of the Civil Rights Act of 1964 as amended, it is illegal for employers, employment agencies, and labor organizations of 15 or more members to discriminate on the basis of a person's race, color, sex, religion, or national origin. Presidential Executive Orders have also been issued with requirements similar to those of Title VII. Within the past decades, various government agencies have issued guidelines designed to help employers interpret and comply with these federal laws regarding employment selection. A great deal of confusion among employers has resulted, however, due to the ambiguities and conflicting standards of the different sets of guidelines. An employer could often be in compliance with one set of guidelines, while violating another. The issuing agencies (EEOC, DOL, DOJ, CSC) eventually recognized the need for a common interpretation and adopted, effective September 25, 1978, the "Uniform Guidelines on Employee Selection Procedures."

Application

Under strict interpretation of the law, all employers are subject to the same selection constraint – to provide equal employment opportunity. However, in practice, the *size* of the organization dictates the degree to which selection procedures must be justified (validated). As a general rule, the larger a firm is, the greater the utility of rigorously applying the Uniform Selection Guidelines. For example, when a large company deviates statistically on selection rates across race, sex, or religion, the company runs a high risk of litigation. This principle (called adverse impact) is *prima facie* evidence of discrimination, and will be the focus of the next section.

When considering the selection process, two important factors are involved, i.e., selection procedures and selection decisions. The Guidelines state that the full range of assessment techniques (also called "predictors") are covered. This includes traditional paper-and-pencil tests, work samples, weighted application blanks, interviews, and so forth. Similarly, virtually all employment selection decisions are covered. That is to say, procedures used to hire, place, promote, transfer, train, demote and terminate employees are all subject to review under the Guidelines.

Obviously, it is critical for the employer to understand both the rights and obligations under the law.

Basic Principle

The spirit of the new Guidelines can be explained in one sentence. The use of any selection procedure which has an adverse impact on employment or membership opportunities for members of any race, sex, or ethnic group, will be considered to be discriminatory, unless the procedure has been validated in accordance with the Uniform Guidelines. At this point, it is necessary to define several terms. *Adverse impact* is a differential rate of selection (for hire, promotion, etc.) which works to the disadvantage of a covered group (EEO-1 group). It is statistically derived by what is known as the "four-fifths rule of thumb." In other words, adverse impact occurs when the *selection rate* for a covered minority group is less than 4/5, or 80% of the rate of the group of candidates with the highest selection rate (usually whites, or males). However, as can be seen in Appendix I, the fact that an employer has complied with the 4/5 rule will not necessarily eliminate the possibility of adverse impact.

When making comparisons of selection rates, two figures are required: the number selected (hired, promoted, terminated) and the number of candidates. The formula for a selection ratio is simply:

$$\frac{\text{\# selected}}{\text{\# applied}}$$

For example, if in a particular organization one (1) out of every three (3) males that apply for a job are selected, but only one (1) out of every six (6) females that apply are hired, then there is adverse impact (adversely affecting females).[1] At this point, the firm has a limited number of options. In general, the only practical solution to defending adverse impact is to conduct a validation study. Of course, the employer may always opt to eliminate the adverse impact by either abandoning or changing the procedure(s) causing the differential rate of selection. Unfortunately, the data gathered from a validation study is usually the best means by which intelligent modifications can be made to the selection system to eliminate the adverse impact. Thus, through the front door or through the back, validation is often a necessary expenditure.

At times, an employer may be able to prove that the adverse impact is necessary for the safe and efficient operation of the business (appropriately called "business necessity"). In this case, justification of the selection procedures is not needed. However, recent court decisions have narrowly defined this option.

For a detailed account of the adverse impact process and the realm of alternatives available to the employer, see Appendix I.

---

[1]Comparisons of selection rates need not be made for subgroups, e.g., white males or black females.

Validation

The process of validation is part of the highly technical and complex field of psychometrics. The major portion of the Uniform Guidelines is devoted to explaining the three types of validity acceptable and their technical standards.

The person often has difficulty understanding that there are many different types of validity. But, by analogy, there are many different types of transportation. Whether one rides a bicycle, drives a car, or flies a plane to some destination depends on practical considerations, e.g., the purpose and distance. The same is true for validation. The overall objective is to demonstrate the job-relatedness of a selection procedure (or procedures). In other words, validation is the effort to show exactly *what* a certain selection procedure (predictor) is in fact measuring, and *how well* it is measuring what it claims to measure. To add even more confusion, validity can never really be measured, but instead, must be *inferred*. As an example, suppose we developed a test of leadership for presidential candidates. To validate this test, we would first have to show that this test really measures "leadership" and not something else. Next, we would need to demonstrate that leadership is a requisite ability for the job of president. Finally, it would be necessary to illustrate that this test can differentiate between "good" leaders and "poor" leaders. Hopefully, it is becoming clear why validity must be inferred. In the final analysis, validity is a value judgment (albeit, statistical techniques are often involved).

As there are many possible ways to travel from one place to another, there are many methods of validation. The assumption is that they all achieve the same end result. The following three sections will briefly present the acceptable validation techniques under the Uniform Guidelines.

Criterion-Related Validity

This first type of validity is merely a correlational relationship between the scores on a selection device and the scores on a measure of on-the-job performance (called a criterion). The general framework is:

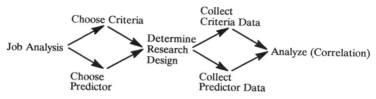

A job analysis is always required by the Uniform Guidelines, regardless of the validation method employed, with *one* exception: when using criterion-related validity with "objective" criteria measures. This sounds easy to implement, but choosing criteria is confounded by many problems. For example, "objective" data measure *outcomes* of behavior, *in lieu* of behavior itself. This means that factors beyond one's control contaminate the relationship between job performance and the predictor. Further, objective measures have limited applicability. There are other complexities to be consider, such as temporal dimensionality, criterion contamination, and composite/multiple criteria problems. Space limitations preclude the discussion of these issues here, yet I strongly suggest that an employer research the literature before attempting a validity study. This will not only help to understand the problems involved, but also assist in determining the research design, i.e., the type of criterion-related validity study – synthetic, concurrent, or predictive. The assumptions, theoretical underpinnings and objectives are somewhat different for each type.

The most important thing to keep in mind about criterion-related validity is that it is a purely statistical technique. Validity is assumed when the correlation is significant.[2]

Before moving on to the two remaining validity techniques acceptable under the Uniform Guidelines, it should be mentioned that the overall validity correlation may covertly discriminate against a covered group. In other words, a predictor may yield different validity coefficients when groups of candidates are analyzed separately. Unfair discrimination cannot be said to exist when inferior test performance by some group is also associated with inferior job performance by the same group. But frequently the validity coefficients obtained for two groups may differ significantly, when job performance of the two groups is equal; in other words, the test may accurately measure one group, but not the other. The variable differentiating the two groups, be it sex, race, etc., is known as a "moderator variable".

For clarification, a few cases are graphed on the next page:

---

[2]Or contributes *unique* variation in a multiple regression equation.

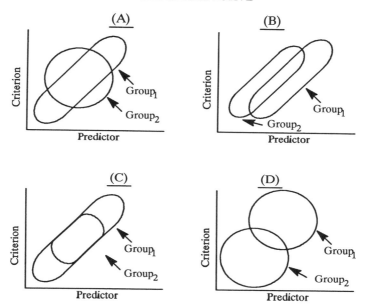

CASE A: This is called *differential validity.* It exists when the validity coefficients are significantly different for two groups, and at least one of these correlations significantly differs from zero. This particular case is often referred to as *single-group validity,* because the predictor is justified (valid) for only Group$_1$. (Group$_2$ demonstrates a zero correlation, i.e., no relationship. For this group the predictor is unfair or discriminative).

CASE B. This is called *test unfairness.* There is a positive correlation for both groups, however, Group$_2$ underperforms on the predictor without exhibiting inferior performance on the job. The employer has two options: eliminate this test for Group$_2$ applicants or use a lower cut-off score for Group$_2$.

CASE C: This situation is both legal and appropriate, because the inferior test performance of Group$_2$ is tied to inferior job performance.

CASE D: This is the most clear-cut case of discrimination. The predictor here has absolutely no predictive value for either group (zero correlations). But, when the data are analyzed in aggregate form, a positive correlation appears to result. This predictor should not be used for two reasons: it probably has adverse impact, and it is not helping the employer select individuals who can perform the job.

The Uniform Guidelines require this kind of analysis when it becomes technically feasible, that is, when the company has a sufficient amount of test-criterion data on minority members. The present status of minority employment in many companies is such that separate validity studies are either impossible, or based on such small samples, that results are quite tentative. The current government requirements appear to recognize this practical problem, but they still do not relieve the firm of the responsibility to eventually do the research.

Content Validity

This type of validity is most often simply a judgmental process. It involves making inferences about the adequacy of the predictor (test) as representing a sample of the significant parts of the job. In other words, given a certain job calling for various activities to be performed in that job, content validity is concerned with whether or not the predictor contains a fair sample of those activities. The basic framework is:

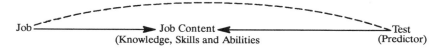

Job ⟶ Job Content ⟵ Test
(Knowledge, Skills and Abilities)   (Predictor)

This is strictly a behavioral approach. In a job analysis the job is broken down into important tasks. These tasks are built into one or more predictors to simulate the actual job. For example, giving a typing test to applicants for the job of typist would be content valid. Still, it should be understood that most jobs require many different behaviors to be performed on the job. Therefore, in order to have content validity, it is necessary for the predictor(s) to adequately represent those different behaviors. This is most often accomplished by using a battery of selection procedures, e.g., an ability test, a role-playing task, an in-basket test and a management game. If the employer is confident that the selection procedures for a particular job are a reasonable behavioral duplication of the job, then content validity can be claimed, at which point complying with the Uniform Guideline's documentation requirements remains.

Construct Validity

Construct validity studies attempt to answer two questions: what is the psychological construct being measured by the predictor, and how well does the predictor measure this construct? The focus is on a description of behavior that is broader and more abstract.

This is not accomplished by a single study. It requires an accumulation of evidence derived from many different sources to determine the meaning of the test scores. It is, therefore, both a logical and empirical process. The theoretical framework for construct validity is:

Job ——————————→ Construct ◀—————————— Predictor

It is first necessary to show that the construct in question is, in fact, an important requirement for successful performance on the job. Then it has to be shown that the predictor measures this construct (e.g., leadership) and not something else (e.g., assertiveness, congeniality, personal power, etc.). Finally, it must be demonstrated that the test can differentiate between individuals possessing varying amounts of the construct. Overall, this is quite a difficult accomplishment!

For a short summary of these validity techniques, including descriptions, appropriate usage, and documentation requirements, see Appendix II.

Discussion

Validation is, at best, difficult to perform, expensive, time-consuming, uncertain in outcome, and often not even feasible due to a small sample size. Thus, both criterion-related validity and construct validity are not *practical* alternatives for many employers. The overwhelming trend is toward content validity for its cost effectiveness. However, a content strategy is not appropriate for demonstrating the validity of selection procedures which purport to measure traits or constructs such as intelligence, aptitude, personality, common sense, judgment, leadership, and spatial ability. This has led to litigation problems for many employers. Today it is much easier for a company to adopt a "numbers game," rather than the more burdensome task of validating and documenting the job relatedness of their employment decision making process. This means that with the increasing difficulty of validation, most employers will attempt to remove adverse impact by hiring and promoting in compliance with the "four-fifths" rule, rather than struggle with the substantive technical standards of validation. This is unfortunate, because *without validation* the employer is naively assuming that adequately skilled people are being chosen for jobs in the organization. Once the emphasis moves from showing job relatedness to equating selection rates, the temptation is great to "fudge" the two figures composing the selection rate. For example, an employer may artificially increase a minority selection rate by throwing out some of the applicant data. There are quite a few other devious techniques, but this is not intended to be a discourse on how to beat the system. Rather, a more ethical and legal alternative is the focus here – a systems approach.

The Systems Approach

The systems approach solution has been suggested by William C. Byham, President of Development Dimensions International, and involves building a selection/promotion system around a set of "dimensions" identified through a job analysis. The basic framework is:

Job ──────────────────►Dimensions◄──────────────────►Predictor

The job analysis, the key element in the legal defense of the accuracy of an organization's selection procedures, is performed to isolate the dimensions. A dimension may be defined as a category under which *behavior* may be reliably classified. If the operational definitions are based on observable work behaviors, a selection procedure measuring those behaviors may be appropriately supported by a content validity strategy. In other words, the use of "dimensions" seems to move the effort from the realm of psychological constructs and places it squarely in the realm of content validity. This is extremely important to the company, because of the cost and time savings of a content validity methodology.

There are three essential steps in this procedure. First, the dimensions must be shown to be job-related and to describe all common and important parts of the job. Secondly, the predictors must be shown to be job-related and to represent the most common and significant job activities. They must also be shown to be comparable in complexity and difficulty level, to that required on-the-job. Finally, the dimensions must be observable in the predictors. In sum, the predictors of the selection system are targeted to specific behavioral dimensions. There is some overlap where data is available from multiple sources and/or where additional information is particularly needed. All the selection subsystems (e.g., hiring, promotion, termination, etc.) use the same dimensions, definitions, and rating scales.

The reader might well wonder how to choose a dimension. It is possible to choose dimensions through factor analytic techniques using incumbent questionnaire data, but a more practical approach for most organizations is a nonstatistical, judgmental, cluster analysis process in which the job analyst groups and regroups behaviors until a logical grouping is attained.

Because rational judgments, rather than factor analysis (or other correlational techniques) are used, it is important to be able to substantiate the accuracy of the rational judgment. This can be accomplished by establishing a "paper trail" in the job analysis report which documents each decision made in the job analysis. Examples of the behaviors that were classified under each dimension should be listed. This procedure stands or falls, therefore, on "expert judgment." For a visual outline of the systems approach applied to employment selection, see Appendix III.

There are many advantages to this type of approach. Communication, training, and administration time is reduced. Managers must learn only one set of dimensions and definitions. They are able to understand more quickly the interrelationships of the subsystems. Further, the selection subsystems deal with common elements (dimensions), and thus support and reinforce each other. This approach is designed to integrate smoothly with the other components of the organization's personnel system. But, most importantly, a content validity strategy is possible, thus greatly reducing costs.

Summary

The Uniform Guidelines have been prepared as a technical guide, not written as law. The courts have, in the past, not acted upon a uniform set of standards. In some instances, tests have been judged solely on the basis of face validity, while at other times extensive evidence is required. The determinant appears to be the sophistication of the judge with respect to personnel testing. This failure of the courts to act consistently or uniformly can be traced, in part, to the psychologists and their failure to develop specific and unambiguous guidelines on many issues in the establishment of content validity.

Naturally, an employer should make every effort to validate selection devices. In this regard construction of a test in accordance with professionally developed standards helps ensure that the selection system is fulfilling its primary purpose, i.e., choosing the most qualified applicants. Often, however, employers are primarily interested in withstanding legal scrutiny and submit to a "numbers game." As a response to cost/time pressures, a systems approach has been developed to provide for *both* equal employment opportunity in the workplace and a truly valid selection system.

Appendix I

Uniform Guideline Procedures

1) Keep records on each covered group, including.
   - # of applicants
   - # hired
   - # promoted
   - # terminated

2) Review the selection system at least annually for evidence of adverse impact:

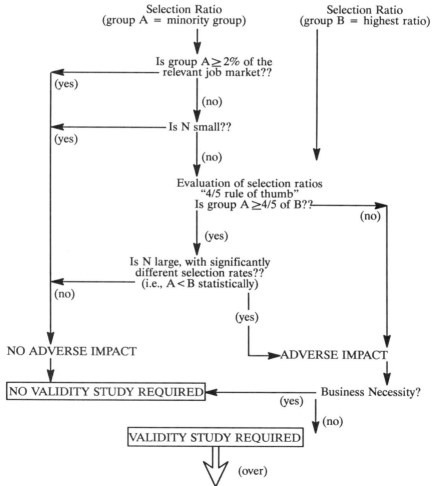

Evaluate each component of the selection process.
Is it possible and desirable to modify or
eliminate the procedure(s) which produce
the adverse impact?

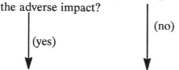

(yes)

(no)

Institute lawful
procedures

Justify Adverse Impact
by validity study
(inside, outside, cooperative)
criterion
content
construct

1) Cease using predictors associated with adverse impact until validity study is completed, unless substantial evidence of validity already exists.

2) Use alternative selection procedures showing less adverse impact while the study takes place (i.e., use screening or grouping *in lieu* of ranking).

3) Investigate the validity and adverse impact of suitable alternative predictors.

4) Compare original and alternate predictors for validity and adverse impact. If validity is substantially the same, use the predictor with the lesser adverse impact.

5) After criterion-related validity study, continue to collect data until it is feasible to test for differential validity and differential prediction (test fairness).

6) If test is unfair to minority, revise or discontinue use.

Appendix II

Appendix II
Validation Techniques

Validity Technique	Description	When Appropriate	Required Documentation — For each Technique	Required Documentation — For All Techniques
Criterion	An empirical demonstration that the selection procedure is predictive or significantly correlated with performance on the job	when it is possible to obtain: sufficient sample size sufficient range of performance on both the predictor and the criterion reliable and valid measure of performance on the job	A description of: selection procedures criteria measures sample statistical methodology statistical results	– location and date of study – description of selection procedures (including why & how they were selected)
Content	A demonstration that the content of the selection procedure is representative sampling of important elements of the job	when the job can be conceived as a meaningful, definable universe of behavioral response and when a sample can be drawn from the universe when it is feasible to develop work samples or measures of KSAs (which are necessary prerequisites to the job) *JOB ANALYSIS REQUIRED	A description of: content of the job, identified from job analysis content of selection procedures evidence that the content of the selection procedure is a representative sample of the content of the job	– description of how the job was analyzed – description of which alternative selection procedures were examined and the results
Construct	An empirical and a priori demonstration that the selection procedure is predictive of identifiable characteristics considered important for successful job performance	when it is necessary to relate mental processes, aptitude, or character traits to the job when the same selection procedure is used for a variety of jobs when expertise is available in the field of test validation *JOB ANALYSIS REQUIRED	A description of: construct how the construct relates to other constructs evidence that the construct is related to the work evidence that the selection procedure measures the construct	– name of a contact person

APPENDIX III

**S Y S T E M S
A P P R O A C H**

Dimensions	Structured Interview	Biographical Data	Business Game	In-Basket Task	Leaderless Group Discussion	Fact-Finding Exercise	Role Play	
Oral Communication Skill	√		√		√		√	
Written Communication Skill			√	√		√		
Reasoning Ability			√	√	√		√	
Interpersonal Skill	√		√		√		√	**For ONE
Ability to Learn			√	√		√		job
Leadership Skill			√		√		√	
Planning & Organizing Skill			√	√	√	√		
Stress Tolerance			√		√		√	
Motivation to Work	√		√					
Energy	√	√	√	√	√			
Management Control			√					

Dimensions	Selection	Training	Appraisal	Career Planning	Promotion
Oral Communication Skill	√		√	√	√
Written Communication Skill	√	√	√	√	√
Reasoning Ability	√		√	√	√
Interpersonal Skill	√	√	√	√	√
Ability to Learn	√				√
Leadership Skill	√	√	√	√	√
Planning & Organizing Skill	√	√	√	√	√
Stress Tolerance	√	√	√	√	√
Motivation to Work	√			√	√
Energy	√		√	√	√
Management Control	√		√	√	√

Implicit Sex Stereotyping in Personnel Decisions

Introduction

It has been my contention for quite some time that university courses, employer training programs, various "human relations" seminars, etc., aimed at educating individuals on the legal aspects of discrimination in various employment decisions, are serving a valuable purpose, they are addressing only half the problem. An individual may be extremely knowledgeable regarding the legal side of employment discrimination and yet, *without consciously being aware of it,* still discriminate in decisions involving selection, placement, promotion, training, and compensation. Based on numerous consulting contacts I am convinced that this persists today, among even the most "enlightened" individuals, and that this implicit discrimination is most likely to be based on race or sex. The present study used sex as the key variable.

Sample and Methodology

To test this contention a sample of 512 soon-to-be-graduated college students, 271 males and 241 females, was used as subjects. All subjects were surveyed during the same semester they took a personnel management course, devoting considerable time to equal employment and fair employment practices. Thus, they were all recently schooled in the legal aspects of employment discrimination and, I felt, were more sensitized to this issue than might otherwise have been the case. Any implicit discrimination found in decisions made by this group might, therefore, underestimate the extent of the problem in the general business community.

Before administration of the survey, the subjects were told that they would be evaluated on the quality of their responses to the various situations presented, and that the evaluation would be a factor in their course. In this way it was hoped that commitment to the exercise would be increased, with fewer subjects simply "going through the motions." Subjects were told to respond to the situations as if they were the personnel manager of a large business organization. They were then given eight separate incidents, each necessitating the making of a typical personnel decision (hiring, firing, etc.), with forced choice responses.[1] Each incident was presented in two forms, one with a female as the individual involved in the incident, and one with a male involved (hereafter referred to as "male and female versions"). Of the 271 males in the subject group, 135 were given the male version of each incident and 136 were given the female version. Of the 241 female subjects, 120 were given the male version of each incident and 121 the female.[2] No subject was given both versions of any one incident, as I felt this would (a) not be realistic to have two identical applicants for selection, promotion, etc., differing only by sex, and (b) make fairly obvious the intent of the survey, thus eliminating the chance of finding any significant difference, since few people would respond in an overtly discriminatory manner. Remember, it was subconscious discrimination that I was interested in measuring.

Survey and Results

The first three incidents involved a conflict between responsibilities on the job and at home. It is my belief that when such a conflict arises, most individuals expect the male to place job responsibilities first, and the female to give first priority to the home.

Jack and Judy Garrison have been married three years. Jack is an aspiring business executive and Judy is a very successful freelance writer. Below is a part of their conversation after attending a cocktail party at the home of an executive in Jack's division.

Judy: Oh, boy, what a bunch of creeps. Do we have to go to these parties, honey?

Jack.   Judy, honey, you know we have to. These things mean a lot to me. Tonight I had a chance to talk to Mr. Wilson. On the job it would take a week to get an appointment with him. I was able to get across two good ideas I had about our new sales campaign, and I think he was listening.

Judy: Is Wilson that fat slob who works in marketing, the one with the dull wife? I spent ten minutes with her and I nearly died! She's too much. Jack, the people there tonight were so dull I could have cried. Why did I major in English Lit. anyway? I prefer to talk to people who know what is going on in the world, not a bunch of half-wits whose main interests are their new cars and spoiled kids. I tried to talk to one guy about Virginia Woolf and he didn't even know who she was. These people are incredible. Do we have to go to another cocktail party again next week? I'd like to see "Look Back In Anger" instead. I've got the tickets. One of my "wifely duties" is to give you culture. What an uncouth bunch in the business world.

Jack: One of my husbandly ambitions is to get ahead in the business world. You know that these parties are required for bright junior executives coming up in the organization. And I'm a bright junior executive. If we don't go, who knows which of the other junior execs will get to Wilson with their good ideas?

Judy.   Can't you relax and work a 40–hour week? That's what they pay you for.

Jack: I guess I'm too ambitious to relax.

Judy: I'd still like to go to the play. At least we could think about real problems.

Jack: And I'd be a mediocre, lower-management nobody for the rest of my career.

Judy.   I want you to be a success, Jack. But the idea of spending more evenings talking to idiots is too much!

The female version had Judy as the aspiring executive and Jack as the reluctant spouse, with all other details identical. Subjects were then asked to choose one of the following three alternatives:

a)   The spouse should go to the parties and stop making such an issue of it.

b)   The junior executive should attend the parties alone.

c)   The junior executive should stop attending the parties.

Agreement results:

	% Agreement		
	Answer		
	A	B	C
Female Version	30%	42%	28%
Male	72%	18%	11%

It is obvious from the above results that the subjects in the male condition expected more support from the female partner. The female was expected to suppress her personal desires and support the male in his work role. Such expectations would make it easier for the male to succeed in balancing career and home demands than a female – that is, he would have more "assistance" and less "resistance" in doing so.

Students' attitudes in the female condition did not reveal significant differences and possibly showed the "mixed feelings" that many people still feel toward career aspirations in women.

The second incident looked at these competing demands from another angle:

Ruth Brown, an accountant in the main office, has requested one month's leave beginning next week. She has already taken her vacation this year. She wants the leave to take care of her three young children. The day care arrangements the Browns had made for the period covered by her request suddenly fell through, and they have been unable to make other satisfactory arrangements. Ruth's husband is principal of the junior high school and he cannot possibly get off during the next month.

The problem is that Ruth is the only person experienced in handling the cost section in the accounting department. We would either have to transfer an accountant with the same experience from the Richardson Division, or else train a replacement for only one month's work. I have urged Ruth to reconsider this request, but she insists on going ahead with it.

I have also checked with the legal department and we do not have to hold the position open for Ruth, if she insists on taking the whole month off.

I would appreciate it if you could give me your decision on this as soon as possible.

The male version was identical except it involved Ralph Brown, whose wife was a principal. Subjects were then asked if (a) this was an appropriate leave request, and whether they would grant leave, (b) with pay or (c) without pay.

Agreement results:

	% Agreement		
	Answer		
	A	*B*	*C*
Female	51%	72%	11%
Version			
Male	31%	56%	3%

In this case the results indicate that sex stereotyping serves to the benefit of females. A leave request for identical reasons is considered acceptable by over one-half the subjects when it is made by a female, but by less than one-third the subjects when it is made by a male. As in the first incident, the evidence suggests that when a job vs. home conflict arises the male is more likely to be expected to somehow accommodate his work schedule, while it is more acceptable for the female to miss work and devote her energies to the home. Such stereotyping is going to create increasing problems for both husbands and wives as more and more wives pursue careers. Women will find it hard to advance as long as the image most employers have of them is that of an employee whose first allegiance is or should be to the home and not the job, while males are going to be subjected to an increasing number of situations where their absence from work is necessitated because of a working spouse, yet where their employers view the reason for such absence as 'unacceptable'. Situation three presented a retention issue, when the other spouse is offered a promotion out-of-town.

As you know, Ronald Cooper is a computer operator in my section. He has played a key role in computerizing our inventory system. Recently Ronald's wife was offered a very attractive managerial position with a large retail organization on the West Coast. They are seriously considering the move. I told Ronald that he has a very bright future with our organization and it would be a shame for him to pull out just as we are expanding our operations. I sure would hate to lose him now. What do you think we should do about the situation?

The alternate form had Rhonda as the computer operator, and her husband offered the job on the West Coast. Subjects were asked to choose from among the following four alternatives:

a) Try to convince the operator that too much has been invested in their career to leave now.

b) Don't try to influence the operator.

c) Offer the operator a sizable raise as an incentive to stay.

d) Try to find an attractive position for the employee's spouse in the organization.

Agreement results[3]:

| | % Agreement | | | |
| | *Answer* | | | |
	A	B	C	D
Female	41%	64%	22%	8%
Version				
Male	88%	19%	28%	8%

It appears from the response pattern that the subjects viewed male employees as worth retaining more than female employees, *even when the qualifications of each were the same.* In the male condition, respondents thought the personnel manager should try to persuade Ronald that the company had a great investment in him, leaving open the questions of his wife's improbable ability to obtain an equal investment from **her** company. In the female condition, respondents chose not to try to influence Rhonda to stay, possibly admitting the devalued contribution of female employees, a company's unwillingness to put forth effort to retain a woman, and the supposed ease of replacement, regardless of skill level. When looking at responses to the first three situations, one begins to get some insight into why absenteeism and turnover rates are higher for females than males, even when they are at the same organization and compensation level. If employers do not make similar efforts to retain females and males and, as seen in situation two, females are more readily granted unscheduled absences, is it any wonder that the government reports slightly higher absenteeism and turnover rates for females than males?[4]

The fourth and fifth situations dealt with unacceptable conduct being exhibited by an employee, with the question being what disciplinary action, if any, should be taken. Situation four follows:

> I have a problem and I don't see how to solve it. It concerns one of the design engineers, Jill Diller, who has worked for me for the past 15 months. Jill persists in arriving late every morning. She is always 10 minutes late, more usually 15 minutes to a half hour. I am at my wit's end. I have tried everything I can think of – private discussions, written reprimands, threats, sarcasm, and more. She is still late every morning.
>
> When Jill walks into the office, the work stops and every one watches. Some of the designers are even joking that Jill's coming in late has something to do with her recent engagement. I don't like to get too tough with a creative girl like Jill, but her behavior is bound to hurt morale in the department.

The male version involved Jack Diller. Subjects were asked to select among the following courses of action:

a)   Suspend for one week for continued tardiness.

b)   Threaten to fire and follow through if necessary.

c)   Don't make an issue of tardiness.

Agreement results.

| | % Agreement Answer | | |
	A	B	C
Female Version	72%	51%	8%
Male	64%	42%	11%

In the case of both the female and male employee the subjects considered the situation serious enough to warrant the more severe types of action. Yet they were slightly more inclined to take such action when the employee involved was a female. This may be connected to the value the subjects attached to employees of different sexes, as exhibited by the responses to situation three. The willingness to risk losing an employee through more severe disciplinary actions and the lesser effort made to retain the same employee (situation 3), when found to be moderated by a variable of sex, both seem to the author to be providing insight into the value the subjects placed on employees. The response patterns indicate that when all else is equal males are viewed as more 'valued' employees – worth more effort to retain, and not as likely to risk losing due to severe discipline – than females.

Situation five involved unacceptable personal, rather than work conduct:

> I would like to get your advice on a matter of great sensitivity involving one of the junior executives in our organization. It has been brought to my attention by an unimpeachable source that Bill Holman, assistant comptroller in my division, is having an affair with a prominent young socialite. I understand it has reached the point where any day now, Bill's wife will publicly denounce the socialite as a homewrecker. I have been reluctant to bring this up, but I know Bill's marital problems will hurt his work. I would appreciate any advice you could give me on this.

The female version involved Renee Holman having an affair with a young playboy. Subjects were asked to select among the following responses:

a) Do nothing unless junior executive raises the issue.
b) Advise junior executive to see a marriage counselor.
c) Confront employee and threaten termination unless affair stops.

Agreement results:

| | % Agreement | | |
| | *Answer* | | |
	A	*B*	*C*
Female	50%	40%	3%
Version			
Male	52%	56%	4%

The only real difference in this situation seems to be in response (b), with subjects more likely to request that a male employee see a marriage counselor than a female. The author would speculate that the almost identical results to response (a) may have to do with the equal number of male and female subjects given each version. It may be that members of one sex (regardless of *which* one) are less likely to approach members of the opposite sex on issues such as this. The author suspects that since this 'opposite sex' situation was present to the same degree in both versions, the results may well be the same in both instances. For response (a) then, it is not a question of the sex of the participant but of the sex of the subject relative to the participant. Response (b) indicates that the subjects were willing to go to greater lengths to correct the unacceptable behavior of male employees than female, even when this behavior was of a personal, rather than a work, nature. When the unacceptable behavior was personal (situation 5) rather than work related (situated 4), the subjects were willing to expend more effort toward male than female employees.

Situation six addresses a situation that is becoming all too common today: by playing a numbers game, the organization has hired enough females to comply with the law, but through subtle forms of unintentional sex discrimination does not allow them to "develop" as managers to the same extent that equally qualified males do. Then when the females do not advance in the organization to the degree that males do, it is used as evidence that they are not as well suited for the work. This failure to advance can then lead to higher rates of absenteeism and turnover, and so the cycle starts again. The difficulty here is that the decisions as to who is promoted may be made on legitimate individual qualifications at the time, and may not be discriminatory at all. The discrimination occurred earlier however, when females, because of subconscious discrimination, were not given the same opportunities to develop as males.

Situation six address this type of situation:

I am pleased that we have the opportunity to send a representative to the Dunbar conference on production supervision. I know from personal experience that it is a high-quality conference, and it has developed such a favorable reputation in this area that it is considered an important form of recognition for those who are selected to attend.

I have reviewed our supervisory staff quite carefully and have narrowed the choice down to two people, both of whom I feel are qualified to attend. Unfortunately, we can send only one person, and I will leave the final selection up to you, depending on what you feel we need to emphasize. The two candidates are Susan Adams and John Elms.

Susan Adams is supervisor of knitting unit A. She is 25, married and has no children. She has been employed by our company for three years. She is a college graduate with a general business degree, and we consider her to have good potential for higher-level positions.

John Elms is supervisor of knitting unit B. He is 43, married, and has two teen-aged children. He has been employed by our company for 20 years. He is a high school graduate. He has been a steady, conscientious employee, advancing gradually from a helper's job to his present position, which may be as high as he will be able to go, judging from our assessment of the information in his file. Selection for this conference would mean a lot to John.

In the alternate form the two names were reversed. Subjects were asked to select one of the two to go to the conference. When all responses were considered collectively, without differentiation by sex of individual involved, the following results emerged:

Send 25 year old: 31%

Send 43 year old: 69%

Hence, regardless of sex, the majority of subjects felt that the older employee should be sent. When the results were sorted by the sex of the individual involved, however, the following occurred:

Send 25-year-old female: 23%

Send 25-year-old male: 39%

These results indicated that the subjects, when selecting younger workers with career potential to participate in "development" of this nature, were more likely to expend company resources if the employee were male, even when all other qualifications were equal.

Situation seven dealt with the selection/promotion decision for a position requiring extensive traveling:

Pursuant to our recent discussion with you about the need to recruit a purchasing manager for the new operation, we have developed a set of brief job specifications and have located some candidates who may be suitable for the opening. Will you please review the attached resume and give us your evaluation?

Job requirements for purchasing manager:

The major responsibilities of the new purchasing manager will be to purchase fabrics, materials, and clothing accessories (buttons, belts, buckles, zippers, and so on) for the production of finished goods.

For the most part, the purchasing manager will have to travel around the country visiting wholesalers and attending conventions and showings. The person hired for this position should have a knowledge of the quality of raw materials and have the ability to establish a "fair" price for goods purchased in large quantities. The person selected for this position will have to travel at least 20 days each month.

RESUME

NAME: Mr. Carl Wood

POSITION APPLIED FOR: Purchasing Manager

PLACE OF BIRTH: Cleveland, Ohio

MARITAL STATUS: Married, four children ages 11, 8, 7, and 4

EDUCATION

B.S. Business Administration, Ohio State University

RELEVANT WORK EXPERIENCE:

One year as purchasing trainee, Campbell Textiles, Inc.

Ten years' experience in various retail clothing stores, in sales, buying, and general management.

INTERVIEWER'S REMARKS

Good personal appearance; seems earnest and convincing. Good recommendations from previous employers.

The female version had Mrs. Karen Wood as the candidate. Subjects were asked to answer the following questions:

a) Would you select this candidate?
b) Is the candidate favorable suited for the job?
c) Does the candidate have the potential to remain on the job?

Agreement results:

	% Agreement		
	Answer		
	A	B	C
Female Version	23%	33%	30%
Male	33%	38%	36%

Subjects apparently felt that employees with this set of characteristics, regardless of sex, were not suited for the position in question. I would contend that the presence of four young children is the main variable in the subjects decision(s).

The final incident addressed the job vs. work dilemma even more directly:

We are at the point where we must make a decision on the promotion of Cathy Adams of our personnel staff. Cathy is one of the most competent employees in the corporate personnel office, and I am convinced that she is capable of handling even more responsibility as Bennett Division Personnel Director. However, I am not altogether certain that she is willing to subordinate time with her family, to time on the job, for the extent that may be required with Bennett. I have had the opportunity to explore with her the general problems of family versus job, and she strongly believes that she would very rarely stay late at the office or participate in weekend meetings.

She believes that her first duty is to her family, and that she should manage her time accordingly. This viewpoint has not affected her performance in the past, but it could be a problem in the more demanding position as head of personnel with the Bennett Division.

The male version involved Gerald Adams. Subjects were given three possible courses of action:

a) Do not promote.

b) Persuade the candidate to make a stronger job commitment prior to promotion.

c) Base the promotion on past experience.

Agreement results:

	% Agreement		
	Answer		
	A	B	C
Female Version	34%	29%	40%
Male	10%	32%	58%

Looking at the responses to (a) and (c), one reaches the conclusion that identical family demands and/or commitments do not disqualify males to the same extent they disqualify females. Hence not only are females *expected* to yield to family demands in the work vs. home dilemma, (as shown in the previous situations), but even when they overcome this and place an *identical* emphasis on the two competing factors as their male counterparts, the males are still given more consideration for the job. Indeed, the effects of this type of sex stereotyping will be difficult, at best, to overcome.

Conclusions

The conclusions to be drawn from this study are obvious. There *is* a large amount of unintentional, subconscious sex stereotyping taking place in the business sector of our society, if the subjects used here are any indication. The author feels quite strongly that, if anything, the subjects used here underestimate the extent of the problem. The subjects were younger, college educated, and were undergoing a learning experience (the Personnel course) that sensitized them to the area of employment discrimination. It is reasonable to expect that responses from such a group would be different from those of a more general sample.

While we as a society can legislate against overt discrimination, equally important and necessary are efforts to eliminate the type of subconscious stereotyping evidenced in the present study. Even if all members of the business community fully complied with the written laws regarding equal/fair employment, the barriers erected by the type of discrimination found in this study would still be imposing. Only after this more difficult type of discrimination is eliminated will *real* equal employment practices be attained. Making people aware of the problem, as this study has attempted to do, is the first step.

Footnotes

[1]These incidents were taken from an earlier survey conducted by Benson Rosen and Thomas Jerdee and published in 1974: "Sex Stereotyping in the Executive Suite", *Harvard Business Review,* March-April, 1974.

[2]In the present study responses were tabulated by the sex of the individual involved in the incident (male and female version), not by the sex of the respondent—although as noted previously the number of respondents by sex was the same for both the male and female versions of the incidents. In a follow-up study I intend to tabulate responses by the sex of the respondent.

[3]In this and certain subsequent situations the responses do not total 100%, since more than one response was possible.

[4]Bureau of National Affairs, Inc., *Bulletin to Management,* information on absenteeism and turnover has been published quarterly in the bulletin.

Trends In Participative Management

Kenneth A. Kovach
William W. Brooks
Ben Sands, Jr.

An important and controversial topic in the field of management is the application of participative techniques for nonmanagerial personnel. Such techniques have been widely used and even more widely debated. The debate involves the philosophical question of whether it is proper for workers to be included in such areas of management responsibility as planning, operational decision making, and performance evaluation, as well as questions of ability and motivation, which challenge the potential effectiveness of participative strategies, regardless of propriety. While the philosophical question broadly embraces virtually all such strategies, the question of effectiveness more pragmatically addresses the results to be obtained by using worker participation in structuring jobs, in defining management/labor relationships, and in managing the firm itself. From the academic perspective, but especially from the managerial viewpoint, the pragmatic question—effectiveness—is of primary importance. A negative finding concerning effectiveness would surely render the philosophical question moot.

While a wide variety of participative techniques have been used in many different job environments, the range of such techniques is basically limited to those which are relatively traditional in concept, representing a "bottom-up" approach and a group of more recently developed techniques which involves "top-down" participation. The bottom-up approaches embody the goal of identifying the worker with managerial values through involving employees in operational decisions, communications, or benefits. These programs include such well-understood and often-used techniques as:

- Job enlargement
- Job enrichment
- Management by objectives
- Team building
- Profit-sharing

The top-down approach envisages the worker or groups of workers in an executive role, participating directly in decision making in strategic areas such as long-range plans and operations. In the U.S., this participation involves the worker in actions and responsibilities traditionally reserved for the board of directors or the chief executive officer. The European experience in this area involves participation mandated by law, with detailed and explicit procedures developed over a long period of time. The American experience, on the other hand, is based on localized programs, usually initiated by management, with a wide variety of bottom-up and top-down approaches to worker participation. This article summarizes the current status of bottom-up and top-down approaches to worker participation in the management of the organization and attempts to draw some conclusions concerning future applications of these approaches in the U.S.

Trends In Bottom-Up Participative Management

Job enlargement is the process of providing more variety in the number of tasks contained in a given job. Moving from the specific, individual job description to an enlarged responsibility for a wider scope of activities is the primary objective of the **job enlargement** process. For example, a machine operator's job may be narrowly defined to consist of merely machining a specific material. Alternatively, this job may be enlarged or broadened by requiring the obtaining materials, maintaining the tools and equipment, and inspect the work. This method of involving workers in a greater variety of activities is viewed by many theorists as the most basic participative strategy. Walker and Guest, in their landmark study in the 1950's, found that worker participation in a wider range of physical activities reduced fatigue and boredom, thereby increasing expected productivity.[1] Job enlargement, however, does not represent an attempt to significantly increase the workers' sense of personal achievement or share of responsibility for results.

Strategies for enhancing the employee's personal identification with a job are called **job enrichment**. Based on a considerable body of theory on worker motivation, this approach is utilized under a variety of titles such as "vertical job loading."[2] This approach, successfully adopted by the Texas Instrument Corporation and other firms, attempts to build employee motivation through loading the job with components of responsibility and autonomy so that the employee identifies with important managerial goals.[3] There is considerable research evidence that job enrichment can exert a positive influence on workers' attitudes and on their productivity.[4] Nevertheless, the potential for generalizing this approach is controversial, some critics claiming that reported results are unrepresentative.

Fein, in summarizing prevalent reservations about the validity of many enthusiastic reports of job enrichment successes, named the following shortcomings of research in this area:

- Selective reporting of results has distorted evaluations of the effectiveness of programs;

- There are too few empirical studies of actual results and they represent a limited range of working environments;

- Published studies reflect the views of managers who initiated the programs of job enrichment, not the views of workers or unions.[5]

The last point suggests that part of the difficulty in implementing job enrichment concepts is that they are viewed as management-imposed, rather than a product of workers' or unions' initiative.

Management by Objectives (MBO) is a strategy for involving lower-level managers and rank-and-file workers in the planning and evaluation process which controls employee efforts toward organizational objectives. The technique was first proposed by Peter Drucker in the 1950's. It has been elaborated and systematized for use in virtually any organization by Odiorne[6] and others, and has enjoyed widespread popularity in subsequent years. MBO has been used extensively in industry during the last decade but observers have noted mixed results.[7] While some firms have embraced MBO enthusiastically, others have found it more difficult to apply than had been anticipated. In particular, the benefits of joint goal setting and review which involve subordinates in the process have been questioned.[8] While MBO has become a popular managerial tool in government as well as business, there have been questions about its efficacy in motivating public-sector employees.[9]

Team building is a concept which assumes that group participation in work activities will develop positive job attitudes and motivation for individual members of work groups. Much attention while training managers has been devoted to this approach.[10] Like MBO, team building approaches are oriented to managerial recognition of the value of contributions by subordinates. Despite a great deal of managerial enthusiasm over these methods, it remains to be seen whether subordinates will prove to be as enthusiastic as their superiors—those individuals who initiate group decision making and problem-solving[11] and normally retain final authority.

Profit-sharing approaches to employee participation vary considerably but share a common assumption, a belief that workers will be motivated to excel in their jobs when their compensation depends on the organization's profits. There have been some notable successes in this area such as the Lincoln Electric Plan.[12] Many other attempts at profit sharing, however, have been disappointing or, at best, yielded mixed results with unclear cause and effect relationships. Many plans which offer profit sharing also include other participative features such as job enlargement, job enrichment, or team building.

We feel that this grab bag of approaches makes it difficult to conclude that any of the participative strategies is deserving of either praise or blame, in the majority of situations where there are clear-cut results that are either beneficial or harmful to employee morale and/or productivity. This is not to say, however, that other individuals have found it similarly difficult to pass judgment on the value of these participative techniques. Labor leaders in particular have been very vocal in their criticism.

The Union Perspective

Generally, organized labor has looked with skepticism on the traditional approaches to participative management discussed above. Most are viewed as the theoretical ideas of academics who lack practical experience in day-to-day contact with nonsupervisory employees. One of the implicit assumptions in particular plans like job enlargement, job enrichment, management by objectives, etc., is that the job can be made a major part of the individual's life—that it can be made challenging enough to effect changes in the employee's attitude toward the position. In certain situations this is true. Traditional participative programs work best when the skills and intellect of the individuals performing the job are at a level high enough to allow them to handle significant enlargement or enrichment features added to their present job description. Further, if the job is at a high enough level in the organization to allow for meaningful and challenging objectives in MBO, or responsibility actually increases in the case of job enrichment and the enrichment is not simply a *facade,* then again the program has a chance of leading to the type of employee attitude change that is desired.

It is for these reasons that traditional participative programs have realized their greatest successes among better-educated, higher-level employees' and have such a poor track record among lower-level jobs, where employees possession of certain characteristics and skills is demonstrably less. Among big-city blue-collar workers, for example, the track record of such participative management programs has been nothing short of disastrous.[13] Thus, in the area where changes envisioned by the introduction of such programs are most urgently needed—for it is at the lowest levels that the greatest motivation and identification problems arise and the potential for increased productivity is greatest—participative management programs have realized the least success.

It is not surprising that unions many times look with disfavor on such programs. The sector of the labor force where the programs encounter the greatest difficulty is precisely that sector where unions have their strongest representation. "You can tell me it works elsewhere, but if it fails often enough where I am, I have reservations about its continual introduction." Thus, while labor organizations may question the practicality of many programs, it is not simply because they see them blurring the traditional us-and-them labor/management relationship (as many have charged), but also because the very people who constitute these labor organizations are the ones holding the jobs where the programs have realized the least success.

This situation causes one to question the cause-and-effect relationship between the variables involved; i.e., is it union opposition that causes these programs to fail at lower organization levels, or do the programs fail for other reasons, and as a result lose credibility among unions? Since the days of Frederick Taylor and Scientific Management, it has been an article of faith among the management of many manufacturing concerns (another bastion of union strength) that for production efficiency, it is best to break jobs down into small increments, assigning a specific task to one worker. This, in turn, has created hundreds of thousands of repetitive, unchallenging jobs. Naturally, these are the jobs where the identification, motivation, and increased productivity—hopefully to be gained through participative management—is most needed, but they are also the types of jobs that, if held by an individual for a number of years, can cause the employee to adopt a very negative mental approach to the work. This mental attitude is manifested in attempts, usually through a union, to get more time away from the job. More holidays, vacations, sick leave, etc., are demanded, since the worker now seeks satisfaction not through the job, but away from it. This same attitude can also result in demands for more monetary compensation for tolerating the job. If the worker likes the job, a given rate of pay may be enough to remain on the job, but if the worker hates the job, the worker will invariably insist on more for the same level of performance. After years of conditioning in this approach to their employment, is it any wonder that many of these employees—who belong to unions by virtue of their positions—are not wholeheartedly embracing participative management?

With this attitude, coupled with the perception that their particular job cannot really be changed in a significant way to make it a worthwhile part of their lives, it is no wonder that the prevailing attitude among employees at "union-level" jobs is one of viewing the job as simply a means to secure a pay–check. Should these factors remain unchanged, and there is every indication they will, then participative management as we have known it in the past will simply not work at this level.

The situation is made even worse by the changing educational, financial, and social level of the typical union member. The blue-collar sector of the labor movement is becoming better educated, wages are rising, and a larger percentage of overall union membership is white-collar and/or professional. The better educated and financially secure these employees become, the more they will resist superficial attempts at participation of the types discussed above. Even profit-sharing plans will suffer in terms of the attitude changes they seek to foster, since, as employees become better educated, they begin to expect more than a paycheck from the job.

In summary, these forces point to the necessity of introducing employer practices calling for *real* participation by employees in the operation of the enterprise. Instead of the previously discussed participative management techniques, that emphasize employee input at the lowest organizational levels (shop-floor or "bottom-up" approaches), we would urge advocates and practitioners of participative methods to turn their attention to "top-down" plans giving employees a collective voice in broad operating decisions traditionally made by upper-level management. The introduction of such plans is crucial not only to improve the mental health and attitude of the individual employee, but also to improve the performance of the firm and consequently, if implemented on a wide-enough scale, the economy as a whole. While not seen as a cure-all in and of itself, we see the emergence of a top-down approach to management as a beacon of hope on an economically bleak horizon.

Trends In Top-Down Participative Management

Bottom-up participative management usually has a relatively short time-period, in terms of actions taken by the employer and employees, and the perception of the results of whatever technique is used. A classic case is Lincoln Electric which uses piecework almost entirely in production runs. The system in Lincoln Electric was carried to such an extreme that meters were attached to the typewriters to count the number of keys struck during the day. The system was discontinued for white-collar workers; one reason being that a creative typist was found eating lunch with one hand and striking random keys on the typewriter with her free hand,[14] an early version of the endless loop that can be programmed into a computer to allow "continuous operation" of the equipment.[15]

Top-down participation by workers normally involves a long period of time, a period limited only by the life of the firm. Actions taken by a worker on the board of directors or in collaboration with the office of the chief executive in strategy and policy areas have, by definition, effects that are more or less permanent in nature. A change on the production line can be made almost immediately, while a change in the product line can be made only after, or in parallel with, changes in marketing and finance, customers and suppliers, and other functional and environmental factors. One immediate, and very valuable, impact of top-down management can be the perception by the worker of some control over his or her life at work, a perception that there is a "friend at court," interested in and involved with conditions affecting workers throughout the firm.

The idea of a top-down approach—techniques that place the worker/employee/member of the community in a position to affect the operation of the unit through input at the highest levels—is not a particularly new idea. Many primitive societies were organized in this fashion. From 1663 to 1858, over 130 communal colonies were established in this country. There were some new settlements in the 1890's, but the leaders and participants in these attempts usually gravitated to socialism and political action in attempting to achieve their goals.[16]

There has traditionally been a hostile reaction to communal organizations in the United States, generated by what has been seen as religious/moral deviations in these communities, but the rapid industrialization of England and America was the major factor in eliminating the conditions that made communal efforts possible. The size of the organizations formed to take advantage of new processes, cheap labor, and heavy demand for the products demanded by developing nations left few niches for communal organizations.

The communes of the 1960's were examples of a continuing need by many in the work force for greater control over their lives as productive members of the community. As was true in the past, these communal efforts had a high degree of what might be called a religious component. Individuals were willing to work for the good of the community and, hopefully, a better life for those who would come after. Most of these communes have experienced the same difficulties and high mortality rates of previous experiments. Perhaps they, too, came before their time.

It can be hypothesized that current conditions in the mature or highly advanced economies of developed countries justify a return of some control of the organization to its members. It can also be hypothesized that this change is desirable from the point of view of both the management and the work force. High incomes, high levels of education, large amounts of leisure time, and an infinite number of ways to organize the processes of production and individual life styles are merely a few of the many factors that cause the labor force in a developed country to differ from the labor force required during the development phase. These factors point toward new methods and techniques of compensation and control. The worker will insist not only upon control of conditions on the floor, but upon control and direction of the policies and goals of the employing organization. This insistence on control and direction of the firm is based primarily upon the employee's perception that there is an increasing need for recognition of "property rights" in the job. A recent article by Peter Drucker discusses this phenomenon and gives many examples.[17]

The "means of production" or sources of wealth inherent in real, personal, or intangible property now reside in the job for the great majority of citizens in developed nations. Pension funds, certainly a "right" of the individual, now constitute one of the largest liabilities of many firms.

On page 68 of Gulf & Western Corporation's last annual report there is a little footnote about $160 million—"the amount by which vested benefits under our pension plans exceed market value of assets in the funds, plus balance sheet liabilities." At AT&T a footnote for 1979 will mention $299 million. At General Motors Corp., another footnote casually mentions $3.9 billion.[18]

This "property right" was recognized in a recent decision in a U.S. District Court in Cleveland, Ohio. Judge Thomas D. Lambros issued an injunction prohibiting the shutdown of the Youngstown Works by U.S. Steel. The injunction was based, in part, on the judge's conclusion that ". . . a property right has arisen from the lengthy, long-established relationship between U.S. Steel, the steel industry as an institution, the community in Youngstown, the people in Mahoning County, and the Mahoning Valley, in having given and devoted their lives to this industry."[19] Although the consensus is that the ruling will not be upheld, the United Steel Workers' Union has raised the plant-closing issue in current steel bargaining. The USW wants contract provisions prohibiting the closing of the plants or major departments during the period of the contract. The United Rubber Workers won a six-month notice-of-shutdown in last year's contract negotiations.[20]

Top-Down Management is usually defined as a situation wherein top management makes decisions, sets the rules, enforces standards, and in general exercises all the traditional powers of the owner/entrepreneur. *Top-Down Participation,* on the other hand, implies sharing by the employee/worker in this process. Major decisions concerning the direction of the firm, products and markets, plans and policies, and conditions of work and employment are set by, or with major inputs from, the worker/employee. The philosophy of a property right in the job underlies the concept of top-down participation and may explain in part the resistance of management to worker participation in the direction of the firm.

Two methods of top-down participation by employees have received wide-spread attention in the past few years. Both methods place the employee in a position to affect and influence the direction and operation of the firm through the presence or the influence of the worker/employee on the policy-making boards of the organization.

In West Germany, *Mitbestimmung* (co-determination) is required by law. In this mandated system, one-third of the "Supervisory Board" (comparable to a board of directors in U.S. corporations) are drawn from the work force. The supervisory board is responsible for the overall operation of the firm, including the development of plans and policies, the allocation of funds, and decisions on issues such as products, marketing areas, etc. It appoints a "management board" to conduct the day-to-day business of the firm. It should be noted that no member of the supervisory board may serve on the management board. Unlike the U.S., West German industry has nothing comparable to the position of "Chairman of the Board/Chief Executive Officer" so commonly seen in this country. The appointive and supervisory power of the supervisory board and its responsibility to make major decisions concerning the goals and objectives of the firm makes membership on the board extremely important to the worker.

"Work councils" (comparable in a very broad sense to union locals in the U.S.) must be formed in any firm employing more than five workers. Blue- and white-collar workers are represented in proportion to their numbers in the company. The work council does not bargain for wages and working conditions normally negotiated on a regional or national basis, but it has a right to co-determination—an equal say with management—in deciding such issues as:

- Job evaluation, piece rates, and wage structures;
- Working hours, overtime arrangements, breaks, and holiday schedules;
- Staffing policies, including guidelines for recruiting, assigning, and dismissing workers;
- Social plans, that is, measures to mitigate the effect of layoffs on workers in the event of redundancy;
- Training, occupational safety, and welfare schemes;
- Allocation of company housing; and
- Workers' conduct on the shop floor.[21]

Hiring, discharge, work allocation, promotion, and demotion decisions require the consent of the council. Unilateral action by the employer in these areas is not allowed.

In the actual conduct of the business of the firm, the powers of the works council are more limited. In firms with more than 100 employees, the works council appoints an economic committee. The committee has the right to obtain information on major issues such as manufacturing methods, automation, production programs, and data concerning the financial condition of the firm. Analysis of this information is the responsibility of the economic committee. The consent of the works council is required for major actions such as plant closings and staff cuts.

Mills saw little potential for European-style industrial democracy systems in the United States.[22] We reached the same conclusion in more recent research.[23] Mazzolini found a clear trend in European countries toward formal participation as exemplified by the West German model, and away from the noninstitutional confrontation. However, he notes that:

> The introduction of participative systems in countries where antagonism is the dominant mode may change little of substance. Both workers and employers may be severely disappointed.[24]

The most recent research in this area has been done by Frieden.[25] He concludes that worker participation in ownership and management holds great potential for improvements in labor relations, efficiency and productivity.

Frieden discusses two specific cases. In 1972 a Kaiser Steel continuous weld mill with 80 employees established a labor-management committee in a last-ditch attempt to prevent a shutdown. The committee was formed at the request of the union, a request reluctantly agreed to by management. In three months time productivity increased 32 percent and the mill was saved. Some workers were displaced, but they were either given other jobs, or took early retirement. Although many beneficial effects were noted, management was apparently embarrassed by the success of the experiment. Information required by the committee was restricted and the committee lapsed into disuse.[26]

In the second case, in 1974, a subsidiary of Youngstown Sheet and Tube Company formed a labor-management committee. The potential for improvement was not as great as had been the case in the Kaiser plant, but the committee was credited with a 5.5% productivity increase during the three years it was in operation. Production delays fell from 10 percent to 3 percent and absenteeism fell from approximately 15 percent to 7 percent. The committee was phased out, ostensibly due to high turnover among committee members. Frieden states that "The primary reason, however, was that increasing tensions within the steel industry made cooperative efforts between labor and management extremely difficult at the plant."[27]

The American system has no clear counterpart in Europe. Industrial democracy in European countries has been fought for and gained in the political arena. Systems such as co-determination are the result of national law, not the normal give-and-take between management and labor practiced in the United States. A review of labor history in our country will reinforce the idea of the voluntary basis of labor/management relations. The system of co-determination in West Germany has resulted in hundreds of pages of manifold, complex legislation bearing little relation to laws in this country and leaving practically no room for the freedom of operation expected and desired by American workers and representatives. In the authors' opinion, these expectations and desires and the traditional adversarial labor/management relationships in the United States will restrict the development of truly effective labor/management committees on the European model for the foreseeable future.

In contrast to the mandated or contractual presence of the worker on worker/management committees are situations wherein the worker(s) actually owns all or part of the firm and has management rights by virtue of ownership.

The Employee Stock Option Plan (ESOP) and its management arm, the Employees' Stock Option Trust (ESOT), is an employee-benefit plan in which the company (usually a small, closely-held, corporation) sells its stock to its employees. These plans work in conjunction with, or as replacements for, the normal retirement plans. San Francisco attorney Louis Kelso, who is credited with the concept, claims that it can

"...redistribute wealth within the framework of our capitalist system, assist in capital formation, motivate workers, promote economic growth, reduce welfare costs, and accomplish a number of other ends that others consider desirable."[28]

Jochim hypothesized that an employee-owned firm (either completely employee-owned, or partially through an ESOP) "... should have (a) increased profitability, (b) a better growth record, (c) increased productivity, (d) more employment stability, (e) fewer work stoppages, and (f) lower turnover of workers."[29] He examined reports on 10 employee-owned firms and found (using both the firms' history of before-and-after ESOP and comparative approaches) that seven of the firms were successes, in that they met one or more of his hypotheses. Two firms experienced insignificant change in any of the indicators. In the final instance the plan failed and the company was sold.[30]

Jochim states that the conditions existing in the successful firms were a small-to-moderate size; a skilled and highly-interactive work force acceptable to good labor/management relations; generally democratic management styles; moderate or cooperative union leadership when a union existed; an economy that was stagnant or growing slowly; project or job-shop production, and; a flat management hierarchy.[31]

A study of 68 representative firms utilizing ESOP[32] supports Jochims' findings. In the 30 firms for which profit data was available, it was found that the largest single correlate of profitability among the characteristics of ownership measured was worker ownership.[33] The data indicates that employee ownership causes improvements in productivity and profits, and improvements in worker and management satisfaction.

Frieden's data supports prior research. Dramatic increases in sales per employee, net profit per employee, productivity, salaries, and other indicators are cited in his study. In some cases, these increases occurred in firms on the verge of bankruptcy where any increase would be dramatic on a relative basis, but there are instances of old, established worker-owned firms in which the firm does far better than the industry average.[34] Democracy in the workplace is justified on the basis of results, rather than some nebulous concept of social good.

Summary

Mills said that "What has happened in America has been open, growing, groping—a *process* without discrete boundaries or manuals or formulas."[35] He quoted John Dewey's definition of political democracy, American-style as:

"...faith in human nature, faith in human intelligence, and the power of pooled and collective experience. It's not belief that these things are complete but that if given a show, they will grow and generate the knowledge and wisdom needed to guide collective wisdom."[36]

This faith in the average person's innate common sense and ability to make decisions that are best for him or her bodes ill for a national application of co-determination as practiced in West Germany. At the same time, the *principles* of co-determination are seen as part of management-labor relationships in the future. Ownership of the firm by the employees and the concomitant responsibilities of ownership will grow. Neither co-determination nor ownership, however, will be mandated. The American system will retain the process characteristics outlined by Mills. Boundaries, formalae, and rules will be developed in individualistic, *ad hoc* ways. Both management and unions will resist the intrusion of the legislative process into labor/management relations.

Footnotes

[1]Walker, C.R. & Guest, R.H., "The Man on the Assembly Line," *Harvard Business Review,* date? (1952), pp. ??.

[2]Herzberg, F., "One More Time: How Do You Motivate Employees?" *Harvard Business Review,* Jan–Feb (1968), pp. 53–62.

[3]Meyers, M.S., *Every Employee a Manager* (New York: McGraw-Hill, 1970).

[4]Paul, W.J., Robertson, K.B., & Herzberg, F., "Job Enrichment Pays Off," *Harvard Business Review,* March–April (1969), pp. 61–78.

[5]Fein, M., "the Myth of Job Enrichment," in *Humanizing the Workplace,* ed. R. Fairfield (Buffalo, NY: Prometheus Books, 1974), pp. 71–78.

[6]Odiorne, G.S., *Management by Objectives* (New York: Pitman, 1965).

[7]Latham, G.P. & Yukl, G.A., "A Review of Research on the Application of Goal Setting in Organizations," *Academy of Management Journal, 18,* 1975, pp. 824–845.

[8]Levinson, H., "Management by Whose Objectives?" *Harvard Business Review,* July–August (1970), pp. 125–134.

[9]Ryan, E.J. Jr., "Federal Government MBO: Another Management Fad?" *MSU Business Topics 24:4* Autumn (1976), pp. 35–43.

[10]Blake, R.S. & Mouton, J.S., *Building a Dynamic Organization through Grid Organization Development,* (Reading, MA: Addison-Wesley, 1969), pp. 84–87.

[11]Dyer, W.G., *Team Building: Issues and Alternatives,* (Reading, MA: Addison-Wesley, 1977), pp. 137–139.

[12]Zollitsch, H.G., "Productivity, Time Study, and Incentive-Pay Plans", in *Motivation and Commitment,* eds. D. Yoder & H.G. Heneman, Jr. (Washington, DC: Bureau of National Affairs, Inc., 1975), pp. 6–51 to 6–73.

[13]Miner, John B., and Miner, Mary G., *Personnel and Industrial Relations: A Managerial Approach,* (New York: Macmillan Publishing Co., 1979), pg. 171, and Wanos, J.P., "Individual Differences and Reactions to Job Characteristics," *Journal of Applied Psychology,* (1974), p. 618.

[14]Straub, Joseph T., *Applied Management* (Cambridge, MA: Winthrop Publishers, Inc., 1979), p. 356.

[15]*Ibid.,* p. 359.

[16]For an excellent discussion of communal settlements in the United States, refer to "Utopia" in the *Encyclopedia Brittannica,* (Chicago, IL: William Benton, 1968), vol. 22, pp. 821–820.

[17]Drucker, Peter, "The Job as Property Right," *The Wall Street Journal,* March 4, 1980, p. 54.

[18]Brophy, Beth, "Unfunded Pension Liabilities," *Forbes, 125:4,* February 18, 1980, p. 54.

[19]"A Frightening Vise on Plant Shutdowns," *Business Week,* March 17, 1980, p. 38. (The case was *Williams vs. U.S. Steel,* 79-2337, U.S. District Court of Northern Ohio, Eastern Division.)

[20]*Op cit.*

[21]*Co-Determination: Worker Participation in German Industry* (New York: German Information Center, 1977), p. 13.

[22]Mills, Ted, "Europe's Industrial Democracy: An American Response," *Harvard Business Review,* November–December (1978), p. 143–152.

[23]Kovach, Kenneth A., Brooks, William W., and Sands, Ben F., Jr., "Is Co-Determination a Workable Idea for U.S. Labor-Management Relations?" *MSU Business Topics,* Winter (1980), pp. 51–55.

[24]Mazzolina, Renato, "The Influence of European Workers over Corporate Strategy," *Sloan Management Review,* Spring (1978), pp. 79–80.

[25]Frieden, Karl, *Workplace Democracy and Productivity* (Washington, DC: National Center for Economic Alternatives, 1980).

[26]*Ibid.,* pp. 33–35.

[27]*Ibid.,* pp. 35–36.

[28]Sullivan, Donald E., "ESOPs Panacea or Placebo?" *California Management Review,* Fall (1977), p. 55.

[29]Jochim, Timothy C., "Employee Stock Ownership Programs: The Next Economic Revolution?" *The Academy of Management Review,* July (1979), p. 441.

[30]*Op cit.*

[31]*Op cit.*

[32]Unpublished report, Survey Research Center for Economic Development, University of Michigan, "Employee Ownership" (Washington, DC: US Department of Commerce, 1977), p. #?.

[33]*Ibid.,* p. 24.

[34]Frieden, K., *op. cit.,* pp. 7–17.

[35]Mills, T., *ibid.* p. 152.

[36]*Op cit.*

HR Strategic Mandates for the 1990's

Kenneth A. Kovach
John A. Pearce II

Significant demographic shifts in the United States will have a profound impact on human resources management (HRM) in the 1990's. Although strategic managers are aware of the general nature of the changes, little progress has been made in identifying their HRM consequences. Since new demographics will require bold new HR initiatives, HR managers must become aware of the coming changes and begin to formulate appropriate strategies. In this article we will look at some of the best information available on the most imposing changes of the 1990's and suggest coping and proactive strategies for succeeding in this highly dynamic new decade.

Younger Workers

The number of workers younger than 25-years-of-age will decrease by 3.4% during the 1990's, a drastic reversal of the trend in the 1970's and early 1980's. As a result, HR managers will face a two-pronged problem.

On the one hand, less competition will come from employee ranks for those jobs with characteristics typically favored by younger workers, such as incentive-pay systems tied to personal performance and task-related programs including job enlargement and job enrichment. This does not mean that these characteristics will cease to influence employees' job preferences, but companies will emphasize them less because of the decreasing percentage of employees in the age group typically most influenced by them.

On the other hand, the smaller pool of younger workers will enjoy increased attention from recruiters seeking to fill entry-level positions. To attract these employees, HR managers will be forced to place a greater emphasis on in-house training and development programs. The younger group's opportunity for rapid advancement will be somewhat limited by the large number of older, baby-boom workers ahead of them in corporate hierarchies. Thus the availability of in-house training and development programs, which will enable younger employees to distinguish themselves from their peers when competing for a limited number of mid-level positions, will be a valuable recruiting tool in the coming decade.

Middle-Age Workers

The 25–54-year age group will be the fastest-growing age segment of the labor force from now until the Year 2000, increasing by 27% between now and then. Given the decrease in the percentage of younger workers and slight increase in older workers, the 25–54-year olds will be "where the action is" for human resources managers in the 1990's. The baby-boomers are the subgroup most responsible for this increase. Consider that by the year 2000, 40–54-year olds will constitute 25% of the U.S. population.

A major challenge for HR managers will be to prepare for the probable job displacement of many of these workers as a result of automation. The 25–40 segment of this age group will not be covered by the provisions of the 1967 Age Discrimination in Employment Act, and the 40–54 segment will have less seniority than the traditionally more job-stable 55-and-over sector. As a result, job displacement because of automation will hit middle-age workers harder than any other age group.

HR managers must, therefore, be prepared to introduce policies in company programs and union contracts that address the issue of job displacement caused by automation. Job security as a trade-off for wage increases became increasingly accepted in the late 1980's, and its acceptance will continue to grow. The deals reached on this issue in the past decade between management and labor in the automobile, steel, and general manufacturing sectors are only a trickle compared to the flood of such arrangements we can expect to see in the 1990's. Such arrangements will be acceptable to both employees and employers because of economic necessity. For example, one of the most popular forms of job security is likely to be a clause wherein employees above a certain seniority level will be retrained for other positions within the company.

Pension portability will also be a response to the impact of automation on middle-aged workers over the next ten years. The older baby-boomers will need to begin long-term retirement planning. Increased solvency problems with Social Security as well as ERISA restrictions on options for vesting of private pensions will make portability of seniority for pension rights a major issue in the near future. Intercorporate and interindustry agreements for pension portability will become commonplace by the turn of the century. Combined employer funding of such plans will become a major concern of human resource professionals.

"Attrition" arrangements, whereby the employer reduces the labor force by not replacing employees who leave, rather than by laying-off employees, will likewise gain wide acceptance. Such arrangements will often be palatable to middle-aged workers faced with the alternative of job loss and will allow employers to address the issue of displacement due to technological advances in a socially-acceptable way.

Employees displaced because of automation will be likely to receive some type of supplemental unemployment coverage. More than 5 million employees are now receiving coverage from a company-financed private unemployment plan that supplements state plans for workers above a certain seniority level. The middle-aged workers of the 1990's will be drawing from such plans, since their seniority level will make them eligible; but unlike older workers, they will not have enough seniority to avoid the technologically-induced layoff. As a result, supplemental unemployment costs will rise as the number of covered employees reaches an estimated 10 million during the 1990's.

Older Workers

The segment of the labor force age 55-and-older will increase by 3.4% during the 1990's, offsetting the decrease in the percentage of younger workers. While the increase in this age segment will be dwarfed by the growth of the middle-age-group, older workers will create unique and serious problems for HR managers. Those problems will be most acute in the areas of retirement and health-care costs.

By the turn of the century a number of factors will combine to increase drastically retirement costs for the typical U.S. employer. The increase in the number of older workers eligible for retirement benefits does not begin to tell the story of the approaching problem with retirement financing. More and more employers will be forced to offer early retirement options, as a result of 1986 changes in the Age Discrimination Act. For many employers the protected group now includes employees over age 70.

Early retirement will be offered in an attempt to replace older workers with younger ones, so as to save on wage costs (when more seniority means higher wages) and insurance costs (when age profiles influence company premiums). Moderating the widespread use of such policies will be increased retirement costs and rapidly rising starting wage rates for the undersized pool of younger workers.

In addition, the practice begun in the mid 1980's of using wages earned during the later employment years, as opposed to income averaging, to figure income for pension purposes can be expected to continue and further increase pension costs.

HR managers should anticipate yet another major factor that will influence retirement costs. The introduction of cost-of-living adjustments (COLA) to pension payments is currently done by only a small segment of employers, and even then it takes place on an *ad hoc* basis. Starting with the organized labor sector and gradually spreading from there, COLA clauses in pension plans will begin to appear during the 1990's, with regularly scheduled, rather than sporadic adjustments.

Such adjustments already take place in Social Security and federal and military pensions, but the federal government has found it possible to operate with huge deficit budgets. Such a luxury is not available to the private sector, and the financial implications of COLA clauses in the pension plans of major employers are staggering. Current estimates are that even a weak COLA clause—one that adjusts for only 50% of the inflation rate—will increase the cost of the average private-sector plan by 30–33% over the next decade. Yet a dramatic increase in the number of those clauses seems probable.

Anyone who doubts that the above factors add up to a serious cost problem for the 1990's, need only to consider that in 1983 a Health, Education, and Welfare Department study found that unfunded, vested-pension liabilities of all public and private pension systems exceeded $600 billion, while Standard and Poors Compustat Services found that such liabilities exceeded net worth in some companies. *Business Week* found that underfunding was almost $22 billion among its top 100 corporations. The factors discussed above will only exacerbate this solvency problem.

In addition to pension issues, the increase in the number of older workers will cause problems in the area of healthcare costs. In 1988, 10% of the U.S. Gross National Product (GNP) went to medical expenses; by the Year 2000 the figure will rise to 15%. This escalation raises serious questions about health-care cost-containment. Since people typically incur 85% of their healthcare expenses during the last two years of life, it is easy to see why even a modest percentage increase in the older segment of the labor force will mean a drastic increase in employer healthcare costs.

Remember also that since 1987, healthcare has been the economic area hardest hit by inflation in the United States. The average employer now spends $2,200 per employee, per year on healthcare, an expenditure expected to increase 15% to 20% this year alone.

Budget analysts, corporate planners, and HR managers will need to devise a corporate strategy for healthcare cost-containment. They should look at policies that curb excessive use of hospitals: utilization reviews, outpatients and surgicenter care, insurance coverage of second and even third opinions on elective surgery, reimbursement for health services at home, greater use of pre-admission testing, and increased private use of professional standards review organizations.

Health maintenance organizations (HMO's) also offer significant cost advantages for the employer. Today only 13% of employer-provided healthcare plans include use of an HMO; by the Year 2000, almost 50% of such plans will have the use of a specified HMO as a component.

Finally, more of the cost of healthcare can be expected to be passed on to the employee. In 1980, 50% of employer-sponsored healthcare plans were contributory; in 1988 the figure rose to 62%, and by the Year 2000 it may well approach 80%.

Female Employees

One of the most striking changes in the labor force during the 1990's will be the increase in the number of women employed full time. By 2000, women will constitute 65% of all labor force entrants and 47% of all full-time U.S. workers—up from 40% in 1989.

The stereotypical family unit of a generation ago, with the male breadwinner, the female housewife, and one or more children, represents fewer than 15% of U.S. families today. Some 62% of all mothers are employed; in fact, nearly 50% of all married women with children under two years are working outside the home. If the current annual 37% increase in the number of working mothers continues, by 1995 more than 80% of all mothers with children at home will be working. Only part of this increase will come from women seeking self-fulfillment through careers; the rest will be the result of economic necessity.

From 1960 to 1973 family income increased every year, but the purchasing power achieved in 1973 has not been matched since. The decline has hit families with young children particularly hard. In 1973 households headed by males over 30 years of age earned an average of $25,253 (in 1968 dollars): by 1988 that figure had dropped to $18,763. Of the married women who worked outside the home in 1988, 40% had husbands whose annual income was less than $15,000. Thus, more and more women are working simply to maintain an economic standard of living equal to their counterparts of 15 or 20 years ago.

As these trends continue through the next decade, they can be expected to produce a different set of circumstances than those produced by the age shifts discussed earlier. While changes in labor force composition by age can be managed through internal company policies, the increasing number of females in the full-time labor force can be expected to draw a legislative response.

The most important Congressional initiative is the proposed Family and Medical Leave Bill (HR 770), a key item on the Democrats' agenda. This bill, already approved by the House Education and Labor Committee and with more than 200 sponsors in the House, will require all companies with 50 or more employees to provide unpaid leaves of up to 10 weeks every two years for parents of newborn or newly adopted children, up to 10 weeks every two years for parents of a seriously-ill child or elderly parent, and up to 15 weeks every two years for employees who are seriously ill. Three years after enactment, the bill would apply to employers with 35 or more employees.

This bill, in its present or amended form, can be expected to pass sometime during the 1990's. Magnifying the cost impact of this legislation is the fact that as a result of the age trend discussed earlier, the females entering the workforce in the greatest number will be of childbearing age, who will disproportionately seek the benefits made available by the new law.

Another legislative response that seems likely is the Act for Better Child Care Bill (S5). Having already cleared the Senate Labor and Human Resource Committee and with a large number of Congressional sponsors, this bill would set federal standards for childcare facilities, establish a referral system, provide financial assistance to low-income families who need such care, and help fund the expansion of existing facilities. When one considers that 36.2 million children now live in households where one or both parents work and only 2.5 million childcare slots are available in licensed facilities, it is reasonable to believe that employers will play a major role in establishing such facilities during this decade.

In dealing with the two big issues tied to female labor-force participation—family medical leaves and childcare—HR managers would be wise to implement new company policies like those discussed above, rather than wait for legislative dictates and then passively complying. In addition, companies should adjust to the needs of their female labor force through internal initiatives such as pooled sick leave, flextime, summer working hours, four-day weeks, split days, job sharing and telecommuting for jobs that can be done at home.

Race and Ethnic Origin

Although whites will remain the major labor group in the United States through the Year 2000, their absolute numbers will increase only 15%, compared with a 20% increase for blacks and a 74% increase for Hispanics. The fertility rate among Hispanics is currently 96 births per 1,000 women, compared with 83 for blacks, and 69 for whites. These facts, coupled with heavy immigration, will make the Hispanic growth rate faster than that of any other race or ethnic group in this country.

Current projections indicate that Hispanics will make up 10.5% of the workforce by the turn of the century and will surpass blacks as the largest racial minority in the next 20 to 25 years. Thus, HR planners and recruiters will have to adjust their mindset on minority employment from "black" to "Hispanic and black." As the relative number of each of these groups increases in the next ten years, their skills and productivity are likely to be an increasingly important element in determining a corporation's future.

The problem employers will face when dealing with this growing segment of the workforce stems from the deprived backgrounds and low education levels that characterize a disproportionate number of these employees. While 86% of white workers now have at least a high school diploma, only 60% of Hispanics and 73% of blacks have this level of formal education. With the fastest growing occupations requiring a college degree or extensive training beyond high school (for example, computer analyst and processor, up 75.6% by the year 2000; medical assistant, up 90.4%; paralegal personnel, up 103%) the lack of highly-educated and trained personnel among the fastest-growing racial and ethnic groups will dictate a greater emphasis on in-house training programs.

Such programs will by necessity be job specific and targeted toward the least-educated personnel in entry-level nonsupervisory jobs. Recall our earlier findings that the decrease in the number of younger workers and the bottleneck created by the baby-boomers will increase the importance of training for the under-25 age group. Now we see that an increasing share of this young age group will consist of lesser-educated black and Hispanic workers. During the 1990's, then, many such training programs will need to be of the job-specific, entry-level nature.

Geographic Location

Since the late 1950's population growth has slowed in the North, while growth in the South and West has increased rapidly. Between now and 2000 the North's population will increase 4%, while that of the South and West will exceed 20%. Current trends indicate that by the year 2030, the population of the South will overtake that of the Northeast and Midwest combined. Of the 32.5 million new jobs created by the year 2000, 18 million will be in the South, 10 million in the West, and less than 5 million in the North. Among the 50 fastest growing metropolitan areas over the next 10 years, 20 will be in the South and 16 in the West, with 11 in California, six in Florida, and five in Texas. Furthermore, the West Coast, especially California and Washington with their extensive production facilities, will dominate the production sector of the economy, as more and more businesses relocate there. The shift of industry follows the population movement, which, in turn, attracts more industry. This cycle is already in motion and is irreversible in the foreseeable future. These shifts will produce an HRM trouble spot in the 1990's. Plant closings and relocations by employers in the North, Northeast, and Midwest will become more common.

The fact that industry is relocating to the South and West, and will continue to do so, seems indisputable. When one considers the number of citizens who will be affected by industrial relocation and the resulting political pressure for regulation of this movement, it is clear that the geographic shift of population and industry will generate a legislative response.

Thus far, organized labor has forced the issue of plant closings in three arenas. At the bargaining table, it has been moderately successful in getting contract clauses (such as advance notice, retraining, relocation allowances, and reinstatement rights) that require management to deal with labor on the effects of plant closings, although not on the closing decision itself. The second arena is the court system; the U.S. Supreme Court has recognized a management duty to bargain over the effects of plant closings (*First National Maintenance Corp. v. NLRB*, 1981) but has removed the actual decision to close from mandatory bargaining (*NLRB. v. Adams Dairy, Inc.*, 1965).

Finally, in the Congressional arena, bills have been introduced in every session since 1974 to eliminate or cushion the impact of employee dislocation. The definitive word on plant closings and relocations can be expected to surface in Congress sometime in the next few years. Congress is presently awaiting a report on plant closing by the Task Force on Economic Adjustment and Worker Dislocation, formed by the Secretary of Labor. It is expected to recommend legislation that would require companies contemplating closing and relocating to (1) give employees three months' advance notice of a plant closing and (2) meet with representatives, if any, of employees to consult in good faith and reach a mutually-satisfactory alternative or modification to the plant-closing plan.

In addition, a 15-member National Commission on Plant Closings and Worker Dislocation will be established to study and report legislative recommendations concerning closings. Thus, employers can be expected to continue to rush to the South and West, but will be required to comply with soon-to-be-passed legislation regulating the conditions of such a relocation.

Planning Ahead

The labor force trends discussed in this article will all have major implications for HR managers during the 1990's. Only by being aware of such trends can responsible individuals begin to formulate intelligent corporate responses. The possible responses discussed above can serve as a starting point for strategic HR planning. In some cases bold corporate initiatives are called for, although in others, simple legislative compliance will suffice. In any event, labor force changes over the next decade will have serious repercussions for those caught unaware.

Do We Still Need Labor Organizations?

It is common knowledge today that organized labor is losing strength in numerical and political terms, as well as in the influence it exerts over the rest of the labor force. Numerically, labor unions have gone from 42% of the labor force in the 1950's, to less than 20% today, with every indication that this downward trend will continue. Were it not for the large number of newly organized public employees, the numbers would be even more ominous for labor unions. Many labor students contend that because of the restrictions on unions in the public sector (many cannot discuss wages and are prohibited from striking), the value to labor as a whole of a limited number of publicly employed individuals organizing is not nearly as great as a like number of privately employed workers organizing. Thus, even the decreasing numbers may not tell the whole story of labor's deteriorating position.

Politically, it should be clear to even the most casual observer that unions are losing their clout. The day when the powerful labor boss could "deliver" the labor vote, and hence was admitted to the inner circles of politics and politicians, is gone. It is hard to imagine a modern day John L. Lewis working closely with the President to draft key pieces of legislation, or inviting members of Congress to his office to "discuss" their votes on upcoming issues, practices that were once a source of pride and status for powerful labor leaders. Labor's present political influence can best be gauged by its track record on such major issues as the Common Situs Picketing Bill, the original Humphrey-Hawkins Full Employment Bill, Labor Law Reform, etc., all defeats.

While organized labor has long been felt to be the trend-setter for wages and terms of employment, with the rest of the labor force following with a certain time lag, even here we are witnessing the declining strength of unions. Except in a few big industries (steel, auto, etc.) where unions enjoy a virtual monopoly, the increasing number of nonunionized firms has reintroduced the cost of labor as a competitive factor in market strategies. More and more frequently unions have had to consider the impact of their economic demands on the employer's ability to attract enough business to maintain employment levels. The construction industry is the most dramatic and widely known example of this phenomena, but it is happening in an increasing number of less publicized instances. The "Southern strategy" of the auto employers, the move to the South of the big steel companies, and the inability of the mining unions to organize new mines are all indicators that even in industries long considered union strongholds, this factor will become increasingly important in the future.

The logical question growing out of the above discussion is, therefore, do we still need labor organizations? Is it not possible that they have outlived their usefulness and are no longer needed? To answer questions such as these, it is important to take a brief look at labor history. Labor history reaffirms one of the more important lessons to be learned from history in general, that if people are pushed hard enough, are subjected to adverse enough conditions, they will take actions they would never have dreamed of, had things been more equitable. It is only within the context of the time that today's labor student can understand why otherwise normal individuals would sit in unheated Michigan and Ohio automobile plants in the middle of winter for 44 days, or why they would barricade themselves in steel mills and vow to fight to the death unless working conditions were improved. Read about what workers did to organize the first textile unions, the first mining unions, the first railroad unions, and then ask yourself if you would be willing or able to endure what they did. I would contend that you probably could, and, furthermore, that you would probably be willing to, if you were subjected to the treatment that those individuals were. The purpose of this article is not to discuss the historical plight of the American worker, yet it is crucial to understand what this plight was. For the first 150 years of this country's independence, the American worker was free politically, but a virtual slave industrially. A look backward at management practices such as company-owned housing, water supplies, stores, etc., with their inflated prices, the payment of workers in company script, the unsafe and unhealthy working conditions, the unbelievably long working week, the ridiculously low wages making it impossible for most families to live on the earnings of a single breadwinner, the completely arbitrary employment and personnel practices, and the company police forces, to mention only a few – in fact, the complete lack of consideration of the worker as a human being – puts the remarkable growth of labor unions in the early 1900's in a different light. Certainly, at this point in U.S. history workers were ready to support any type of organization that promised them relief from their miserable industrial existence. Thus, labor unions filled a real need—they brought humanitarianism to the workplace and a degree of dignity to the American worker.

Ironically enough, because of their success, unions have eradicated most of the conditions that led to their formation. Thus, an often heard argument today is that while unions were necessary once, they are no longer needed. Proponents of this argument contend that the American worker today enjoys a higher standard of living than ever before, that we now have laws such as the Fair Labor Standards Act, the National Labor Relations Act, the Occupational

Safety and Health Act, etc., which set a floor for wages, working conditions, and general treatment of employees below which no employer is entitled to go.

While there is much support for this point of view, I must take exception to it. While laws and subsequent conditions of employment may have changed, basic human nature has not. While it may be a pessimistic assessment of humanity, and one with which the reader will likely disagree, I firmly believe that a high percentage of 20th century people will take advantage of you, if the price is right. Through the ages, history has repeatedly proven this to be a truism, and anyone who does not realize it is either uninformed, extremely idealistic, or naive. While the laws provide deterrents in the form of minimum acceptable standards, it would certainly be unacceptable to the majority of our working population to exist at these minimum standards. For many even a small retreat backward (e.g., compensation, working conditions, safety standards, etc.) would be completely unacceptable. Yet if the law were the only minimum, the only deterrent, there would be plenty of room for retreat in the standards enjoyed in the workplace by the majority of the U.S. labor force. The biggest single deterrent, besides the law, to the reduction of standards in the workplace, is the combined action of the workers—call it a *union* or any other name you wish. This action does not even have to come to pass to serve its purpose, for in many instances the mere *possibility* of such action is sufficient. (There can be no doubt that the level of benefits received by many nonunion workers is in part buttressed by their employers desire to reward them at such a level that they remain unorganized.)

Thus, while unions may have outlived their usefulness in terms of their original objectives, they are still needed because of what I have been referring to as their *deterrent* effect. If they are truly the instrument prohibiting exploitation of the worker, not in the traditional browbeaten sense, but in today's more humanistic, less extreme sense, then they are definitely needed. The irony is that even those individuals in the blue-collar sector who would suffer first and most if unions were to disappear tomorrow, do not realize the vital role labor organizations play in today's economy. It is not necessary for them to be as strong as they once were, for the problems they are trying to correct are not as severe, and the government has taken over part of their original purpose through various pieces of legislation. Yet it is still vital that they continue to exist, not only for those who benefit directly from them, but also for those who believe in the need to maintain the dignity of the worker. Unions find themselves in the same peculiar position as the military, in that what they cause to happen may not be nearly as important as what they cause *not* to happen. Thus, while I hope that the American public is never forced by events to realize why we still need labor unions, I do emphatically contend that they are, in fact, an absolute necessity.

Organized Labor's Deteriorating Condition

Any serious student of organized labor is aware that the American labor movement has experienced, and will continue to experience, hard times. Its membership is declining, the industries upon which its strength was built are in serious trouble, and unfavorable demographic, economic, and political trends have seriously weakened the once unparalleled influence of organized labor. Many who work in the field view this as a favorable trend, destined to mitigate problems from high inflation and unemployment to an unfavorable balance of payments, while others see it as a threat to the "checks and balances" necessary for reasonable labor management relations. Regardless of one's perspective, there can be no doubt that the deteriorating position of organized labor and its resultant effects in other sectors of the economy is one of the major socio-economic trends in the U.S. over the past fifteen years.

I propose to examine this phenomenon by: dissecting the problem itself and discussing its various components; exploring the major factors contributing to the problem; looking at the response to the problem by management, the government, and independent consultants, and; finally assessing labor's potential for rectifying the situation.

The Problem

There are three equally important components of labor's present unenviable condition, one being numerical, one political, and one jurisdictional. Numerically, the picture could not be worse for labor organizations. Despite the growth in the labor force over the last fifteen years, unions now have fewer dues-paying members than they did in 1980. In the last seven years alone, total membership has dropped from twenty million to barely over eighteen million, and there is every indication that this trend will continue. Obviously, with the increasing number of jobs and the decreasing number of union members, the percentages present an even more ominous picture.

Organized labor's percentage share of the labor market has dropped from 42 in 1954, to 28 in 1975, to 18.8 today.[1] This numerical decrease (which translates into dues, which translate into economic clout) is the independent variable that drives all the other dependent variables discussed in this article. Organized labor has long dismissed this trend as attributable to demographic factors, but the validity of this claim is undermined when one considers the magnitude of the numbers. Any institution that loses ten percent of its membership while the universe from which it can draw increases twenty-five percent, is in serious trouble. The numbers, as they say, speak for themselves.

Politically, the loss of influence by organized labor is obvious. Every American who follows the news is aware that labor poured more than ten million dollars and deployed thousands upon thousands of volunteers to support the Democratic candidate in the latest presidential election. Their politically stated goal was to deliver sixty-five percent of the union households for the Democrats, while holding the Republicans to thirty-five percent. Exit polls showed that nearly one-half the labor households voted Republican, which is better than they did in 1988.[2] Yet, one must look beyond this well-publicized failure to understand the severity of the political component of labor's deteriorating condition. The failure to wrestle a new Labor Law Reform Bill out of Congressional committee, the revision of the Davis-Bacon Act, and the lifting of import quotas on Japanese automobiles despite labor opposition, the fact that two more states have Right-To-Work laws than was, the case in 1986, and the high probability that the Administration's subminimum wage for teenagers will weather the AFL-CIO's attack, all speak loudly and clearly to labor's political condition. Regardless of what advances it achieves at the bargaining table (an area to be discussed later), unless labor reverses its political direction, it may well "win a few battles, but lose the war."

Jurisdictionally, the overwhelming percentage of organizing successes has come in the public sector. Over twenty percent of total union membership is now in this area. In the federal sector, sixty-one percent of the workforce is now represented, while in the non-federal public sector, thirty percent are represented. Even in these sectors, however, the growth is slowing markedly since the big increase in the late sixties to mid-seventies. More important is the fact that these new public members are being recruited to replace (not in addition to) private-sector members. With many in the public sector being prohibited from negotiating over wages and technology, from striking, and from covering their union with a security clause, one must question whether public-sector employees give labor organizations as much clout as an equal number of their private-sector counterparts would. Thus, the numbers may tell only part of the story regarding labor's deteriorating position. The jurisdictions covered by the numbers may provide additional insight.

The Factors

The five major factors contributing to the present condition of organized labor are the outcome of certification and decertification elections, the shift from blue- to white-collar jobs in the economy, the increasing number and percentage of women in the workforce, the biological and philosophical generation gap between union leaders and members, and the present Administration and the National Labor Relations Board.

Regarding union elections, even among the decreasing number of workers receptive enough to listen to labor's message, the numbers bode ill. Over six hundred bargaining units decertified their unions in each of the last three years. Unions won less than one-half of the certification elections in each year since 1986, and have lost three-quarters of the increasing number of decertification elections during the same time period. When studied longitudinally, one sees that these trends are, in fact, accelerating, and I have every expectation that they will continue into the foreseeable future.

Another contributing factor is the shift we have seen in this country away from blue-collar manufacturing jobs to white-collar, service-oriented jobs. While the blue-collar manufacturing worker has traditionally been the cornerstone of the movement, there was only a .4 percent growth in such jobs from 1984 to 1990, and no growth since then. The blue-collar base of organized labor has been dependent upon industries that are shrinking, automating, closing, moving, or going international. The millions of new jobs created have been almost exclusively in the white-collar service-oriented sector, where union organizing success has been mediocre at best. While efforts to organize this sector have increased drastically in the last decade, the successes have not been of such a magnitude to offset the losses in the blue-collar sector. Thus labor, while it is making progress in the white-collar area, is not advancing rapidly enough to keep pace with the industrial shift from blue- to white-collar work.

Additionally, the increasing number and percentage of females in the workforce is a factor that should not be underestimated when diagnosing labor's present condition. Since 1985 the percentage of women who have unionized has fluctuated between thirteen and sixteen, compared with twenty-eight percent for men. As women, who are organized at approximately one-half the rate of men, constitute an increasing percentage of the labor force, unions have increased their efforts to organize this "pink collar" sector. Effort should not be confused with results, because, as stated above, the percentage of women who have organized has not increased noticeably over the last seven years.

I believe the most significant problem in this area has been unimaginative union leadership. Fortunately for organized labor, groups such as the Coalition of Labor Union Women, The National Education Association and the Service Employees Union, with their female leadership and large female membership are working hard from *within* the system to educate the traditional white, male hierarchy as to the importance of organizing drives aimed at women and to the issues essential to such drives (pay equity, health and safety issues, equitable job classifications, etc.). Despite the best efforts of such groups, however, it does not appear to me that women will become full-fledged members of the labor community in the near future, since they are concentrated in the job fields where unions are not well entrenched: administrative, service, part-time, and high-technology industries with many small and union-resistant companies. For these reasons, the increasing number and percentage of females in the workforce is a contributing factor to organized labor's deteriorating position.

The biological and philosophical generation gap between union leaders and members must also be recognized as a factor. The union workforce, in addition to becoming smaller, is becoming younger and better educated. Many old-line union leaders have failed to recognize the fact that this change makes it impossible to conduct business as they did twenty years ago. The civil rights and antiwar activists of the 1960's have become disenchanted with their ossified and lethargic leaders, and they see the traditional union structure as incapable of responding to their needs and desires because of the type of individual who holds key hierarchical positions. Additionally, young workers, unlike their parents, take a living wage as a given, not something that needs to be fought for. They see work as more than just a financial necessity, and the relative generosity of state and supplemental unemployment benefits exacerbates this feeling. The postwar baby-boomers are, and will continue to be, labor's dominant age group in the 1990's. The fact that they are confounding labor s establishment with values and needs different from their parents is even more threatening than the normal young-versus-old split. Their increasingly middle-class outlook, made possible by the struggles of the two preceding generations of union members, makes them less likely to devote themselves to the labor struggle. Their present is no longer measured by fears of the past, but by hopes for the future.[3] The changes of this generation gap are critical, because it is in the industries with the most union growth potential that the problem is most acute. Better-educated workers in the high-technology industries may well come to regard the unions as bureaucratic entities that are as much of a damper on their aspirations as any unenlightened corporation. One of the most serious threats to future union growth may come from this generational schism.

The final contributing factor to labor's condition is the present Administration and the National Labor Relations Board. The President's campaign promise to "get regulators off the backs of business" has had a direct effect on unions, in that the way labor laws have been interpreted and enforced has changed drastically since 1988. Labor leaders have been unable to protect their members from what they perceive to be, and what under previous Administrations would have been, violations of the National Labor Relations Act, the Railway Labor Act, the Labor-Management Relations Act, and the Labor Management Reporting and Disclosure Act.

The reasons for this are twofold. First, the number of enforcement personnel, as well as the budgets of the agencies administering these acts, has been cut drastically. This creates a backlog that discourages the filing of charges, and it means that, among those filed, a smaller percentage can actually be heard and, if need be, prosecuted. Second, present appointees to political positions within the regulatory agencies have shown no reluctance to reverse previous and, in many cases, long-standing decisions.

In no agency has this been more evident or important than in the National Labor Relations Board. To mention just one of many important examples to illustrating this point, the Board reversed a long-standing decision and ruled, in Milwaukee Spring Division II,[4] that an employer may relocate operations from a union to a nonunion facility during the term of a labor agreement, even if the move is solely designed to escape the higher labor costs of the unionized plants, so long as such relocation is not specifically forbidden in the existing labor agreement.[5] Decisions such as this have become commonplace under the present Administration, and while differences of opinion arise concerning their propriety, there can be no argument that they weaken the position of organized labor and, in turn, make unions less attractive to potential members. While this factor is not as readily apparent and visible as those mentioned previously, it is equally important.

The Responses

Responses to the situation discussed in the first section of this article have come from three main sources: management, local governments, and independent consultants. Management's most direct response has been to relocate to the Southeast and Southwest. In the last twenty years, the number of manufacturing jobs grew by forty-five percent in the Southeast and sixty-seven percent in the Southwest. It is crucial for the reader to realize that the *jobs* moved first, then the well-documented population shift was pulled along. It is somewhat of a chicken-and-egg phenomenon, but large numbers of individuals cannot relocate, unless there are jobs available at the new location. Certainly, their very presence will create some new jobs, particularly in the service sector, but with the sophisticated logistics system in this country today, it is not as imperative as it used to be that most jobs be performed within the immediate geographic market they serve. Hence, in the classic economic push-pull situation, the jobs *pushed* first and the population was then *pulled*.

As a result, for the first time since Reconstruction, the Northeast and Mid-west, once our industrial heartlands and solid union strongholds, no longer hold the majority of the American population. A response favored by other companies has been to transfer jobs overseas, or to subcontract work to countries with lower wage scales. The average consumer would be hard pressed to notice the differences in quality between the work of a unionized American seamstress and a Taiwanese seamstress, yet a company will surely notice the ten-to-one wage differential. The result is that management shifts union jobs not only to the American South but to foreign countries as well.

A final management response has been to seek "give-backs" at the bargaining table. Many times, unions were faced with the alternative of either granting these concessions or losing some or all of their jobs. Major contracts settled during 1989 produced wage increases of 2.8 percent over the life of the contract, versus 6.6 percent increases three years earlier. In fact, nonunion wage increases have been exceeding those of union workers during recent times.[6]

Local government has been another respondent to unions' deteriorating condition. As management's response is to relocate, many local governments have begun to compete to be the beneficiaries of this relocation. In an attempt to retain or attract private capital, state and local governments have begun to give present or prospective industrial citizens some tax and labor-law relief. The creation of a **probusiness climate** is one of the major marketing points local jurisdictions are using to attract industry. Conversely, jurisdictions presently housing these industries have been forced to grant similar relief, in an attempt to hold onto what they have. One need only look at the tax base and resultant city services and physical plants in industrial centers across different geographic regions, to realize the magnitude and implications of this particular response.

Finally, a new breed of independent consultant has surfaced as a response to labor's plight. Use of these **union-avoidance** consultants has become fashionable, widespread, and effective. Such consultants as Stephen Cabot, Anthony McKeown, Alfred DeMaria, and Scott Myers are making fortunes teaching management how to keep a company union-free. Their success is based on their ability to convince employers that treating employees properly makes good economic sense. Stephen Cabot states that employers should blame themselves if their workers unionize, because it may well be an indication that they have not been fair, even-handed, or open-minded.[7] Success rates approaching 90 percent in keeping unions out are an indication of the effectiveness of such consultants. In addition to their success rate, the high fees paid to such experts are easily justified, when one stops to consider the economic advantage to a large company of remaining union-free. Rational economic thought connects the economic benefits to the company, to the high fees they are willing to pay for this service, to the high number of individuals attracted to this line of work. Hence, the final response is simply the end result of economic evaluation.

Conclusion

The next logical question is "what can labor do now?" Given the magnitude and diversity of the factors contributing to the problem, there will not be any simple answers. Addressing one or two particular aspects of the problem at a time will not be sufficient.

First, there must be a philosophical rapprochement between organized labor's leadership and the work force of the 1990's. These leaders must recognize that the nature of American business has changed, and that things will never be as they were when they were young workers. The reality of a better-educated, high-technology or white-collar, service-oriented work force must be considered. Extensive use of simple attitude surveys among present and potential union members would go a long way toward making decision makers within the unions aware that the use of self-reference criteria is no longer appropriate. Unlike thirty years ago, when today's decision makers were in their positions, today's workers and potential union members have a middle-class outlook that gives rise to different objectives, images, and behavior than their unionized parents.

Until today's union leader realizes this and reacts accordingly, little will be done to improve the unions' position. Attitude surveys are a quick, inexpensive way to find out about respondents' desires, attitudes, etc., so that the labor organization can bring itself and its actions in line with those of the individuals it is trying to attract. I believe that such surveys will show that today's worker expects more than wages from the job, regards demands for wage increases beyond a certain point as job threatening, and sees incessant union bickering over trivial work rules as needless and unproductive. Health and safety, job enlargement and enrichment, quality of work life, and pay equity may well emerge as issues labor should be addressing more vigorously at the bargaining table. Progress in these areas, as opposed to wages (which, in many cases, only further exacerbates the existing problem) may well be the key to enrolling the new, better-educated, and female members the unions need so desperately to attract.

Additionally, more emphasis must be placed on retraining programs for workers displaced by automation, and less on the lock-step protectionist policies of the past. For example, if one-half the money spent by labor to lobby for import quotas on automobiles had been spent on retraining existing workers for the new jobs in that industry, not only the union, but also the industry and the entire economy would be much better off.

Another tactic labor should try is to play economic hardball through the use of the billions of dollars in union pension funds. Shifting, or threatening to shift, these monies to encourage companies or local governments to modify their thinking and actions in the area of labor relations holds tremendous potential. The dollar value of corporate stock and local government securities held by union pension funds makes this, like the use of attitude surveys, a direct and immediate response by labor to its present situation.

While attitude surveys, retraining programs, and pension funds all offer hope for the unions, I must close on a pessimistic note. These and many other polices that could be recommended must still be implemented through those at the **top** of the hierarchy. In a recent survey of seventy-nine top labor officials,[8] several agreed that arrogance, inability to prepare successors, dogmatism, adherence to outdated ideas, and shortsightedness are problems with the leadership of organized labor today. The movement has lost its role as a *cause* for many leaders, and is now simply a *job*. Many are more interested in holding union office for money and power, than they are in effecting significant change.

If in fact this is the attitude of many union leaders, and I think it is, then it is too much to expect them to run the attitude surveys and respond accordingly, to shift bargaining emphasis to retraining and enrichment, and to use the pension fund as indicated. Proposed solutions are fine, and I have presented what I feel are the best and most immediate ones in this article, but one must be realistic enough to realize that human beings must be willing and able to implement them. Given the current composition of labor leaders and their attitudes toward their jobs, I do not attach a high degree of probability to the application of any of these ideas on a large scale; and, given the magnitude of the problem, piecemeal implementation by individual leaders will not suffice.

Thus, the *human factor* becomes the overriding one in this situation, and that causes me to be pessimistic about any reversal in the condition of organized labor in the foreseeable future. Those species and institutions that do not adapt over time become *at worst* extinct, or *at best* lose their position of dominance. Organized labor has not adequately adapted to economic, environmental, or sociological changes. As a result, it has lost much of the strength it enjoyed thirty or forty years ago. The real problem for labor today is not that this has occurred, for these things go in cycles, but that there is no effective, coordinated attempt being made by the leadership to reverse the situation. The most ominous question for a labor leader to consider today is: "given present trends and your inability to combat them, what in the world will you look like in ten or fifteen years?"

Footnotes

[1]David S. Broder, "A 'New Day' For Unions," *Washington Post*, March 10, 1985.

[2]Mark Erlick, "Hammer Out A Warning," *The Progressive*, October 1989, p. 18.

[3]Gus Tyler, *The Political Imperative: The Corporative Character of Unions* (MacMillan Publishing Company: New York, 1968), p. 290.

[4]1983–84 CCH NLRB ¶16,029, 268 NLRB No. 87 (1984).

[5]Arthur F. Silbergeld, "How Recent NLRB Decisions Have Tilted Toward Management on Critical Issues," *Management Review*, July 1989, pp. 14–15.

[6]Carey W. English, "Why Unions Are Running Scared," *U.S. News and World Report*, September 10, 1989, p. 62.

[7]Carey W. English, "Business is Booming for 'Union Busters'," *U.S. News and World Report*, May 16, 1988, pp. 61–64.

[8]Harry Graham and Brian Heshizer, "Are Unions Facing a Crisis? Labor Officials are Divided," *Monthly Labor Review*, August 1989, pp. 24–25.

Women in the Labor Force: A Socio-Economic Analysis

"...Assist members in their endeavor, to secure and maintain wages and conditions of employment by every honorable means; to cheer them in times of industrial trouble and to assist them to secure what is considered by all fair-minded persons to be their rights...to further the recognition of women industrially...with equal pay for equal work."

> Platform of the Ladies' Auxiliary to
> the International Association of
> Machinists, 1955

The numerical growth of women in the work force and their entry into traditionally male-dominated industries has revolutionized work attitudes shared by men and women alike. The Equal Pay Act of 1963, Title VII of the Civil Rights Act of 1964, and The Equal Rights Amendment proposed by Congress in 1972 have provided a framework of law within which much of the movement toward equality in hiring and pay has been accomplished. The Women's Liberation Movement has altered the manner in which many Americans look at social, sexual and job equality, and the emergence of women's groups, such as the Coalition of Labor Union Women and the newly established Women's Department at the United Auto Workers clearly demonstrate progress toward job equality and the need for recognition of women's participation within organized labor.

Changing employment trends, such as a higher percentage of white-collar and service-industry jobs in our economy and a lower percentage of manufacturing and blue-collar jobs will effect the employment possibilities for women, who traditionally have been concentrated in low-skilled, low-paying retail trade and service industries with only minimal representation in the professional and technical job classifications.

While much progress has been achieved in hiring practices, pay equality, and recognition of women's skills in the labor force, there are other less promising developments and facts which serve to present a contrasting story. While nearly 40 percent of the civilian work force is comprised of women, fewer than 2 percent of the 40 million working women have entered skilled crafts and trades, one reason that the earnings gap between male and female workers is widening. In California there were only 147 female apprentices in 1975, among a total of 38,708 in State programs.[1] Despite the fact that more women are earning college degrees, large numbers of college-educated women, lacking professional preparation and experience, are relegated to office work and retail trade positions such as department store clerks. About 1 in 6 working women is in a profession, but normally in lower-paying subcategories like nursing and public-school teaching. Only one-in-20 is an executive or holds a middle management position in private business. The ratio of male-to-female corporate chief executives stands at a "blatantly sexist" 600 to 1.[2]

The concentration of women workers in lower-skilled, lower-paid professions is not merely a sign of the times. The reasons for the massing of women in particular industries—and their exclusion from the skilled trades, blue-collar, and professional/technical vocations—is traceable to a socio-economic fiber that is pervasive at all levels of government and industry. Although only theories may be advanced as to its causes and empirical documentation cited as evidence, I will present several aspects that have resulted in the concentration of women in lower-skilled and lower-paid occupations and industries.

It is within this overview that several areas relating to women workers warrant analysis. The areas include how women tend to define a career, why pay differences persist despite the protection of new laws, and why they belong to labor unions traditionally representing a majority of skilled-trade blue-collar industries.

Women and Careers: Changes in Attitudes and Expectations

The most recent statistics regarding women workers reveal that more than half of the 7.2 million families with women-heads-of-households are in the labor force.[3] Although families headed by women constitute a small portion of America's population, they are, nonetheless, significant because of their growth in the last 25 years. Between 1940 and 1975, families headed by women doubled in number and now represent 1 out of 8 American families.[4]

The manner in which working wives and family heads view themselves has been changing as dramatically as their representation in recent years. Expectations regarding marriage and child bearing are most evident. Traditionally, child bearing has brought with it not merely a temporary absence from paid employment but a complete withdrawal from the work force for a period of years (the time being extended by the birth of each successive child). Of crucial importance to a woman's career development is the fact that this withdrawal generally occurs during those years in which job advancement would be most rapid. Thus, women lose the opportunity to establish their careers or to gain seniority or experience prior to withdrawal. Whereas wives 18–24 (years of age) in 1950 often expected to have 4 or more children, in 1972 the commonly expected number was two. From 1965–73, the average number of children per husband-wife family dropped from 2.44 to 2.18.

Acceptance of childless marriages is increasingly widespread. As women find paid employment more appealing, the tendency toward smaller families is enhanced.

Mature women are in the work force far more frequently than they expected to be in their earlier years. A longitudinal study of young women aged 18–24 in 1968 over the 1968–70 period indicated that about two-fifths of those surveyed would alter their plans for age 35. Overwhelmingly, they moved in the direction of labor force entry. Occupational aspirations of this same group of women are indicative of an increasing commitment to careers. About three-fourths of the white and two-thirds of the black women indicated preferences for white-collar occupations, with half of the white-collar aspirants looking forward to work in professional, technical, or managerial jobs.

Some of the strongest evidence of the commitment of women to their careers has emerged from the survey of women aged 30–44. Among women in this age group, 60 percent of the white and 67 percent of the black women reported that they would continue to work *even if they could live comfortably without their earnings.* The findings are reinforced by the fact that the same women displayed considerable attachment to their current jobs.[5]

While this report deals primarily with married working women, it would be inappropriate to exclude two additional segments of women in an analysis of changing attitudes and expectations. These segments are the single woman, and for the purpose of discussion, working-class women (as opposed to professional and technical) who may be either married or single.

The single woman is likely to be younger, less educated, and have less work experience than the average working wife, and consequently her expectations will differ. Her social attitudes are more likely to be strongly influenced by "economic necessity;" and for many women, husband-finding may be secondary to job-finding. The following is an example of what I would term economic necessity:

"When I was a young girl, I imagined I'd grow up to marry a doctor and walk down Michigan Avenue in fancy clothes and smoke imported cigarettes. Now I'm single and a clerk on Michigan Avenue, and I have problems affording a polyester suit."

"This Chicagoan reflects many of the hopes and anxieties of a growing Army of 8.6 million single women in the U.S. Often by choice, but sometimes not, they are carving lives for themselves outside traditional mating patterns... Few seem greatly concerned about discrimination and sexual harassment—minor problems, many say in comparison with dull jobs and career doubts.[6]

In addition to married wives who seek professional and technical careers, and the single women who may end up working in the occupation of a retail trade clerk, a large number of working-class women contribute substantially to the labor force. They are likely to be factory and service workers, employed in textile plants, furniture factories, food-processing plants, or countless other industries where they fill working-class occupations. The needs of working-class women and their reasons for employment are primarily, as are those of single women, based upon compelling economic necessity. They work to maintain their standard of living and to provide the opportunity for their family to survive the impact of inflation and/or unemployment of the husband, who is also likely to be employed in manual and semi-skilled labor. The working-class wife may not have a working husband or even a husband at all—the incidence of women as heads of households,[7] although not broken down by the Department of Labor, is probably higher for working-class female employees than their professional counterparts.

The growth of families headed by women has doubled in 25 years, while families headed by men have grown at a 70 percent rate over the same period. Unfortunately, the incidence of poverty among families headed by women is substantial, and hence is likely to affect the attitudes and expectations of working-class women. The accelerated growth of families headed by women has been a serious social problem because 1 out of 3, compared to 1 out of 18 families headed by men, is living at or below what is generally defined as the poverty level.

In 1974, for nonfarm families headed by women, the poverty cutoff was $5,014 for a four-person family (11% higher than in 1973 because of inflation), $3,822 for a three-person family and $3,167 for a two-person family. By these standards, about 2.2 million families headed by women were living in poverty. Typical characteristics of these families included having a family head who was likely to have graduated from high school, had little or no work experience during the previous year, or worked in a low-paying occupation. A disproportionate share of all children under 18 in families headed by women lived in poor families.

A study performed by Dr. Burleigh B. Gardner, Chairman of the Board of Social Research, Inc., Chicago, Illinois, analyzed the image working women have of themselves regarding attitude changes which may be developing from the impact of job and pay equality, and the women's liberation movement.

"Women – many blue-collar workers themselves – are getting, often unconsciously, a new image of themselves and new goals. Formerly, the working-class woman accepted with little question the idea that women must be subservient to their husbands and, in the working world, must accept lower pay and fewer opportunities than men. And she firmly reared her daughter to likewise accept this woman's role.

Today, the working class woman is rejecting such limitations. She feels women should have free choice of careers or homemaking or of both, and should have equality with men in pay, in choice of jobs, and in opportunities-and not be restrained just because they are women. When she hears these demands made in the name of women's lib, she heartily concurs. This represents one of the most significant changes in attitude we have witnessed in more than a quarter century of probing the attitudes of working-class women."[8]

The "Why" of Income Differential and Hiring Discrimination

A summary perspective of vital economic statistics shows a widening of the earnings gap, continued concentration of women in low-paid, low-skilled industries, and a high poverty rate for women family heads. The news is not encouraging for women workers, especially during a time when major social and legal changes have been brought about in an effort to break the economic bonds which have restricted them. The reasons for a continuing and pervasive inequality are an unfortunate commentary on the ability of our nation to recognize and solve a serious economic and social plight. The reasons are complex, certainly not obvious, and probably interrelated with strong institutional forces that, at best, are slowly reacting to public attention.

The "whys" of our social dilemma over inequality in the work force have been carefully studied for clues as to its nature and persistence. The following theory strongly suggests that three social and economic forces contribute to the dilemma:

"Economists have exhibited increased interest in the relative economic statuses of the sexes. A number of facets of this problem have been examined, but one of the thorniest questions has been the role of sexual differentials. Although literature on this subject can be traced back more than half a century, it has been only in the last few years that there has been the...theory, statistical techniques, and data necessary to begin answering the question in a meaningful quantitative fashion. To date, however, little progress has been made in sorting out the complex set of sociological and economic factors behind male/female income differences. The conclusions reached by various researchers sometimes have differed strikingly – a rather distressing situation given that this has become an important issue of social policy...The debate about these causes involves essentially three broad questions...

1. What part does occupational distribution play in explaining the observed sex differential in income?
2. How much of the sex differential is attributable to differences in male and female productivity?
3. How much of the observed sex differential is attributed to discrimination?"[9]

An analysis of occupational distribution by the median wage of male/female employment shows that women are paid substantially less, regardless of the industry and occupation:[10]

Major Occupation Groups	Median Salary		Women's Median, Expressed as a Percent of Men's
	Men	Women	
Professional, technical	$13,945	$9,095	65.2%
Managers, administrators	14,737	7,998	54.3
Sales workers	12,031	4,674	38.8
Clerical workers	10,619	6,458	60.8
Craft & kindred	11,308	6,315	55.8
Operatives	9,481	5,420	57.2
Service workers, non-household	8,112	4,745	58.5
Private household	—	2,243	—
Non-farm labor	8,037	5,286	65.8

It is clear from these statistics that a substantial income differential by sex exists despite the occupational group. The empirical data by occupation must be combined with a distribution of females by occupations, to see exactly how serious the weighted differential is. For example, a closer examination of the professional and technical occupational group reveals that women are heavily concentrated in such lower-paid subcategories as nursing and elementary school teaching. In general, the more one dissects the figures, the more obvious it becomes that differences in occupational distribution are an important factor underlying the observed sex differential in median incomes. A much larger percentage of female workers is concentrated in the lower-paid occupational groups than is the case with male workers. Fifty-three percent of female workers are found in two relatively low-wage occupations, clerical workers and service workers. In contrast, only 14% of male workers fall in these categories. Thus, not only do women seem to find their way in disproportionate numbers into the lower-paid occupations, the lower-paid occupations tend to be those traditionally regarded as "women's work."[11]

A more recent analysis of trends by occupational groups brings into perspective the relationship between lower pay and low-paying occupations;

the statistics are important because they include married or formerly married women, and this group accounted for the largest share of the increase in payroll employment of women.

From January 1964 to January 1973, the number of women on payrolls in nonagricultural industries expanded from 19.1 to 27.9 million. Most of the 8.8 million labor force entrants or reentrants found jobs in the four major industry divisions that were the fastest growing:

Division	Women Workers
Services	2,500,000
Government	2,400,000
Wholesale, retail trade	1,900,000
Manufacturing	1,100,000

In the late 1960's, the service industry maintained its position as a principal employer of women, and by 1973 had more female workers, 6.8 million, than any other industry. In 1973, the trade industry was the second-largest employer of women, 6.3 million, most of whom held jobs in retail stores. Women were only one-fourth or 900,000 of the employees in wholesale trade, but nearly half or 5,400,000 in retail trade. Within retail trade, women made up two-thirds of the employees in department stores, clothing and accessory shops, and drug stores, and over half in restaurants and other eating and drinking establishments.

Services provided by government agencies were responsible for the soaring employment of women on government payrolls, especially at the state and local levels. In January 1973, the state and local education industry accounted for nearly 60 percent of the 6.1 million women on government payrolls.

The industry division encompassing finance, insurance and real estate became predominantly female during the 1960's, and by January 1973, women accounted for 52 percent of the employees.[12]

What the occupational distribution clearly shows is that the concentration of women in the labor force is greatest in the major occupational groups which have the highest median income differential. The service industry, the major occupational group which employs more women than any other group, has a median income for women that is only 58.5% of the male median income, or $4,745 for women versus $8,112 for men. The trade industry, the second-largest occupational employer of women, has an even greater income differential. The median income of women is a meager 38.8% of the same figure for men, or just $4,674 versus $12,031. The differential among clerical workers is a substantial $6,458 for women and $10,619 for men, or 60.8 percent.

The third question—how much of the observed sex differential is attributable to discrimination—is somewhat more difficult to evaluate. Pin-pointing reasons for employer discrimination in hiring and pay practices is virtually an impossible task. Although it is highly unlikely that an employer would specify the manner in which hiring and pay discrimination occurs, certain noninstitutional myths and inherent assumptions about women workers on the part of employers probably contribute, at least in part, and possibly unintentionally, to discrimination. The biggest of these assumptions is that women are paid less because of differences in important nonsexual characteristics that exist between both male and female workers, including absenteeism and turnover, age and job experience, and length of the work week. The first of these appears to be the most widely held, that is, that female workers tend to be less productive and more costly because they have higher rates of absenteeism and turnover.

Government research indicates that age, occupation and salary may be more important determinants of absenteeism than sex is. In 1967, men between the ages of 25 and 45 lost 4.4 days per year due to illness, while women in the same age bracket lost 5.6—a difference of only 1.2 days per year. In the 45-and-over age bracket, female employees lost fewer working days due to illness than men, making the overall averages 5.3 days per year for men and 5.4 per year for women. To be sure, illness does not account for all employee absenteeism. In particular, because of the different family roles typically assigned to men and women, women are probably more likely to take days off to care for sick children or to meet other household responsibilities. However, Labor Department data show that, during the average week in 1971, 1.4 percent of women and 1.2 percent of men did not report to work for reasons other than illness or vacation, certainly a small difference.

The problem—or presumed problem—of employee turnover may have its greatest impact on female occupational distribution, but it might also affect relative pay. Employers, believing that there is greater risk in investing on-the-job training for female workers, might attempt to recoup their expected loss by paying women less. If the sex differential in turnover rates is an important factor in explaining the sex differential in pay, it is a testimonial to the power of myth over economic fact, for the existing data show the differences in turnover to be small. Labor Department figures reveal that voluntary "quit" rates for the sexes are not very different—2.2 per hundred male employees per month and 2.6 per hundred female employees in 1968.[13] Furthermore, it has been asserted that about one-half of this quit rate differential is attributable to the greater concentration of women in occupations where quit rates for both men and women are above average. Employers may magnify the quit rate differential in their minds, perhaps showing greater sensitivity to a woman quitting to have a baby, than a man quitting to take a better job, but whatever the cause, there seems little basis in fact for the popular view of the size of the quit rate differential. Unfortunately, employers may act on their mistaken impressions, and there is a tendency for them to practice "statistical discrimination."

A discussion of the impact of on-the-job experience upon hiring and pay differentials is difficult because data in terms of training experience is not readily available. Job training programs as a means of attracting employees are well publicized because they provide an opportunity to learn a skill and gain employment. But data on male/female job experience rarely provides an insight into training as part of that experience, and one might generally conclude, therefore, that job experience and age are factors that employers may subconsciously lump together regarding attitudes and assumptions toward hiring and pay. Since women are more likely to have fewer years of job experience at any given age than their male counterparts, female job experience probably contributes to the pay differential. Women, at least in past years, have tended to enter and leave the labor force at earlier ages and then reenter at later ages. Women who have never married tend to have an age-earnings profile much like that of men, but for married women with spouse present the differences between male and female average hourly earnings increase with age. It seems likely that as women interrupt their careers to raise children, differences in work experience will give rise to a significant sex differential in earnings.

Income differences, and the accompanying pay discrimination, are also partially explained by the weekly overtime pay data. In 1971, women employed full time on nonfarm and salary jobs worked an average of 39.9 hours per week—considerably less than the 43.6 hours averaged by similarly employed males. Only 15 percent of women with full-time jobs worked overtime in May 1971, compared with 30 percent of men. These disparities are in large part attributed to the relatively greater concentration of men in the blue-collar occupations. The Council of Economic Advisers recently estimated that the length of the work week differential accounted for about 6 percentage points of the 1971 sex differential in median income—a smaller share than in 1949, but still very significant.[14]

An analysis of changing attitudes and expectations of women workers clearly shows that women now expect more, and statistically—because of the widening earnings gap and concentration in low-pay, low-skill areas—deserve more. Even a comparison of male and female employment by occupation shows that women are paid less for the same work.

An analysis of absenteeism, turnover, age and experience dispels the commonly held view that women are paid less because they are absent more. Even though women are likely to have less job experience—although job training records are not readily available—at a given age because of absences from the work force, the pay differential can hardly be justified within low-skill occupations like retail trade and the services industries where experience does not necessarily equate to performance.

The final area of concern is the woman worker as a labor union member

Women In Labor Unions

In 1972, 4.5 million women belonged to labor unions, accounting for 21.7 percent of all union members. They accounted for more than half of the membership gain between 1970 and 1972 of unions affiliated with the AFL-CIO and at least 6 large AFL-CIO unions now have more women than men members.[15]

Although women comprise an increasingly larger percentage of the work force, nearly 80 percent of women who work do not have the protection of a union contract. Women are concentrated in two of the largest unorganized sectors of the economy, the clerical and service sector and—the fastest-growing sector—banking, insurance and finance. As a result of the large percentage of women in unorganized fields, they generally lag behind male workers with respect to wages and working conditions, and often suffer the additional burden of hiring and pay discrimination. The absence of union representation denies working women the strong deterrent against low wages and job discrimination that a union working agreement supposedly provides.

In June of 1976 at the Teamsters' General Election Convention in Las Vegas, Nevada the following resolution was introduced by Local 743, Chicago, Illinois on behalf of Teamster women, to recognize

...equal opportunity on the job...to deal with the employers tools of discrimination (i.e., wage differentials based on sex, dual seniority, etc.)... greater participation of women members at every level of the International Brotherhood of Teamsters;

...acknowledgement and appreciation of the valuable contributions of Teamster women over the years.[16]

At the United Auto Workers' Convention in June, 1975, President Leonard Woodcock of the UAW issued a proclamation on International Women's Year in support of their goals.

...promotion of equality between men and women, support for the integration of women in the total economic, social and cultural development effort; recognition (and encouragement) of the role of women in the development of international cooperation.[17]

As is the case across the labor force, the earnings gap between men and women workers who are union members varies according to the industries in which they are employed. In 1970 the earnings gap between men and women was narrower among union members who were white-collar and service workers, but wider among union members who were blue-collar workers. Within any given industry, men are more likely than women to be union members. This holds equally for white-collar and blue-collar workers and where adequate data are available, for service workers as well. Both men and women are more likely to be labor union members if employed in industries predominantly composed of male workers; an industry is more likely to be unionized if most of its workers are men. In these industries, with increasing percentages of women covered by a labor contract, problems such as wage discrimination based on sex disappear.

Within the labor movement, some joining of forces between women union members and the women's liberation movement outside of organized labor has come about in common support of protective legislation such as the ERA. But the goals of the two groups are dissimilar and may roughly be summarized as economic opportunity for the women's liberation movement versus economic necessity for the working women. The middle income woman's interest in work as a career, or as a device for self-actualization is something only remotely related to the blue-collar women's interest in improvement in the quality of her work life. Women in the middle-income group, who largely compose the liberation movement, have choices that working women do not have: to work or not to work, the kind of work, part-time or full-time work, to further their education and thus upgrade their occupational level, etc. Most women in blue-collar jobs have no choices, i.e., they work because they must do so. To them, many of the issues so important to the women's liberation movement seem removed and even frivolous compared to their own bread-and-butter issues.[18]

Additional Considerations

While the rights of working women are to a certain degree protected by union membership, the Equal Employment Opportunity Commission (EEOC) has filed many discrimination suits against both corporations and unions, to afford them additional protection. A classic example is the landmark case of *Patterson v. The American Tobacco Company*, an EEOC action brought to end hiring discrimination. A federal district court required the company to appoint a woman or a "minority individual" to the next position vacated at the supervisory level at one of its facilities. Unlike previous rulings, where a company was given a number of years to comply, American Tobacco was ordered to name a minority member to the very next management post to become available and to continue to fill supervisory jobs with females and blacks until the percentage of those minorities approximated that of the company's local area (Richmond, VA).[19] Rulings such as this, while they may be branded as "reverse discrimination" by some, are essential to achieve parity in the foreseeable future.

Women have also experienced job discrimination because of "health hazards." Working women have traditionally been sheltered in "women's jobs" because they were the "weaker sex." But what about standards of safety and health as women increasingly penetrate what have traditionally been called "men's jobs?" As women, with the force of law behind them, move into "men's jobs," they share men's exposures to the full range of safety and health hazards. And again the question comes up: do men and women react differently to job stress and environmental factors such as toxic substances?

Because of the lack of information, many of the stereotypes about women workers rest on shaky foundations. Dr. David Wegman of the Harvard School of Public Health suggests that common beliefs, e.g., women are too weak to do heavy work, women cannot tolerate temperature extremes as well as men, women are more susceptible to toxic substances are mostly well-cultivated myths. Studies show that on the average, women's absolute strength is about two-thirds that of men. Other studies reveal more differences in strength between working and non-working women, than between working women and working men. And although the temperature regulation mechanism apparently is different in the two sexes, women can regulate their body temperatures equally as well as men. Therefore, Wegman urges employers to set criteria on work strength and hire regardless of sex.[20]

Conclusion

The contribution of working women to national productivity cannot be over-estimated: forty percent of the work force is women, women increasingly are heads of families, and they work out of economic need, not for discretionary income. Women comprise approximately 22 percent of the membership in labor unions, yet their representation in the work force is concentrated in the service, retail trade, and banking/finance industries where the percentage of organized workers is low, compared to the blue-collar sector. And, most unfortunately, the income gap between men and women is widening despite protective laws.

The future is brighter, however, as the country shifts from a predominantly production-oriented economy toward a service economy. White-collar jobs will grow faster than blue-collar jobs and women should find the trends more favorable than what they have been forced to accept in the last several decades. It is well to keep in mind, however, that socio-economic changes of this magnitude are, by necessity, gradual ones. From an historical perspective it is obvious that the majority of employers have not been, and to a certain degree are still not, receptive to the emerging role of women in the labor force. Sad commentary on our society though it may be, forceful legislation has thus far been the only effective technique for initiating change in the traditional "women's role" in the world of work. In my opinion, it is this vehicle that must continue to be used if the progress made to date is to be continued. Additionally, efforts on the part of individuals or groups for more favorable legislation should not be directed, as they have so often in the past, at specific instances of injustice. While favorable settlements in these areas may prove a valuable point, the time and effort would be better spent in the long run, if directed at the passage of basic pieces of legislation such as the Equal Pay Act, Title VII of the Civil Rights Act, and the Equal Rights Amendment. Once more legislation of this nature is activated, the specific battles and cases can be fought. Now, however, specifics should be of secondary importance. Favorable conceptual legislation is the hope of the future for women in the labor force.

Footnotes

[1]"Women's Rights—Why the Struggle Still Goes On," *U.S. News and World Report,* May 27, 1974, p. 40.

[2]"The American Woman", *U.S. News and World Report*, December 8, 1975, p. 58.

[3]U.S. Department of Labor, Women's Bureau, *1975 Handbook on Women Workers.*

[4]"Women Who Head Families: A Socioeconomic Analysis," *Monthly Labor Review,* June 1976, p. 5.

[5]"The Changing Economic Role of Women," Manpower Report of the President, 1975, pp. 64–65.

[6]"The American Woman," p. 54.

[7]"Women Who Head Families: A Socioeconomic Analysis," p. 3.

[8]"Women's Rights—Why the Struggle Still Goes On," p. 41.

[9]"The Incomes of Men and Women: Why Do They Differ?" *Monthly Labor Review*, April, 1973, p. 3.

[10]"The Earnings Gap," U.S. Department of Labor, Women's Bureau, March 1975.

[11]"The Incomes of Men and Women: Why do They Differ?" p. 5.

[12]"Where Women Work—An Analysis By Industry and Occupation," *Monthly Labor Review,* May, 1974, p. 5.

[13]"The Incomes of Men and Women: Why Do They Differ?" pp. 3–4.

[14]*Ibid.,* p. 6.

[15]"Women in Unions," *U.S. News and World Report,* March 17, 1975, p. 70.

[16]Proceedings, 21st Convention, International Brotherhood of Teamsters, Las Vegas, Nevada.

[17]Cable: UAW Detroit (Solidarity House), "UAW Proclaimation on International Women's Year," May 1974, p. 5.

[18]"Working Women and Their Membership in Labor Unions," *Monthly Labor Review,* May 1975, p. 32.

[19]"Women Executives Are Different," *Dun's Review,* January 1975, pp. 47–48.

[20]"Women Workers and Job Health Hazards," *Job Safety and Health Magazine,* April 1975, p. 2.

Blacks in the U.S. Labor Force

There have been increases in membership and power, but these are minor compared to changes that are yet likely to be made.

Between 1965 and 1968 the cause of black labor was aided by the civil rights movement. Such organizations as the Southern Christian Leadership Conference (SCLC), the National Association for the Advancement of Colored People (NAACP), and the Negro-American Labor Council (NALC) were key actors in this movement. The NALC changed its leadership in 1966, and with it came a change in policy. The new policy "stressed that black masses had to assume a greater leadership role in the alliance than in the past," in the words of leader Cleveland Robinson. The idea was not to work in the highest levels of union administration, but to organize as many black workers as possible. These masses then could bring pressure to bear to have their demands met. In a sense, this was a social class movement as much as a labor one.

Martin Luther King, Jr., must be mentioned here not specifically as a labor leader but as the figurehead for a racial upsurge. More than any other black leader, he helped blacks realize that bringing organized pressure to bear on the establishment (unions) could achieve equality.

The greatest victories for King, the NAACP, and the NALC were the Memphis, Tennessee, sanitation workers' strike and the Charleston, South Carolina, hospital workers' strike. Both were real tests of Cleveland Robinson's policy of organizing black service workers to reach pay parity with whites. In both cases, the grievances were black pay rates equal to approximately half the pay of whites on the same jobs, poor working conditions, and biased behavior on the part of "lily-white" administrations. Neither group was organized when it struck, and they probably would have failed, had it not been for the support of the SCLC and the black social and labor movement. Several important unions also backed the strikers. United Auto Workers, United Steel Workers, and United Rubber Workers, as well as some AFL-CIO locals in the Memphis and Charleston areas. It is significant that these strikes were bitterly opposed by the power structure in the communities and were not readily supported by local white workers. Despite this opposition the black workers were able to ally themselves with social movements and use labor support to win outstanding victories in both cases.

The successes of the civil rights movement gave the impetus to black labor to try for total equality with white labor. After 1966, with the escalation of the Vietnam war, many more blacks found employment in industry, especially young blacks. Cleveland Robinson used the word *power* in a speech to the

NALC Convention in 1968, and immediately the idea of *black power* was used by friend and foe of the black labor movement. Robinson was emphasizing that union membership of blacks was increasing by leaps and bounds, but their representation on local, international, and executive councils was not. As Wayman Benson, head of the Chicago Transit Workers, pointed out: "This is nothing different than the old plantation system. Here you have a union with about 65–70 percent blacks and the leadership is virtually all white. How long do you think we can stand for this?"[1]

As a result of this frustration, many black extra-union organizations were formed to put pressure on the unions. These groups were concentrated in the northern industrial cities, specifically, Pittsburgh, Detroit, and Chicago. These organizations (Ad Hoc Committee to the USW, and Chicago Transit Workers of Local 241, Amalgamated Transit Union, to name just two) did not want to disband and form black unions, for they realized they would be cutting their own throats. What they wanted was an active role in union policy formation.

The younger black unionists were more militant than older leaders in their attacks upon management. They criticized older blacks for not attacking union bias and for not forcing union management to allow blacks a greater role in union leadership.

> It was not long before these young black workers were challenging conditions that other auto workers had learned to live with or had concluded, after many years of fruitless efforts, were impossible to change. . . . Before the auto corporations realized it, they were confronted with a new, and in some ways more basic opposition.[2]

It is interesting that the UAW, probably one of the most egalitarian unions of its time, had such problems. One group, the Dodge Revolutionary Union Movement (DRUM), was highly critical of both the union and Walter Reuther, its president. How many people joined the movement is difficult to ascertain, but the numbers are not important. What is significant is the fact that union leadership and older black caucuses felt compelled to accommodate this angry, primarily young, militant movement. The revolutionaries were helped in their cause by the Ad Hoc Committee of Concerned Negro Workers, which stated that the younger people wanted the UAW to pay more attention to the needs of blacks and not attack groups such as DRUM.

Some of the revolutionary movements even courted white employees. They argued that management and union leadership could also treat whites, arbitrarily and unfairly. These groups did not advocate dissolving the unions, for they realized that the unions were their lifeblood, too. They just asked for equal treatment, both in working conditions and union representation.

Federal Contract Compliance
Required of Unions

The Office of Federal Contract Compliance (OFCC) was established in 1965 to ensure that minorities would not be discriminated against under any federal contract. At first this seemed a logical way to alleviate racial discrimination. However, the general nature of this office's responsibilities has caused it to become a "toothless lion."

One of the major reasons for OFCC ineffectiveness is that much of its responsibility has been waived for a hometown policy:

> But instead of enforcing the law, instead of obtaining compliance with federal guidelines in the construction industry, the U.S. Department of Labor, at the insistence of the politically powerful building-trades unions, is promoting and funding so-called "home-town" solutions. These local plans . . . do not establish contractual duties and obligations, they do not state time limitations, they do not contain legal sanctions, there are no guarantees of anything, nothing is spelled out. In short, the "home-town" solutions are a fraud.[3]

The hometown plans have been used in many cases to circumvent the Philadelphia Plan, which stemmed from *Ethridge v. Rhodes* in a district court in Ohio. In the case, the idea of hiring tables was developed, establishing "the legal principle that government agencies must require a contractual commitment from building contractors to employ a specific number of black workers in each craft at each stage of construction."[4] Many black leaders believe that hometown solutions merely perpetuate the *status quo* in whatever trades and areas are affected. The Federal Contract Compliance doctrine is little more than a law on paper. The NAACP felt that "cancellation of a single contract would have provided real evidence of intent to use enforcement powers embodied in the Executive Orders. . . . This failure destroyed not only the real power of governmental authority in this field, but the symbolic power as well."[5]

Most of the states have fair employment practice agencies with extensive powers. However, most have declined to use them. A big part of the problem is that they do not approach employment bias as a broad pattern to be settled as a class action, but instead settle each individual complaint as if it were separate and distinct from all others.

The best argument in the OFCC's favor is that, at least, the government is making an attempt to solve a problem that white labor refuses to solve, and that black labor cannot solve without help. Some successful steps have been taken under the compliance doctrine. On January 15, 1973, Labor Secretary James D. Hodgson ordered the Bethlehem Steel Corporation to open job classifications formerly restricted to whites only. The directive was issued under Executive Order 11246, which requires government contractors to follow nondiscriminatory employment practices and to take affirmative action to ensure that job applicants and employees are not discriminated against on the basis of race, color, religion, sex, or nation origin.

Seniority

The concept of seniority has evolved with the trade union movement. Unions have pushed it as a defense against arbitrary dismissals by management. In many cases, it has forced management to change its old policy of displacing experienced workers with new employees at lower wages. The need for protection in this area has made the seniority system a vital part of the trade union movement.

Now these systems, even though they contribute to the strength of organized labor as a whole, are often found to be discriminating against blacks. There is approximately a 20 percent difference in job tenure between white and black men,[6] which means that blacks suffer disproportionately from layoffs made according to seniority. The phrase "last hired, first fired" applies well. All seniority systems function on this principle. The more discriminatory seniority systems, however, ensure that the minorities are the last hired. A recession becomes a depression for black workers, who have unemployment rates much higher than do whites. In August 1975, for example, the official unemployment rate for blacks and other minorities was 14 percent, compared to an overall rate of 8.4 percent. This 14 percent did not include the people who had given up looking for jobs.

In cases of discriminatory seniority systems, the employer often has discriminated by hiring minorities into subordinate positions and then limiting their prospects to a specific group of jobs through the operations of the seniority system. Damage remedy, a method to repay those who have been discriminated against, can lower the conflict between white and black workers, which should reduce the tensions between the civil rights and labor movements at the institutional and political levels. It may involve an equal opportunity fund—provided by the employer—to aid those who have been victims of seniority discrimination. These funds would be similar in function to automation funds.

Seniority gives an order of priority for promotion and layoff based partly on length of service. In 1944 it was declared illegal (Steel v. Louisville + N. Ry.) to restrict blacks to lower-paying jobs through the seniority system, whether by written rule or by common practice. Unions and companies were required to treat all employees fairly and not to discriminate on the basis of race. Under President Kennedy's Executive Order 10925, discrimination by government contractors was outlawed.

There are many ways in which seniority systems may discriminate. First, blacks may be hired into jobs from which there can be no advancement. Second, in many cases job seniority discriminates against black workers because they are always behind white workers in promotion. Third, when blacks are hired to all-black units, e.g., in janitors' or laborers' jobs, they have no realistic chance to transfer without losing benefits. Fourth, in cases of plant seniority, where whites and blacks are considered separate groups and are under separate collective-bargaining contracts, blacks lose seniority when they transfer to the predominantly white union.

Many contradictory rulings have been made on seniority systems. Some courts have voided the seniority system and have encouraged other approaches that they consider less discriminatory, including work-sharing and voluntary retirement. Many appeals courts have reversed these decisions, upholding decisions against existing seniority systems only when the company previously had been ordered by the court to end its discriminatory employment practices. In cases such as these, the courts sometimes ordered reinstatement of the dismissed employees and reduced workloads for others as a way of preventing loss of jobs. Such measures could lead to imposed affirmative action programs. In general, the courts do not seem to be heading in any single direction.

Apprenticeship Programs

The U.S. Department of Labor has sponsored an Outreach Program through which blacks may acquire apprenticeships needed for skilled jobs in the building trades, where most jobs are union controlled. Descriptions of the main programs follow.

The interest of the Joint Apprenticeship Program is placement of blacks in skilled jobs, not the setting of precedents. This program is concerned with the building trades and was instituted because a very high percentage of blacks in these trades worked as laborers. The Workers' Defense League, with the support of the A. Philip Randolph Educational Fund (AFL-CIO-sponsored), thought they deserved a higher proportion of skilled jobs. Thus the apprenticeship program was instituted in 1963 with an on-the-job training grant from the Department of Labor and grants from the Ford Foundation.

The Philadelphia Plan (1969) provides "clear but flexible" guidelines for employing a certain number of minority workers in the skilled jobs of the building industry. Labor unions claim it is a discriminatory quota system. The plan proposed to raise, over a four-year period, black membership in six unions from 2 percent to 20 percent. The unions were those of the electricians, elevator constructors, iron workers, plumbers, steam fitters, and sheet metal workers. The effort was unsuccessful because (1) it applied to only six unions, (2) it applied only to federally assisted projects costing more than $500,000, and (3) the labor movement did not cooperate.

The Chicago Plan (1970) resulted from street demonstrations by blacks. It has managed to get the full backing of the trade unions and is therefore more effective than its Philadelphia predecessor. It creates a pool of skilled labor, which the Philadelphia Plan never did. Also, it was negotiated at the local level rather than the federal and, therefore, stands a better chance for survival. One strength is that is was derived from negotiations between blacks and the building trades, rather than being federally imposed.

The Pittsburgh Plan came along a few months after the Chicago Plan and is modeled on it.

In the Pittsburgh Plan, four major groups use apprenticeship training programs: manufacturing, construction, utilities, and trades and services. Where there is a union shop, management and labor decide the terms of apprenticeship through joint apprenticeship committees. Where there is no union shop, management sets up the program. Apprentice pay usually begins at half that of journeymen.

Even with the Outreach Programs, blacks and other minorities were still limited in certain ways. Since building is a seasonal industry and one of the most vulnerable to ups and downs in the economy, craft union members have tried to tighten the labor supply by limiting the number of apprentices. The main problem lies not in apprenticeship, however, but in getting black workers with journeymen licenses into the trade unions and the union-controlled jobs, since these unions resist changes in hiring practices.

The basic, and largely unrealized, flaw of the Outreach Programs is that even if lull racial integration is achieved in the apprenticeship programs, no great integration of the craft unions will result, because most whites become journeymen without the apprenticeship programs. More than 70 percent of the whites learn directly on the job: they learn by doing. It is very discriminatory for 100 percent of blacks to be required to go through apprenticeship programs when less than 30 percent of employees hired in the building trades have undergone apprenticeship.[7]

Coalition of Black Trade Unionists

The Coalition of Black Trade Unionists (CBTU) was organized in September, 1972 at a meeting in Chicago attended by more than a thousand union officials and rank-and-file members from thirty-seven international unions. It was decided that the CBTU:

> ... will work within the framework of the trade union movement. It will attempt to maximize the strength and influence of black workers in organized labor....as black trade unionists, it is our challenge to make the labor movement more relevant to the needs and aspirations of black and poor workers. The CBTU will insist that black union officials become full partners in the leadership and decision-making of the American labor movement.[8]

The president of the CBTU is William Lucy, who is also the Secretary-Treasurer of the American Federation of State, County, and Municipal Employees, which is affiliated with the AFL-CIO. In addition to annual conventions, there are more frequent meetings of the executive council. They deal with the same issues, but the council meets on a continuous basis and thus is able to cover more ground and remain current. Most issues raised are of national interest, such as consumer protection and revenue sharing. Some problems involving localities, such as the desegregation of Boston schools and the Joan Little murder case, also are of national interest and thus receive attention.

Some CBTU goals are: (1) to work for the election of a Congress that will fight for programs needed by blacks and other minorities, (2) to offset the impact of an ailing economy on the black worker and the black community, and (3) to continue to increase organizing efforts—the most important issue now. The coalition believes that the labor movement, since it includes more blacks than any other mass organization in the nation, is the only one with enough power to help the black worker. However, William Lucy notes that neither the unions nor the Congress has been very helpful to black workers. He believes that neither completely understands "not only the need but the opportunity to do something substantial."[9] The CBTU is vital and generally influential now, but when it is able to make these groups better understand the importance of the black worker's needs, it will become a much stronger force.

The Outlook

As the U.S. labor movement has progressed, would it be accurate to say that the black worker has been an integral part? Based on the preceding pages the answer would have to be *no*. Black laborers have been maligned by white workers trying to maintain their supposed superiority. Black laborers have been excluded both formally and informally from union membership. Their own unions were kept out of full federation membership until the mid 1950's and left to be the "whipping-boy" of locals. At best, they were affiliated with the AFL, CIO, or AFL-CIO as unions *in name only* and were almost powerless.

For many years black labor has tried to use formal union machinery to advance its own interests within the labor movement. That approach left blacks sadly behind. When there is only one black on a lily-white Executive Council (Philip Randolph was for many years the only black on the AFL-CIO Council), no practical policy decisions can be judged in favor of blacks. The seniority and apprenticeship arrangements of unions have made it extremely hard to get adequate advancement for blacks in unions. Labor leadership for years has had the power to enforce unions' antiracist policies, yet has preferred to "sit on its hands" and let problems be solved at the local level. Such a do-nothing policy leads to no measurable change.

The greatest changes in black labor have come with the combination of black agitation (black power) from militant young blacks and external pressure brought to bear on the unions by civil rights groups and the federal government. The NAACP, Southern Christian Leadership Conference, and the Urban League have combined with various labor groups, primarily the NALC, to pressure local organizations and stage demonstrations. On the national level they have brought test cases before the Supreme Court which have laid a foundation for blacks to become more active in the labor force. These groups also helped to raise the total consciousness of blacks to the point where they began demanding parity with white workers—not begging for it. It is the former, not the latter, type of action that brings results.

The federal government has tried to provide access to jobs and union membership through affirmative action policies and federal contract compliance. Affirmative action is slow at best, for if there is a complaint that discrimination exists, it must be settled in the courts. Federal contract compliance has relied heavily on hometown solutions, which have suffered the same fate as did early union locals dealing with blacks—accomplishing almost nothing.

Blacks also have turned to forming their own congregations of black business people and contractors to generate black union membership and advancement. Significant among these are the National Afro-American Builders Conference and the Coalition of Black Trade Unionists.

The black labor movement has been referred to by leader Philip Foner as a "sleeping giant who is awakening." Slowly blacks' percentage of the total labor force is increasing, and they are finally becoming aware of the benefits that organized labor can *and should* assure them. Blacks are no longer going to settle for the "last hired, first fired" doctrine. They are now found in large numbers in several major unions—the United Auto Workers, the United Steel Workers, and the Teamsters—and will not take a back seat in deciding their futures. However, for their own sake, they must use the tools that social movements and government legislation have allowed. If used effectively, and not against unionism but supporting union organization of blacks, then the giant will most certainly finally awaken.

Footnotes

[2]Philip S. Foner, *Organized Labor and the Black Worker* (New York: Atheneum, 1972), p. 412.

[3]Herbert Hill, "Racism and Organized Labor," *Ebony Handbook* (Chicago: Johnson Publishing Co., 1974), p. 275.

[4]*Ibid.*, p. 274.

[5]National Association for the Advancement of Colored People, 1968 Annual Report, p. 110.

[6]Coalition of Black Trade Unionists, "The Seniority System and Affirmative Action," September 1976, mimeographed, p. 2.

[7]Thomas R. Brooks, *Black Builders: A Job Program that Works* (New York: League for Industrial Democracy, 1970), p. 53.

[7]William Lucy, "The Black Partners," *Nation* 219 (7 September, 1974), pg. 31.

[8]*Ibid.*, p. 33.

Cases

Recruiting Techniques to
Achieve Affirmative Action Goals

The Resdex Laboratories of Cleveland, Ohio, has for many years relied on college recruiting and executive search teams as their only methods of recruiting. The company needs to recruit 197 highly-skilled personnel that will require a concerted recruiting effort by the personnel department. The program was planned along with the company's newly organized affirmative action program. As part of this new program the company president stated, "We will meet and exceed the recommendations of the personnel manager to insure equal employment throughout this company."

The personnel manager plans a college search in the numerous universities throughout northern Ohio. Going over this strategy in his mind, he realizes that since it is the fall of the year he will only be able to attract a few professors and have a very limited number of graduating students. Additionally, he realizes that the university placement services will not be as receptive to him as they would be to one of their regular college recruiting companies. Despite these obstacles, he estimates that he must fill at least 50% of his positions through this means.

In discussing the remainder of the personnel needs, the president suggested that the cheapest and widest distribution of the company's personnel requirements might be newspaper ads. He realized there would be a large number of resumes received and that the company's personnel department would have to sort through these resumes and develop an application form that could facilitate the interview process. The company, therefore, began to advertise in the Cleveland, Columbus and Akron/Canton newspapers.

In addition, the personnel manager made several recommendations to the president. The first of these was the use of private employment agencies as a beneficial means of searching for qualified applicants. The president ruled out this source, as the company could not afford to pay the compensation charges, not, and at the salaries paid, could the clients be expected to pay. The second recommendation was more favorably received. It involved the promotion and intended promotion of those present employees who had either completed or would soon complete their advanced degrees. This progression of employees allowed the company's recruiters to devote greater attention to undergraduate degrees.

The company's executive search team was sent to various other laboratories to observe and recruit personnel. This was viewed as a positive step since the company now holds a long-term government contract and could afford to entice those selected candidates.

A final recruiting method was to publish a notice to all the company's present employees, providing them a breakdown of those positions that were available. It was felt that since highly-skilled personnel normally associate with other skilled personnel, all these people could be used as another form of executive search.

All of these methods were considered necessary and would, hopefully, provide the company with the required number of personnel.

Questions

1. Can a personnel manager expect such a high percentage from college recruiting?

2. Did the personnel manager consider a geographic area wide enough for recruiting such highly technical personnel? Should it have been statewide or nationwide?

3. Is the newspaper campaign wide enough to attract the highly skilled minorities and women necessary to meet the affirmative action goal?

4. Should the president have considered a private employment agency, with the client paying the fee, since there would be no cost to the company?

5. Is it legal for the personnel manager to hire or advertise for minority job applicants?

"Word-of-Mouth" Hiring Referrals

TRA, Inc., has been providing restaurant services to buildings housing large corporations for the past 26 years. What initially began as a single contract to provide luncheon facilities for the central office of GMG Corporation, has now expanded into a nationwide service employing over 100,000 people. Each unit is tailored to the needs and specifications of the building it serves. All of the TRA units are equipped to provide cafeteria services, executive dining rooms and banquets for conferences. Each pays rent to the company it is affiliated with and, in turn, takes pride in providing good, yet relatively inexpensive food served in an efficient and tasteful manner. TRA must be prepared to effectively handle a heavy influx of customers between the hours of 11 a.m. and 2 p.m. and provide service to their customers within the limitations of their lunch breaks. Their customers include only employees of the affiliated corporations and their guests. None of the TRA services are open to the general public.

Each TRA unit is individually managed and personnel policies are left to the general manager of the unit. Recently, problems have developed in the Morristown, NJ unit, located within one of the larger Tricor buildings. Most of the employees, including waitresses, bus people, kitchen help and general maintenance crews work between the hours of 9 a.m. and 3 p.m. This time period is ideal for mothers with school-aged children and others who desire part-time work. As a result, TRA consistently has a surplus of applications. All applications are accepted and kept on file, but are seldom used, as it has become a practice to hire referrals from employees of Tricor. It is felt that this relationship with people who work in the building will facilitate a higher degree of loyalty, than could otherwise be expected. Most of the lower-level positions are filled in this manner, and TRA has found that their employees tend to have a significantly lower turnover and absenteeism rate than the industry as a whole.

A year ago the top-level management position for the unit became vacant and was filled by a recent MBA graduate. One of the first things that she noticed was the unit's hiring practices. She did not feel that they were in compliance with EEOC regulations, especially when she discovered that not even one employee who dealt directly with the customers was black. Furthermore, when she referred to the personnel files, she found that 12% of the applicants were black. On this basis, she instituted a selection program designed to hire minorities. She considered applicants connected with Tricor personnel last, in an attempt to fill the payroll with a better representation from the general public. After a period of several months, the turnover and absenteeism rate began to increase noticeably. The quality of the services dropped and the new manager has just been presented with a memorandum from the president of Tricor to that effect.

Questions

1. Was the method of selection used previously by this TRA unit ineffective? Why or why not?
2. Were the new manager's concerns warranted? What legal basis did they have?
3. What mistakes, if any, did she make in his selection procedure?
4. What policies should have been instituted at the central headquarters of TRA concerning personnel? Discuss various methods of selection that could have been implemented, their advantages and their disadvantages.

Application Blanks and Job Relatedness

P. Everready was a director of personnel at a medium-sized department store. He had been in this position for a number of years and had lived through many changes in the composition of application blanks. Because of the implementation of Title VII of the Civil Rights Act, it was getting harder and harder to get the information he wanted without fear of violating Title VII or any of the other antidiscrimination acts.

Everready liked to hire healthy people if he could, figuring they would be on the job more often and thus contribute to better job performance. Over the years as personnel director, Everready knew that older, married women whose children had left home had exhibited excellent job performance.

In addition to the application blank, which asked for sex, age, the number and ages of dependent children at home, and marital status, Everready liked to have the job applicants answer an inquiry about any health impairments they might have—physical or mental—which might hamper their job performance, and check off a list of diseases they might have had, or might have now.

The department store P. Everready works for is located near an all-male college and many of the students from the college fill out application blanks at the department store.

Lately, the initial screeners in the personnel office have been telling Everready that several applicants, mostly male, have been complaining that, "all this store hires is old ladies," and, "what business is it of the store's, if they have ever had the chicken pox?"

Everready, never wanting to be at a disadvantage these days, asked his people to prepare a summary of weighted application blanks using the "Horizontal Percentage Method" on information collected in the past, so he could prove that even though he was asking non-neutral questions, they were in fact, job-related. After this was done, he wanted an expert on the legal aspects of Title VII to review the data and tell him where he stood, in case he had to defend his position.

This is a summary of some of the absenteeism data gathered from the weighted application blanks:

		High	Low	Total	% High
Ques. I	male	30	20	50	60
	female	40	10	50	80
Ques. II					
(female)	age				
	18–25	25	75	100	25
	26–40	40	60	100	40
	41–65	75	25	100	75
Ques. III					
(male)	age				
	18–25	20	80	100	20
	26–40	50	50	100	50
	41–65	30	70	100	30

The data on absenteeism showed that out of a possible 363 working days per year, females missed an average of 81 days, and males missed an average of 83 days.

The Title VII consultant looked at the department store's weighted application blank and their figures on absenteeism. He also looked at the geographic area from which Everready could reasonably recruit and select his work force. He found the area to be white-dominated with a median age of 23. Everready's work force was 15% white male, average age 30. Also, the consultant found that, according to the Department of Labor, the figures for days missed for a department store comparable to Everready's showed his store to be well above the average.

Question

1. Based on the information above, what advice and recommendations would you offer P. Everready in regard to how he is using the application blank and health inquiry to select his job applicants? Explain.
   Would you suggest any changes? Explain.

Weighted Application Blanks

The Ajax Power Company has for many years relied on a single application blank for their selection process. Over the course of the years, it has come to the attention of the Equal Employment Opportunity Commission that the company has been hiring blacks in a disproportionately low number, relative to their availability in the surrounding labor market. The EEOC office also knows that the power company uses several questions on its application blank that are not neutral in nature and figure prominently in the selection process. With this information in hand, the EEOC has brought the Ajax Power Company to court on charges of discrimination in selection, in violation of Title VII of the 1964 Civil Rights Act.

Realizing the potential danger of their situation, Ajax Power Company called in a consultant to weight their application blank and to show that the three questions under consideration were not discriminatory, but were in reality related to job performance. The main emphasis in the court hearing was placed on the question concerning the applicants' possession of a high school diploma. The EEOC contends that this question was placed on the application blank because a disproportionate number of blacks in the geographic regions where Ajax hired, did not finish high school. Ajax contends, however, that a high school education is necessary to run the complicated machinery in the power plant, and that the question is job related. The other two questions are also believed to be discriminatory in nature by the EEOC, yet are felt to be job related by the employer.

The consultant took the 1,000 application blanks the power company had on hand, and the periodic supervisory evaluations of past and present employee performance and came up with the following:

Supervisory Evaluations

	answer	total	high	low	%high	weight
High School Ed.	yes	800	424	376	53	
	no	200	94	106	47	
Question 2	A	275	198	77	72	
	B	340	224	116	66	
	C	385	266	119	69	
Question 3	A	407	155	252	38	
	B	314	132	182	42	
	C	279	126	153	45	

Questions

1. Weight the questions above using a 2, 5 and 10 percent spread.
2. Which set of weights would the power company use before the court to show that the questions are related to job performance? Why?
3. Which set of weights would the EEOC use to show that the questions are discriminatory? Why?
4. Do you believe the questions are related to job performance or discriminatory? Explain.

Introducing the Polygraph
as a Requirement for Employment

The Baltimore Company is a medium-sized department store chain operating in the Baltimore, MD, area with eight branch stores. The Company has approximately 950 employees and a payroll and accounting department of 15 people. In addition, each store has two employees who consolidate each store's monetary intake and forward it to the central office. All of the employees involved in handling funds have been working for the company for some time, and have been promoted into their current position of trust as a result of excellent work and dedication to the company. There has not been a reassignment to the fiscal positions for over two years and all personnel are considered very experienced.

Approximately one year ago an employee, who had worked in the payroll and accounting department for eight years, was caught embezzling funds from the company. The company policy staff has been reviewing security measures for control of funds and has made several changes. One of the changes is to require polygraph examinations, on an annual basis, of all personnel who handle large amounts of company funds.

Mr. Robert Delly has been a member of the payroll and accounting department for 15 years. He has held numerous positions within the department and has always been a trusted and valued employee. Never has a shortage of funds occurred in his area and he is diligent in assuring his subordinates are trustworthy and thoroughly perform their duties.

When recently asked to take his first yearly polygraph examination, Mr. Delly objected and has filed a complaint with the Grievance Committee. He asserts that he has never given the company any reason to distrust him and, after 15 years of faithful service, he feels the company has committed a breach of trust by now asking him to take a polygraph, or be faced with dismissal for not adhering to company policy.

Question

1. Should Mr. Delly be required to take the polygraph examination as a condition of continued employment? Why or why not?

Aptitude Tests for Selection

The United States Air Force, along with the other military services, uses the Armed Services Vocational Aptitude Battery (ASVAB) as an entry examination. The ASVAB gives the Air Force five scores. Four are aptitude scores, Mechanical, Administrative, General, and Electronic, scored 0–95 in increments of five. The fifth score is a Qualifying Test, AFQT, scored 0–100 in single increments.

Aptitude qualifying varies with the occupational series for which an individual is enlisting, with minimum qualifying scores within a specific skill of 40, and some skills requiring a minimum of 80. In addition, the four aptitude scores must total 195.

The AFQT is an intelligence score and a score places an applicant within one of five categories. The lowest eligible score varies with service, and sometimes with supply and demand. In general, only the top three intelligence categories are accepted into the Air Force, i.e., those achieving an AFQT score of 31 or higher.

Questions

1. Discuss possible reasons for heavily Spanish-speaking areas having an 83% failure rate. Does this indicate a poor test, a poor educational background, or some other variable?

2. Discuss the interplay between the aptitude scores and the AFQT. For instance, a person wanting to be an aircraft mechanic receives a Mechanical score of 90, Administrative of 0, General of 40, and Electronic of 45, with an AFQT of 44. Is he eligible for the Air Force? If not, is the Air Force possibly missing a good mechanical prospect?

The Privacy Act's
Relationship to Applicants and Employers

Juanita Walpole just moved to the Washington, DC area from the South. The recent move forced Juanita to quite her old job. She requested that her employee file be made available to her, but her employer refused. After Juanita arrived in Washington, DC she searched the newspaper job advertisements in the *Washington Post*. A bank manager position interested her, but the job advertisement listed a doctoral degree as a requirement. Unfortunately, Juanita only had a bachelor's degree. Desperate to start work, Juanita applied for the job anyway and discovered that the advertisement only asked for a doctoral *candidate* to attract a higher class of people to the position. The bank's actual job description revealed that the job could be performed by a college graduate. Juanita proceeded to fill out the job application and found that one question asked about arrests, "Have you ever been arrested?" Juanita answered this and all other questions on the application blank, but after returning home began, to reflect on some of the things that had happened to her.

Questions

1. According to the Privacy Act, was Juanita legally denied the right to see her former employee file?

2. Was the newspaper advertisement that Juanita responded to legal, as far as its requested qualifications being related to job performance?

3. Does the application question dealing with arrests violate any law and, if so, which one? How might the question have been worded differently, to obtain the same information and yet clearly not violate the law?

Individual Rights and
Equal Employment Opportunity

Mr. I. Ben Hadd has been an employee of a large chain of hardware and lumber stores for the last three years. He began as a clerk in one of their major departments, home building and lumber supplies. After the first three months, and every six months thereafter, he received wage increases as called for in his union contract. Mr. Hadd had shown great managerial potential and began to slowly move up the ranks. Within six months he was placed in charge of the department's scheduling of employee hours, the general condition of his department, and was bestowed the title of assistant manager of the home building and lumber supply department. After eight months in this position he was enrolled, at the company's own expense, in a two-week seminar, where he was taught how to maintain the books, and how to run an accurate inventory system for his department.

Two months later he was named manager of the department, in charge of all purchasing and coordination of the chain's advertised promotional sales related to his department's inventory. During the first month of his third anniversary with the company, Mr. Hadd was offered the position of an assistant management trainee for an entire store. Although the new position did not offer an immediate increase in salary, the opportunity for later advancement and salary increases was apparent. However, the new position entailed moving to another state, 400 miles away, and working with all new personnel. Mr. Hadd weighed the pros and cons of the offer and decided to accept it, because it represented an opportunity for future advancement.

At the new store Mr. Hadd worked under the store manager, Mr. Kenneth Large. Mr. Hadd experienced problems during his first two weeks working under Mr. Large, most of which seemed to arise due to personality differences between the two. Mr. Hadd felt, however, that, as far as output of work was concerned, he was still productive for the company. During his third week at the new store, Mr. Large called him into his office and informed him that he was no longer a candidate for the assistant manager position, citing as the reason a new corporate policy calling for more positions of responsibility to be filled by female employees. Mr. Large stated that within the two-and-one-half weeks since Mr. Hadd had moved to the store, this new policy position had developed and quotas had been established that had to be filled. Mr. Hadd was informed that he would be back in the building and lumber supply department of Mr. Large's store, and his salary would remain the same. Mr. Hadd requested to be sent back to his position at his previous store, but was informed that his position had already been filled, and that there were no other vacancies at that store to match his salary level.

For the next two weeks Mr. Hadd worked in the building and lumber supply department at the level of responsibility that he had when he first joined the company, three years earlier. He felt that the store manager was belligerent toward him and that he had been denied an opportunity for advancement, through no fault of his own. He therefore decided to terminate his employment and inform the union of his unjust situation, in hopes of being rehired at another store at an assistant manager level.

Questions

1. Legally, or through union petition, can the company be forced to rehire him?
2. If the answer to #1 above is *no,* would he be eligible for state unemployment using the defense that he *quit with cause?*

Subjective Choices
Based on Employment Interviews

Illinois College is an open-admission school which operates on the quarter system. The admission, registration, and registrar functions are all performed by the Records Office, necessitating the use of various skills and abilities in the successful performance of the jobs. The Personnel Office of the school collects all employment applications and sends them out to the various departmental offices when there is an opening. It is the responsibility of each office to review the applications for interviewing and selection. The State requires that three people be interviewed for each vacant position, before a selection can be finalized.

In August an opening for a full–time file clerk position occurred in the Records Office. This job required that the person hold a high-school diploma and have the ability to organize material for the students' academic records. The individual had to learn the responsibilities of recordkeeping and the confidentiality of records as set down by the Family Educational Rights and Privacy Act. The job also required considerable overtime during registration periods.

Joni Jones, a young Afro–American, applied for a job and her application was routed to the Records Office. During her interview, it was discovered that she was presently employed by another firm in a nearby town. It was determined that she had worked with the other company for three months as a telephone receptionist. General philosophies and polices of the Records Office were discussed by the interviewer. The candidate did not ask any detailed questions about the job she was seeking. She stated that if she were hired, she would need to give the company where she was currently employed a two week notice.

The second interviewee was a middle-aged woman who was returning to the work force after eighteen years spent raising children. After the description of the office and the notice of overtime she voluntarily withdrew herself from consideration for the position.

Pricillia Mudd was the third candidate interviewed. She had just graduated from high school and had no prior office experience. She had worked at a fast-food restaurant during the summer between her junior and senior years of school. Pricillia asked several questions and seemed very eager to find a full–time position. During the interview, the possibility of temporary registration work was explored. Pricillia was made aware that this temporary employment did not guarantee that she would have a full–time job with the college in the future.

Pricillia accepted the temporary position and worked during the two week fall registration period. During that time she proved to be very energetic and patient with the registrants. She also recognized and corrected errors. Since she demonstrated her ability to handle a varied work load, she was hired for the file-clerk position.

Questions

1. Should the interviewer have offered Joni the same opportunity for temporary employment?
2. Since Joni did have prior office experience, was she discriminated against? If so, does she have any recourse under Title VII?

Discrimination in Selection

Director of Health and Public Welfare for the State of Virginia, Mr. John Brown had received only two applications for the position of Environmental Protection Officer. One applicant, Dr. Harold Schmidt, had a chemistry degree but had very little training in environmental impact. Schmidt, who was white, did not appear to be the most qualified candidate since he had very little experience besides his teaching and research position at Johnston University. The cutoff date of August 1st had to be extended even to consider his application.

The second applicant, Susan Dixon, a black female, seemed to be fully qualified on paper. She had five years of experience within the department, had taken several courses that the State recommended for their "Personal Growth" program, and had demonstrated good, conscientious work habits. However, a colleague of John Brown had met Susan at a workshop in the past month. According to him, Susan lacked effectiveness and easily became sarcastic when frustrated. After some informal inquiries by Brown, several of Susan's coworkers confirmed this. Mr. Brown suspected, though, that the reason they objected to her possible appointment was that there had never been a black or female supervisor in that department.

So much dissension was being voiced that Mr. Brown decided to select Dr. Schmidt (even though he would have to change the job specifications and extend the application deadline). Mr. Brown felt that the Department of Environmental Protection's effectiveness was dependent upon its staff's cohesive abilities.

Questions

1. Obviously, Susan Dixon could claim discrimination on the basis of sex and race, but how does this affect staff cooperation and organization maintenance?

2. Miss Dixon has challenged the hiring and promotion practices of Virginia's Health and Public Welfare Department. Discuss affirmative action.

3. Discuss counseling and probationary procedures that Mr. Brown could use if he hired Susan Dixon.

Job Performance
and Discrimination in Selection Decisions

The Liberty Plastics Corporation is located within a city with a population of 300,000. Liberty employs 425 injection-mold operators. For the past ten years its personnel department has been using a delayed selection procedure to maintain an adequate number of injection-mold operators.

The top-level management of the company became dissatisfied with the delayed selection procedure which, with a growing work force, had become an increasingly expensive selection method. With a view to simplifying the selection process and stabilizing the work force, the personnel office was tasked with developing a more cost-effective selection procedure. Part of the guidance given to the personnel officer by the company's president was to reduce absenteeism by utilizing the new selection procedure.

A survey over the past 6 years involving 880 employees who held injection-mold operator jobs was used in the search for selection tools. Five of the questions or test results weighted in the areas of productivity and absenteeism appear on the attached chart (see chart, page 176).

The selection procedure put to use by Liberty's personnel office utilized a structured interview that included questions on marital status and parenthood. All applicants were also required to take the psychomotor portion of the General Aptitude Test Battery, and score 80 or more to be considered for employment as an injection-mold operator.

This new selection procedure came to the attention of the state Equal Employment Opportunity Commission after a black, unwed mother charged that she was not selected for an injection-mold operator's job because of her status as a single parent, declaring that this discriminated unfairly against blacks who had a higher proportion of illegitimate births than whites.

Questions

1. Is the Liberty Plastics Corporation in violation of Fair Employment Practices by selecting on the basis of parenthood and marital status?
2. To what extent is absenteeism a valid factor in establishing job performance?

		Productivity				Absenteeism			
		High	Low	High	Weight	Low	High	Low	Weight
1.	Sex								
	a) Male	155	215	42%	4	205	165	55%	5
	b) Female	285	255	53%	5	235	275	46%	4
2.	Married								
	a) Yes	308	242	56%	5	253	297	46%	4
	b) No	132	198	40%	4	187	143	57%	5
3.	Children (Married)								
	a) None	184	156	54%	5	188	152	55%	5
	b) One or more	107	103	51%	5	86	124	41%	4
	(Single)								
	c) None	134	146	48%	4	154	126	55%	5
	d) One or more	21	29	42%	4	12	38	24%	2
4.	General Aptitude Test (psychomotor)								
	a) 0–79	86	134	39%	3	112	108	51%	5
	b) 80–110	192	208	48%	4	201	199	50%	5
	c) 111–150	162	98	62%	6	127	133	49%	4
5.	Race								
	a) White	255	235	52%	5	265	225	54%	5
	b) Nonwhite	185	205	47%	4	175	215	45%	4

Racial Composition of the Geographic Area in Hiring Discrimination

The Grand Food Company is a supermarket chain with 100 food stores in the Washington DC metropolitan area, all located in Maryland and Virginia. The chain does not operate any stores within the District of Columbia's city limits. The retail work force of Grand Food Company consists of 3,000 workers, 53% male and 47% female. By race, 12% of the work force is black, while 88% is white. The management positions are department heads like produce and meat, etc., are held by women 15% of the time and 5% of the time by blacks.

Since the retail food industry in the Washington area is highly unionized and the pay scale is very high, Grand Company has five times as many applicants on file as jobs available at any one time. The high pay and low turnover of the industry have resulted in a situation where Grand Company has no need to advertise job openings. With a ready supply of workers, they rely entirely upon word-of-mouth advertising.

The interview process consists of a standard math test for cashiers, and a standard questionnaire about past experience, schooling and general information. If there are no blatant reasons why an applicant is undesirable, such as having been convicted of theft, or questions which require further research, such as having been fired from their last job, the person's application is filed with the others. As an opening occurs in the general vicinity of an applicant, the person is called and informed of the job. This is done by going through the file arranged by application date, and calling the first applicant in the vicinity of the job. If an applicant already has obtained work and turns down the offer, that application is taken out of the file.

The sexual and racial makeup of the area where the Grand Company operates is relatively close to the makeup of the workforce. The sex makeup of the suburban areas of Virginia and Maryland where Grand Company operates is approximately 52% female and 48% male and the racial mix is approximately 85% white and 15% black. However, if the District of Columbia were included in the operating area, the racial mixture would be 70% white and 30% black.

Questions

1. If Grand Food Company were accused of unfair hiring practices would the EEOC be likely to prosecute under their guidelines? If yes, for what specific reasons?

2. What do you think Grand Food Company would contend is their operating area? What do you think the EEOC would contend is their operating area?

3. Should the promotion practices of Grand Food Company be examined? Why, or why not?

Relevant Factors in Findings of Sex Discrimination

The ABC Chemical Company sought to fill a sales trainee position. ABC placed an advertisement in a local newspaper which read: "Sales Trainee, male or female, no experience required. We are looking for an aggressive, career-minded individual." Jane Smith applied for the position. During her employment interview she was asked several questions which she felt were prejudicial toward women. Some of the questions included "What are your plans on marriage?", "Are you really intent on making a career with ABC Chemical?", and a statement "You know, there aren't too many women in the chemical field."

After the interview, Jane was informed that the company would give preference to someone with a background in chemicals, which she did not have, and would notify her within the next few days about the status of her application. Two days later Jane was notified by letter that she was not selected for the job. She charged ABC Chemical with sex discrimination in their failure to hire her.

When questioned by an Equal Opportunity Specialist of the Equal Employment Opportunity Commission, ABC Chemical's Personnel Director stated that the company had a firm policy of no discrimination and had an affirmative action program to recruit minorities and women. He stated that the sex discrimination charge had no merit, since the individual selected was more qualified, due to his having taken a chemistry course in high school. He further indicated that Jane had shown a negative attitude during her interview by refusing to answer questions about her personal plans for the future. Such questions are asked of all applicants, because the company is interested in their attitude toward a career. Lastly, he contended that statements relating to the number of women in the chemical field were not made to discourage Jane, but merely to inform her of factual information relative to the chemical industry.

During EEOC's subsequent investigation, it was learned that, at present, no women were employed by ABC Chemical as sales trainees or sales representatives – out of ten trainees and 35 representatives. Although the individual hired had taken chemistry courses in high school, seven currently employed trainees and 24 representatives did not have a background in the chemical field. It was for this reason, as a matter of fact, that ABC's in-house training program was very extensive, lasting in excess of six months. In conversations with other applicants for the same position, it was learned that all were men and none had been asked questions concerning their marital status or plans.

Questions

1. Was Jane Smith unlawfully denied employment because of her sex?
2. What factors would contribute to a finding of sex discrimination?
3. What remedy is available to Jane Smith in this situation?

Compliance with Title VII:
Numbers are Not Enough

Stalo, Inc., is a large multiline manufacturing company, with headquarters in New York City and plants located in fifteen states. Stalo also has six wholly-owned subsidiaries located in the southern part of the country. The company carries electronic equipment for distribution and also manufactures electronic toys, household items and desk-top calculators.

For many years Stalo has provided its employees with excellent benefits, working conditions and wages. The company has always cooperated with its unions and has never had a strike close its plants. In all its union shops, Stalo only hires people from union apprentice programs and union hiring halls, in accordance with their contracts. The high level of compensation has kept turnover to a minimum. With the low turnover rate, Stalo has generally filled job vacancies with people recommended by current employees. Employees who bring in qualified replacements are given a ten-dollar bonus for each person hired who satisfactorily completing company training programs.

Stalo uses a decentralized personnel department structure and the main office personnel staff is small, because hiring and recruiting is done at each individual plant. The Vice President of Personnel is John Bowers, who possesses a general business degree from a small Midwestern college and very limited knowledge in personnel administration.

A year ago Stalo was investigated by the EEOC, because the commission received numerous complaints against the company and its hiring practices. The company had never been in this position, and they knew very little about the existing laws regarding fair-hiring practices. John Bowers decided to hire more women and blacks at the entry-level positions that opened in the next year to comply with the laws as he understood them. He instructed the personnel offices at each plant to make an effort to hire these two classes of people.

At the end of the year the EEOC representative returned to Stalo to conduct a follow-up investigation. Mr. Bowers explained that the company had every intention of obeying the law and proceeded to show the investigator the results of his progress in complying with the law. The company had hired thirty-two women in the various production lines throughout the company and seventeen black men to work on the loading docks and to drive the company trucks. The investigator stated that Stalo was still violating Title VII of the Civil Rights Act and that the case would be turned over to the Justice Department in six months, if Stalo did not comply.

Questions

1. What must Stalo do, in addition to the steps it has already undertaken to comply with Title VII?
2. What statistical information determine compliance?
3. Should Mr. Bowers investigate the union apprenticeship programs and hiring halls? If so, why?

Sex Discrimination and Universities

When Cemaron University, a small college in Tupolo, Oklahoma, hired its women's resident supervisor from among 100 female applicants, little did they realize the situation which was to follow.

The chosen applicant, a college graduate and school teacher, had two years of work experience in student counseling. After an intensive interview and recommendations from previous employers, the applicant was selected as the women's resident supervisor to supervise approximately 150 female students in the college dormitory. Immediately thereafter, a male was interviewed and hired to supervise the men in the dormitory complex.

The position required a college degree and live-in status as part of the conditions for employment. However, the men's supervisor did not have a college degree, but was in fact attending classes to complete his degree at the university. The men's supervisor was paid a higher salary due to being responsible for 50 additional students and the fact that the male students caused greater disciplinary problems than the female students.

In the spring of the school year the men's supervisor started doing his practice teaching, which meant he was not available during the day for student counseling and other responsibilities. Consequently, the women's supervisor assumed some of his responsibilities. When the women's supervisor was asked to substitute teach at one of the local high schools from 8:00 a.m. until 2:00 p.m. each day for eight weeks, she assumed there would be no problem, since the men's supervisor was being allowed to do his practice teaching all day. However, the Director of Housing, the immediate supervisor, flatly denied her the opportunity to substitute teach, justifying the action by saying that both supervisors could not be away from their duties at the same time.

Questions

1. Was the university discriminating against the women's resident supervisor because of sex, as indicated under Title VII?
2. Assuming that identical job descriptions existed, would the BFOQ requirement have any effect on the type of applicant who was hired and the salary?
3. Would the women's supervisor be entitled to the same amount of compensation under the Equal Pay Act?
4. In a recent case, the Supreme Court has ruled that "Academic competence shall no longer be the supreme determining factor in faculty, professional appointments." Would this imposed policy be considered in this case? Why?

Non-profit Organizations and Title VII

Camp Olympia is owned and operated by the Mountain Area Council of the Boy Scouts of America. The purpose of the camp is to provide a summer program of camping and educational recreation activities and to fulfill the objectives of scouting in general. In addition, the camp is a facility that can be utilized by individual troops throughout the year on a first-come, first-served basis.

The land and the buildings of the camp were purchased over a period of years. From 1954 to present, the funds for the property and building acquisition were raised by the scouts of the area. The revenues necessary to operate and maintain the camp come from many sources. From the period of August 22 to June 2, the camp is for rent to any organization other than BSA. Presently there is a boxing club operating in the camp. Local industry and the United Fund also provide income to the facility. There is a fee charged to each scout who attends the camp during its summer session, primarily to pay for food, utilities and supplies.

Up until 1954 all of the staff, except the ranger and camp director, were volunteers. In the fall of 1954 an extremely wealthy individual left a vast sum of money in trust to the camp to pay the wages of the summer staff. The trust provided that any person from 15 years of age and over, members of BSA and nonblack, could be compensated out of the budgeted fund. Today the camp operates in the red and this fund.is a source of financial relief.

Up until 1974, the camp was able to maintain its policy of an all-white staff without too much difficulty. During the summer of that year the camp enrolled in an international staff-exchange program which was organized by the BSA. The staff member sent to the camp was from India. The only compensation other than his room and board was to be his fare to and from India. When the camp director applied to the local bank where the trust fund was set up, the request was denied because this staff member was dark-skinned. Other measures were provided for the payment of the fare.

In the two years that followed, some qualified blacks applied for summer employment, and because the payroll for the summer staff was budgeted based on the trust fund, were denied jobs. These individuals knew that they were qualified and that the camp would be forced to hire less-qualified people. They filed suit against Camp Olympia and the Boy Scouts of America.

Questions

1. Should the camp be forced to hire the blacks and provide for their compensation from other sources?

2. Is the present situation counter to state and federal law? If so, which particular legislation?

3. Does the fact that the BSA is a nonprofit organization have any bearing on this case?

Sex Discrimination and Federal Employees

Erin Patrick, an employee of the ABC Agency in the United States government, rapidly rose from a GS-6 to a GS-11. She transferred to the MTK Agency in April of 1965, as a GS-11. In June of 1966, she was promoted to a GS-12, and in October of 1968, she became eligible for a GS-13 position in the economics department, after a Civil Service exam.

Erin's educational background consisted of a B.S. degree in economics. She also had taken several university-level courses in a variety of subjects from 1961 to 1966. During her career, she completed many courses which were offered by her employer.

At the MTK Agency, Erin applied for promotion to a GS-13 in March of 1970, and again in July of that same year. In November of 1971, Erin applied for a GS-13 position as a Computer Systems Analyst. Although Erin was qualified by the Civil Service Commission for all three positions, she was not selected. On each occasion, the selecting official was a white male.

When Erin was turned down for the Computer Systems analyst position, she filed an EEO complaint of discrimination on the basis of sex and race. She claimed that she had not been selected because she was black and female.

A white male, Terrance Klein, was chosen for the Analyst position. He had only a high-school diploma, and had completed three computer courses. Terrance received a promotion to GS-9 in 1967; Erin was promoted to a GS-12 in 1966. His performance was rated high in motivation. Erin had received very good performance ratings from 1961–1972, and her performance was rated satisfactory to superior in motivation. Both employees were rated high in the technical skills area.

Since 1969, the MTK Agency had promoted only one Spanish female, and no black females, to GS-13 positions. During the same period, ten white females, 103 white males, and three black males were hired or promoted to GS-13. After Erin's complaint was received, the agency responded by stating that opportunities for advancement were uniformly available to all employees and that Erin was not discriminated against because of sex and/or race. The agency also maintained that Terrance was better qualified for the Computer Systems Analyst position, because he was rated high in both technical skill and motivation. Erin, on the other hand, was rated high in technical skills, but slightly lower in motivation. This rating was based on a new agency rating form rather than on objective criteria. Erin's supervisor was a white male.

Question

1. The court ruled in favor of Erin Patrick. Based on your knowledge of the EEO guidelines, list three reasons why the MTK Agency was charged with discrimination.

Weight-lifting Ability as a BFOQ

Marsha Thompson was recently discharged from the United States Army. Upon discharge Marsha returned to her home town of Springfield, Virginia. During her four years in the Army, Marsha was a truck driver. Hoping to use her skills in trucking operations, Marsha applied to Ben-Hurst Trucking Company after arriving home.

It was a well-known fact in town that Ben-Hurst was expanding operations considerably and had a need for fifteen new truck drivers. Since Marsha had four years of experience, she thought her chances of employment were excellent.

Ben-Hurst was an excellent company for which to work. They paid their truck drivers excellent wages and had a good benefits plan. As a result of this, many applicants turned up for the fifteen new jobs. Of the thirty-five applicants applying for the jobs, all were men except Marsha. This did not discourage Marsha, however, because as she talked to the various men, few seemed to have as much experience as she. Although some of the men complained to her that this was not women's work, she told them to mind their own business.

Marsha and the others were given a written test on Friday afternoon and told their results would be given to them Monday morning. On Monday, Marsha was informed that she passed the written test with an excellent score and was told to report to the trucking area for a driver's test. Upon arriving at the trucking area, Marsha noticed that there were now only about twenty applicants left. As far as Marsha could tell, she drove the trucks as well as any of the men.

After the driving test, all applicants were told to report to the docks for a weight-lifting test. The test required each applicant to lift one hundred pounds. Although Marsha was a fairly large woman, she was not able to lift the required one hundred pounds. All of the applicants were told that they would be informed by Wednesday if they were to be hired. When Wednesday came, Marsha did not receive a phone call. Upset over this, she called Ben-Hurst to find out why. Ben-Hurst told her that she qualified in all aspects, but since she could not pass the weight-lifting test they could not hire her. They told her that this was a *"bona fide* occupational qualification," and they, therefore, had the right to reject her.

Marsha did not think that the company should be able to discriminate against her, just because she could not lift the weight.

Question

1. Is the amount of weight to be lifted (100 lbs.) a legitimate BFOQ in this case? What arguments can you give for and against it being considered as such?

Physical Appearance as a BFOQ

Sally Jones is a college student looking for a job as a sales clerk in a dress shop. On March 19th she was in Washington filling out applications, but all positions seemed to be filled for the summer. However, her day brightened when she applied for a job in a tiny dress shop in Georgetown which actually had a sign in the window reading, "Help wanted—experienced salesgirl—good looking only." Sally was very pleased—she was experienced in the field and felt herself to be attractive, although she didn't understand why it was necessary to be good looking to be a salesgirl.

Sally applied for the position in question, and heard nothing for a few weeks. As she expected, there were no openings available in the other shops she had investigated. However, three weeks after she'd applied at the dress shop in Georgetown, she received a call requesting her to come in for an interview. Sally was thrilled, since she badly needed a job.

During the interview Sally felt sure she would get the job—the manager of the shop seemed to like her qualifications and was very friendly. He told her he would let her know in a day or two. He never called. Sally became angry and called the shop herself, asking to talk to the manager. The manager seemed evasive to her questions on why she hadn't been contacted. Finally, the manager told her she hadn't been selected because she was not attractive enough. Sally was outraged, and demanded to know how it was decided who was or was not attractive enough to work in a tiny dress shop? The manager had no answer and hung up the phone.

Questions

1. Is this a case of discrimination, or does the dress shop have the right to choose only "attractive" salesgirls, regardless of other qualifications?
2. Can attractiveness be classified as a BFOQ, in general, or in this case?
3. Could Sally have taken legal action to stop the dress shop's hiring practice?

Title VII and Job-related Educational Requirements

The Brett Consulting Firm, a growing consulting firm specializes in government contracts in the Washington area, is facing a quota problem in fulfilling its minority hiring policies. Its staff at the present time has a very high ratio of Ph.D.'s and it is having difficulties recruiting qualified blacks with electrical engineering or physics backgrounds.

The Brett Consulting Firm has eleven white, male professionals, seven white, female professionals, and three white, female clerical staffers. They have doubled their number of employees in the last four years.

The benefits program with Brett consists of a profit-sharing retirement program, extensive health and dental insurance coverage, liberal salary increases and bonuses for overachievers. There is no cash-flow problem with this young growing company. Through excellent employee selection and good business practices, Brett is a solid investment in anyone's future.

The firm is too small to have its own personnel staff and recruitment is done by middle managers using personal referrals from their alma maters and word-of-mouth sources. The cost of campus recruitment is too high and has not been successful. The area universities have not been too successful referring candidates that fulfill the strict requirements for the open positions. There isn't a pool of black graduates with a solid background in EE or physics in the geographic area. Additionally, Catholic and George Washington Universities don't have graduate departments that could supply the firm with job candidates.

A problem exists for the middle managers: they must get a more racially balanced firm without actually reducing their high educational requirements and abilities. James Conrad, a middle manager, has been working for months trying to come up with a solution to this problem. He has decided that the only logical solution is to hire a private employment agency to recruit candidates for his department. Based on previous failures, he realizes he may have to lower the educational requirement to a bachelor's degree; electrical engineers have the labor market cornered right now, and can pick any job they want.

Questions

1. How can James Conrad specify a preference for only black candidates to the private agency?
2. Must the Brett Firm lower their high standards for applicants, to achieve a racially balanced staff?

3. What antidiscrimination laws must be considered in any recruitment policy?

4. Would a private employment agency be the best source of new employees for Brett?

A High-School Diploma as a Job Requirement

Mike Jones was a young Puerto Rican who had dropped out of high school to help support the family after his father died; he did manage to attend night school for two years to become a computer operator. This was his first interview and it seemed that the interviewer, Mr. Clark, was impressed with Mr. Jones.

"Mr. Jones, I am impressed with your performance at computer school and your work record at your present job," Clark said. "I know that you applied for the programming job, but I can give you one of the vacant positions as a keypunch operator."

"I am anxious to get my career started," Jones said, "But I was applying for the programming job."

"Well, I'm afraid that the programming position requires that you have a high school diploma," Clark said, "and you did not finish high school."

"I know that I don't have a high-school diploma, but I was near the top of my class in computer school and was highly recommended by my instructor."

"That may be true," Clark said, "But we have always required a high-school diploma for that position. Perhaps you should have finished high school and then entered computer school."

"That doesn't seem fair," Jones said. "You seem to be saying that I am qualified for the programming, but can't get that job because I don't have a high school diploma."

"I don't make the rules, Mr. Jones," Clark said. "I can't make exceptions to company rules. After all, you can advance to the programming position once you get a high-school diploma. This is only fair to everyone."

Questions

1. Can this be considered discrimination under Title VII, since it is a rule that is applied to all applicants?

2. Would it be discriminatory if the company had data that showed the majority of those with high-school diplomas had considerably higher job performance records?

3. If this requirement proves to be discriminatory against minorities, Jones was ultimately given the job, and later a white male applied under the same circumstances, could he be refused on the high-school requirement?

National Origin as a BFOQ

The Bali Hai Corporation started as a small Chinese restaurant in Boston, Massachusetts in 1959. The restaurant was an exact replica of a Chinese pagoda. Over the years, the restaurant, owned and managed by Arnold Sing, became known for its food and atmosphere. Customers were made to feel as if they were actually in China.

In the last few years Sing decided to incorporate and open other similar restaurants throughout the country. Sing, who had come to the United States from China in the early 1940's, was very strict in keeping up his reputation of good food and atmosphere, and had a policy of hiring only waiters of Oriental descent. He felt this added to his customers' dining pleasure and made for a more authentic environment. For kitchen positions, though, Sing hired any applicants who were qualified.

About a year ago in Sing's Bali Hai of Washington, DC there was a shortage of waiters. An advertisement was placed in the paper for waiters, and the manager of the store was instructed by Sing to hire only Orientals. The manager was also reminded of Bali Hai's commitment to a reputation of good food and atmosphere.

Two young men, one black and one white, both with considerable restaurant experience, applied for the waiters' jobs. The manager explained the policy of hiring only Orientals to the young men, and he also told them he could get them work in his kitchen.

The two men declined the positions and instead went directly to the area Equal Employment Opportunity Office and filed a complaint. Sing's defense was that the policy was only to preserve the atmosphere of the restaurant. He said the Oriental waiters were needed to make it more authentic. Sing also added that he hired blacks, whites, and other races for his kitchen help.

Question

1. Is Sing's defense a good one under the law? Why, or why not?

Job Qualifications and Task Performance

Giant Airlines advertised for four flight officer positions. The requirements were a college degree and 500 flight hours. Five persons with the following qualifications applied for the positions.

Candidate A: White male; degree in chemical engineering with 500 flight hours in a standard aircraft

Candidate B: White male, degree in biology with 350 hours in a jet aircraft

Candidate C: White male, Master's degree in mathematics with 200 hours in a jet rotary-wing helicopter and 250 hours in a standard aircraft

Candidate D: White male, degree in astronomy with 600 flight hours in a standard aircraft

Candidate E: Black male, degree in English with 500 hours in a standard aircraft (Mr. Johnson)

Mr. Johnson was turned down for one of the available positions with the explanation that he was not as well qualified as the other four candidates, due to his degree and flight time.

Mr. Johnson sued Giant Airlines on the basis of racial discrimination. The plaintiff stated a college degree was not related to the type of position he had applied for and, in addition, he had the required flight hours, while some of the other applicants had not.

To establish that Giant's flight officer qualifications resulted in discrimination against blacks, the appellant showed that out of the approximately 5900 flight officers in Giant's employ at the time of the trial, only nine were blacks. Appellant contended that these statistics established a *prima facie* case of racial discrimination. Giant claimed that these bare statistics established nothing, unless accompanied by similar information on the number of qualified black applicants for the flight officer position.

The two job qualifications that appellant challenged were the requirements of a college degree and a minimum of 500 flight hours. The evidence at the trial showed that Giant did not train applicants to be pilots, but instead required that their applicants be pilots at the time of their application. It could not seriously be contended that such a requirement was not job-related. Giant also showed that applicants who had higher flight hours were more likely to succeed in the rigorous training which Giant flight officers went through after they were hired.

The statistics showed that 500 hours was a reasonable minimum applicant requirement to insure their passing Giant's training program. The evidence also showed that because of the high cost of the training program, it was important to Giant that those who began the training program could eventually become flight officers.

With regard to the college degree requirement, Giant officials testified that it was a requirement which could be waived if the applicant's other qualifications were superior, especially if the person had a lot of flight time in high-speed jet aircraft. The evidence showed that Giant flight officers went through a rigorous training course upon being hired and then were required to attend intensive refresher courses at six-month intervals. Company officials testified that the possession of a college degree indicated that the applicant had the ability to understand and retain concepts and information given in the atmosphere of a classroom or training program. Thus, a person with a college degree, particularly one in the "hard" sciences, was more able to succeed in the initial training program and the unending series of refresher courses.

Question

1. Do you agree with the company's defense? Why, or why not?

Age Discrimination in Employment

Johnnie Walker has worked for General Cement Company for eighteen years. He joined General as an engineer and subsequently was promoted to operations manager for the northeastern region. He has served in this capacity for the past ten years. Recently, the General company was acquired by the Red River Corporation. Mr. Walker and several other upper-level management personnel have been notified that they will be replaced by Red River employees.

In light of his present situation, Mr. Walker is in the process of seeking employment elsewhere. Upon the advice of a close friend who works at the Harbour Cement Company, a newly established, up-and-coming cement company in the area, Mr. Walker applied for a managerial position with that firm. He filed an application and was interviewed by the personnel director the following day. Mr. Walker was informed that he would be notified of the company's decision, pending the completion of interviews with the remaining applicants.

Several days later, he was notified by letter that he had not been selected for the job. In talking with his friend a few days later, Mr. Walker was told that the person who was hired to fill the position at the Harbour Cement Company was not as qualified as he was. The new employee had only ten years' experience, as opposed to eighteen years for Mr. Walker. His friend also related that he felt the primary reason for Mr. Walker's not being selected was his **age.** It was his friend's opinion that the personnel department felt the other applicant's age (fifteen years younger than Mr. Walker') would be a greater asset for the company in the long run.

Encouraged by his colleagues, Mr. Walker sought legal advice as to the possibility of filing suit against Harbour Cement Company under the 1967 Age Discrimination in Employment Act. In discussions with his lawyer pertaining to the application and interview, Mr. Walker recalled on the application form an inquiry as to his specific age. His lawyer advised him that he had legal grounds for filing suit against Harbour Cement Company on the basis of age discrimination.

Questions

1. Was it legal for the application to contain a question regarding the specific age of the applicant?
2. Is *age* a *bona fide* occupational qualification in this situation?
3. Is quality and/or quantity of job-related experience a *bona fide* occupational qualification in this case?

4. Would Johnnie Walker be eligible for state unemployment compensation in your state, if he did not find another job before he was laid off?

Age Discrimination and Physical Job Requirements

G.M. Enterprises, a small company employing 22 persons, had a vacant position after a recent resignation. Bob Blake, 43 years old, and Tom Boswell, 53, applied for this position. Both men had worked for the company for an equal number of years, but Tom had experience which was similar to that required for the new job. Both Tom and Bob had been to a company-paid school for a training course relating to this new job. Tom had much better course scores but Bob had passed with a score acceptable by company standards.

The new job required operating a rather complex piece of equipment and, at times, involved some heavy lifting. The younger man was given the job. The supervisor called Tom into his office to inform him of the decision.

"Well, Tom," said Duncan, the supervisor, "I'm sorry we could not promote you to the position, but Bob just seemed the best choice under the circumstances."

"I don't understand," Tom said. "I have had some related experience and had excellent scores in the training course."

"What you say is true, Tom," Duncan said, "But Bob is younger and you may not be able to do the heavy lifting several years from now. Besides, you only have a few years until you are eligible for retirement. It just makes sense to promote Bob. He's younger and will be around for a longer time. It just makes economic sense from the company's viewpoint."

Questions

1. Would this situation fall within the purview of the Age Discrimination Act?
2. If the company could show that several past employees had to be reassigned after reaching between 55 and 60 years old and were unable to perform the above job, could this be a legitimate basis for hiring the younger man in this situation?

Reverse Discrimination

The Millers, Brad and Mary, moved to Tallahassee, Florida for Mary to attend law school at Florida State University. Brad graduated from Georgetown University with a degree in business administration and worked in retail management for five years. Brad graduated with top honors from Georgetown and had excellent recommendations from his former employers.

Tallahassee, Florida is basically a college town, centering around two universities and the Florida State Legislature. The two universities are Florida State University and Florida A & M University. There is only one large shopping mall and a few department stores in Tallahassee, and as such, jobs in retail management are quite scarce.

Upon arriving in Tallahassee, Mary started classes at the law school and Brad began looking for a job. There were absolutely no openings anywhere in town for a retail manager, and Brad eventually had to settle for a teller position at a local bank. Brad kept abreast of the retail job market in Tallahassee, and finally an opportunity arose.

T. H. Sandy, a women's discount sportswear retailer advertised in the local newspaper for a store manager. Brad immediately made an appointment for an interview and sent in a resume, as requested in the ad. Brad arrived early for his interview and was given an application form to complete. The application form was a long one and included a question concerning sex of applicant. While completing the application form, Brad noticed that all of the employees of T. H. Sandy were female and all of the other applicants waiting to be interviewed were also female. Brad was finally called in for his interview, which he thought went very well. The interviewer told Brad that they had two more days of interviewing before a decision would be made, and that he would be hearing from them in about a week. The next week Brad received a letter from T. H. Sandy informing him that he had not been chosen for the position and thanking him for his interest in the company. The letter gave no reason for the decision. Since this job was so important to Brad, he decided to visit the store and talk with the lady who had interviewed him.

In his meeting with the interviewer, Brad found out that the company had been very impressed with his experience and credentials, but had decided against hiring him because he was a male. The interviewer showed Brad a job description for the manager's position and pointed out that one of the duties of the manager was to supervise all areas of the store, including the dressing room. Because of this particular duty, the company felt that the position should be filled with a female. Brad left the store upset and discouraged.

After discussing the situation with his wife, who was now studying Fair Employment Legislation, Brad considered filing suit against T. H. Sandy for discrimination based on sex under Title VII of the Civil Rights Act of 1964.

Questions

1. Was T. H. Sandy's decision concerning Brad Miller in conflict with Title VII of the Civil Rights Act of 1964?
2. Was it legal for T. H. Sandy's application form to include a question concerning sex of applicant?
3. Is sex a *bona fide* occupational qualification in this situation?
4. Legally, would it have made a difference if there had been no job description for the position of store manager?

Selection for a Position Without a
Specific Job Description

The president of the Itty Bitty Machine Company approached Kirk Johnson, the personnel officer about the need to fill a soon-to-be-vacant position as the president's administrative assistant. Discussion between the president and Kirk indicated that the position was used as a stepping-stone for higher executive positions and as such, would require a higher degree of education and experience than what would normally be required for an administrative assistant.

The position was then advertised within the company via the company newspaper.

Three applicants made application to Personnel for the position.

Frieda Spiher had worked for Itty Bitty for fifteen years. She had a degree in secretarial science, and had been an administrative assistant to the Vice President for Production for the last five years.

John Moscella joined the company five years ago right out of George Mason University, with a degree in business administration. He has been attending night school working on his MBA, with about one year to go. He has been the assistant personnel officer for the last two years.

Richard D'Aleo is in charge of the computer room and has been with the company since it was founded twenty years ago. Richard is five years from retirement. He has a bachelor's degree in engineering, but has not pursued any further education.

Aside from working with John for the last two years, Kirk has been good friends with both Richard and Frieda since he came to Itty Bitty ten years ago.

Questions

1. What recommendations should Kirk make to the president regarding selection for the position?
2. If Frieda were not picked for the job, would she have any grounds for charging discrimination? If so, what defense could Itty Bitty Machine Company use?
3. If Richard is not picked for the job, would he have any grounds for charging age discrimination? If so, what defense could Itty Bitty Machine Company use?

Married vs. Maiden Surnames and Title VII

June Garcia, 28 years old and married, worked for Goliath Electric as a line worker, testing and inspecting electrical semi-conductors. She had a very favorable record and had worked her way up from packing clerk to being a valued employee, one of the most consistent and best on the line. She also worked her way through college at night.

Mr. Bollin, personnel director, was considering either June or Tom Henly, a 32-year-old white male, for the position of line supervisor. Mr. Bollin wanted to promote a minority, especially an Hispanic, and felt Garcia would be excellent for the job.

Occasionally, Goliath received contracts that required their supervisors to have a secret clearance. Mr. Bollin checked out both candidates' backgrounds to determine if either had anything that would preclude them from obtaining a secret clearance from the government. Mr. Bollin discovered that June had been arrested three times while in high school for being with someone caught stealing (her old boy-friend).

Even though the company did not currently have a government contract, Mr. Bollin felt that Tom Henly should be promoted, since he had a perfect record.

There was another supervisory position opening up soon in another department that June would qualify for. Mr. Bollin knew from past experience that an arrest record would keep Garcia from obtaining a secret clearance. One month after Tom Henly was promoted to the job, June filed an EEOC claim, stating that she should have been promoted and should be given back pay for the period that Tom Henly had been in the position.

Questions

1. Should June be promoted, even though her stay in the supervisory job may be of short duration, if a government contract comes along?
2. Can a secret clearance be denied due to an arrest record?
3. If Garcia's maiden name was Smith, could she still be considered a Spanish surname minority?

Employment Rights of Single Parents

Major Jim Jones is a career Army officer who has spent 17 years in the service. Last year Major Jones' wife died, leaving him to care for their two daughters, aged 7 and 10. The Major does not want to give up his daughters and is keeping them with him. The nature of Major Jones' job requires him to work shifts ranging from 4:00 p.m. to 12.00 a.m., 12.00 a.m. to 8:00 a.m. and 8:00 a.m. to 4:00 p.m., as well as weekends and holidays. While his wife was living this was not an inconvenience for Major Jones. In addition, as a military officer Major Jones is always faced with the possibility of mobilization in the event of a military crisis.

As a result of this schedule, the Army has required Major Jones to sign a document stating that he has taken adequate steps to assure the Army that his family obligations will not interfere with his ability to work odd hours or mobilize on short notice. In effect, this document states that Major Jones' parental responsibilities will not inconvenience the Army or affect his job performance.

Failure to sign the statement will result in Major Jones being forced to resign from the Army or face discharge. Furthermore, failure to perform his shift work could also result in a discharge. This, of course, would mean the loss of 17 years earned toward a pension as well as the right to use military benefits such as the commissary, PX, health care, etc.

So far Major Jones has not missed any of his duties. The girls are in school during the week, but Major Jones is having a great deal of difficulty finding someone to watch his daughters on week nights and weekends. Major Jones is trying desperately to be reassigned to an office where the hours are more stable.

Questions

1. In view of court rulings forbidding the military from discharging its pregnant female members, is Major Jones being unfairly discriminated against, because of his single parent status?

2. When Major Jones was required to sign the statement about the care of his daughters, was this an invasion of his privacy?

3. Did the Army bring undue pressure upon Major Jones by asking him to sign the documents under the threat of an immediate discharge?

4. Obviously, an argument could be made for the Army's view if it were a wartime situation. However, since the U.S. is at peace, does the Army or any employer have the right to delve so thoroughly into an employee's personal life, especially when the employee's job performance is satisfactory?

Equal Pay for Equal Work

A local hospital is directed by a single administrator. Due to the growth of the facility several years ago, she changed the organizational structure, organizing the hospital into four divisions: professional services, ancillary services, nursing services, and a financial division. Each of these divisions was headed by an assistant administrator. It was the responsibility of each of these individuals to appoint department heads to manage the areas within their responsibility. For example, the Assistant Administrator, Director of Ancillary Services, had department heads for Engineering, Housekeeping, Laundry, Materials Management, and Safety and Security. Each of these department heads had the title of "Director" of their area of responsibility; i.e., Director of Housekeeping.

Within the nursing services division, the Assistant Administrator was also considered Director of Nursing. She had, therefore, designated her department heads as supervisors, to have a distinction of titles. Although called supervisors within their division, they were considered department heads on the organization chart. The function of these supervisors was identical when compared to the Directors in other divisions; the job description was the same. However, the department heads in the other divisions were all males, while the supervisors (department heads) in nursing were all females.

The hospital salary scale identified department heads as a grade 16, while supervisors were a grade 14. During the growth of the hospital, much contact was necessary between divisions. The department heads in nursing service began to realize that confusion was being caused by the fact that they were called supervisors while their counterparts in the other divisions were called directors. As a result, titles were changed; responsibilities remained the same.

As the Assistant Administrator of Nursing Service was writing her report of the change to the Administrator, she discovered that her department heads were being paid less than department heads in other divisions. She included this information in her report, with a request that the salaries be changed.

The Administrator reviewed the report and called a meeting of all Assistant Administrators and the Director of Personnel. She was concerned with possible violation of the Equal Pay Act of 1963.

Questions

1. If you were the Director of Personnel, what would your recommendation be regarding the salaries?
2. If an increase for the Nursing Services supervisors is in order, should the change be retroactive? If so, to when?

3. Has the hospital violated the 1963 Equal Pay Act?
4. What should be done regarding the "Department Head" and "Supervisor" titles?

The Fair Labor Standards Act and Eligibility for Unemployment Compensation

Bob worked at a fast-food restaurant. He knew he was being taken advantage of by the manager, his boss, because Bob often was asked to work overtime, but only got his regular pay, $3.50/hr. However, he never really realized it until a friend told him he should demand his right to the minimum wage, if not time-and-a-half, for overtime work. Besides, he was not earning any tips, since "overtime" at the restaurant meant vacuuming, cleaning counters, etc., after the business was closed for the night.

Bob finally decided to get his nerve up the next time the boss insisted he work overtime. Sure enough, two days later he was asked to close up, which meant another two hours of work after an eight-hour day. Bob went to his boss and asked him if he could get minimum wage or time-and-a-half for working overtime—after all, $3.50/hr. and no tips wasn't enough to live on.

The manager didn't agree to this. Instead, he just laughed and said Bob should be glad he got paid at all for overtime, since "some places make you work for free."

Bob was very angry. The next time he was called to come in to work, he told his boss he quit. The next day he was talking to a friend who also worked in a fast-food restaurant, and the friend told Bob that he got a little over minimum wage for overtime work. Bob was even more angry now. How could his boss tell him some places made employees work for free? He decided to call and find out if he was eligible to get unemployment compensation while he looked for another job. When he told the office why he quit his job, they told him he did not qualify.

Questions

1. Did Bob have the right to claim overtime pay?
2. Did his boss have the right to conceal the possibility of getting overtime pay, or was he legally required to tell Bob that he was entitled to it?
3. Did Bob qualify for unemployment compensation, or had he quit without cause?

Implicit Overtime Under the
Fair Labor Standards Act

Glen Miller became the Assistant Pro to Head Pro Melvin Rowe at the Holly Hills Golf Club about three months ago. Mr. Rowe had hired Glen on an informal basis. The terms of employment were all verbal. However, Glen had been working about sixty hours a week and not receiving any overtime compensation. Every two weeks, Glen received the salary that he and Mr. Rowe had agreed upon for a normal forty-hour work week. Glen wasn't the least bit upset about the long hours, as he felt it was just part of the job.

One evening after work, a group of the members asked Glen to play gin rummy at the clubhouse that evening. Glen welcomed the chance to get to know the members better. As the evening progressed, Glen innocently mentioned the long hours he was working to a member. The member became rather upset and began threatening to turn Melvin Rowe into the State Labor Department. Glen thought the gentleman was just kidding. He didn't think anything of the situation and went on home to bed.

The next day, Glen saw the member and was told that a formal complaint had already been sent to the Labor Department! Glen panicked at first, but he eventually calmed down and decided it was best to remain silent about the entire situation.

About two weeks later, Melvin Rowe found out about the complaint and became angry and concerned. Mr. Rowe called Glen into his office the next day and chastised him severely. Glen tried to explain that he had no part in filing the formal complaint, but this had no effect on Mr. Rowe. The once close relationship between Mr. Rowe and Glen began to deteriorate as they waited for the investigation to begin.

Questions

1. How would you conduct the investigation for the Labor Department? State your arguments against Mr. Rowe.
2. How would you defend Mr. Rowe's viewpoint?
3. What legislation dealing with working hours is Mr. Rowe violating, if any? Explain.

Job Grade and Eligibility for Overtime

Mason, Davis & Dulaney, a successful civil engineering firm based in Northern Virginia, currently employs a fulltime staff of over four hundred civil engineers and supporting staff. As with any large company, MD & D has, for legal and administrative purposes, set dollar compensation limits relative to job positions. That is, a detailed wage structure has been computed for each job type. In addition, in compliance with federal regulations and their own wage structure, certain job types pay overtime at the rate of one-and-one-half times the normal hourly rate, while other job types allow for overtime pay at the rate of exactly one time the normal hourly rate. The third category is composed of salaried management staff, thus receive no overtime pay at all.

MD & D perform job evaluations once each year and use these as supportive information for the salary reviews that follow shortly thereafter. As of the last salary review, several individuals reached the base-pay dollar mark (maximum level), sending them out of the first overtime pay category and into the second, which pays overtime at a straight time rate.

These individuals are not professionals, nor do they have supervisory status. Furthermore, they do not work independently.

All five involved individuals refused to continue working the overtime that management insisted had to be done, to meet the demanding production schedule. Their refusal stemmed from the fact that they could show how, based on past years, they would lose money annually by continuing to work the same number of overtime hours, but now at the lower rate. This seemed, on the face of the matter, to be a *bona fide* complaint, even in light of the recent increase in their base pay at the time of the salary review. For these individuals, their base pay was not what made their job monetarily worthwhile, but rather the abundant supply of overtime pay. The employees felt that they deserved not only a base pay increase for a job well done, but also to be left on time-and-one-half for overtime.

Questions

1. Federal law dictates certain criteria for job types that determines whether or not these individuals must receive overtime pay and at what rate. One of the criteria is base pay. If these employees are receiving base pay substantially higher than required by federal law to take them off time-and-one-half overtime pay, should they also have to meet all the other standards before the employer is allowed to remove them from this overtime pay status?

2. At the ever-increasing rate of providing fringe benefits and state and federally required compensations, the government has not made it very attractive to hire new people into the firm, only to take up the slack created by employees who refuse to work overtime. It could be cheaper in the long run for MD & D to just continue paying these individuals time-and-one-half. However, this would create ambiguous guidelines and would definitely stir emotions among other workers who have been previously removed from this status. What can be done to keep the employees happy, to keep the government happy, and to maintain the wage structure set up by the company officials?

Compensatory Time and the Fair Labor Standards Act

A small government contracting firm has a staff composed of technical engineers, clerical support personnel, and corporate administrative employees. Because of the restriction by the government of not reimbursing a contractor for premium overtime pay, this organization instituted a policy of compensatory time earned for overtime worked, in lieu of direct overtime payment. All employees, regardless of salary level, position, or responsibilities, earn compensatory time for overtime hours worked. Earned compensatory time is available for use as time off at a later date. Compensatory time and ensuing time off require prior approval by supervisory personnel.

This compensatory time policy obviously benefits both the company and the employees. The company is paid for overtime hours worked on its government contracts without having to pay the employees working the overtime, until a future date when time off is taken. The employees earn an extra fringe benefit in the form of time which they can use in lieu of their vacation or sick leave (unused vacation may be requested as cash payments by the employee, which adds to annual compensation). However, unused compensatory time is forfeited by the employee upon termination from the company.

All personnel hired by the company, including clerical employees who are normally classified as nonexempt in other organizations, have the compensatory time policy fully explained, prior to commencing fulltime employment.

The firm's compensatory time policy comes into direct conflict with federal and state wage and hour legislation. Local laws particularly, classify employees of companies within their jurisdiction into exempt/nonexempt categories according to specified criteria, including job responsibilities, salary level, educational background, and degree of working independence. Regardless of the company's overtime policy, and the acceptance of this policy by the employees, the wage and hour laws direct that employees meeting certain criteria must be paid premium overtime pay.

While the firm was technically in violation of the minimum wage laws of the state in which it conducted its business, there was no problem until a dissatisfied nonexempt employee registered a complaint. When this complaint was registered against the company, a total review was conducted by the state Minimum Wage Office of the three preceding years, including all overtime worked by employees determined to be entitled to premium overtime pay. The company was forced to pay a substantial sum of back wages to the employees affected, even to individuals who had left the firm months or years before.

Questions

1. What are the potential effects on motivation and production arising from the company's compensatory time policy?

2. Should the company be bound to the state minimum wage laws, even though:
   (a) the majority of employees prefer to earn compensatory time?
   (b) the federal government will not reimburse contractors for overtime premiums?

3. Is there a possibility that supervisory personnel can manipulate the compensatory time policy to favor certain employees (thus discriminating against others)?

4. Will employees tend to manage their individual compensatory time earned, to ensure total usage prior to termination, so they will not have to forfeit any unused time? Can this affect the reliability of employees?

5. Will employees tend to create overtime work in order to earn compensatory time? Does this put an unnecessary extra burden on supervisory personnel?

6. Will certain long-term, valued employees' productivity and morale be affected by being reclassified as nonexempt personnel, rather than professional, exempt employees following the minimum wage office investigation?

Abuses of Compensatory Time

The Speery Univac Corporation sells, rents, and services electronic data processing equipment and employs a large staff of servicepeople to keep its customers' equipment in order. The 30 servicepeople who work out of the St. Paul district office (which covers most of the Midwest) all live in the St. Paul area and are often required to travel to customers in distant locations; usually they travel by air.

A given trouble call may take several hours or even days of work. A problem has arisen from the fact that, when an assignment is completed, the workers fly back to St. Paul and often arrive home late in the evening, or even after midnight. Under these circumstances, management has always allowed the servicepeople to take a few hours extra sleep and not report to the office the first thing in the morning.

Recently there have been signs that the workers have begun to abuse this privilege. A few people have developed the habit of taking the entire morning off after every out-of-town trip, even if they arrive back at their home by 5:00 p.m. the previous evening.

Management has considered imposing a hard-and-fast rule that all servicepeople must report for work at 9:00 a.m. regardless of what time they arrived the night before. But, in some cases, this would impose an obvious hardship, and it might encourage the servicepeople to spread their work out, so that instead of finishing their job in the afternoon and returning home late, they would slow down and work through the next morning, returning home in the afternoon.

Above all, management is anxious not to disturb the employees' high morale and interest in their work. These servicepeople are paid a salary, receive liberal fringe benefits, and are treated almost like members of management.

Question

1. What action could management take to alleviate this problem?

Increased Responsibility
Without Compensation Adjustments

Late in the afternoon on August 18, 1979, Don Chamberland began to think about his future. Don was a staff operations researcher and had worked for Transoil for about a year. He had been hired by Dave Scott, head of the Analysis Department, in September 1978. About three months later, Scott was replaced by Jack Townsend—another staff member in the department. A replacement had been hired to fill Townsend's old position. Don Chamberland thought he was going to be selected for Townsend's old position—which represented a promotion. He was feeling a bit confused about his place in the organization and was thinking of resigning.

Jack Townsend had been Director of the Analysis Department for about eight months. Over that time period, his relationship with the Staff Director, Ralph Ortega, blew hot and cold. Ortega had a high regard for Jack's technical skills and experience, but was dissatisfied with his lack of attention to office matters. Ortega had commented to his secretary, "I recognize Jack's shortcomings, but in a pinch, he will come through for me. We will just have to watch that he tends to business."

Jack Townsend had steadily grown to rely on Don Chamberland's taking care of normal office matters. Jack traveled frequently and when in the office, provided only general guidance to Don or worked on projects which Ortega personally assigned to him. Don made sure that all finished products leaving of the office were reviewed and approved by Jack.

Don found himself in a rather peculiar position. Other offices were beginning to interface directly with him. Don often represented Townsend at staff meetings but felt uncomfortable under what he thought was Ortega's disapproving eye. Ortega had once stopped the staff meeting and asked directly, "Where is Jack this morning?" Don mentioned the comment to Jack. Townsend responded, "Don't worry about it. You're doing a good job, you keep me informed and Ortega's getting the service he needs." Don recalled almost telling Townsend then that he was bothered by doing work which was not his responsibility, or for which he did not get the recognition.

About four months ago, Townsend had been given approval to fill his old position. He called Chamberland in and told him the news. "I know you have been loaded down with your own work plus the things I've sort of delegated, but maybe the situation will soon improve. I'm going to talk to Ortega about promoting you into a senior position and having you act as my assistant. We will hire somebody else to fill your job."

A month later Townsend mentioned to Chamberland that he might have difficulty hiring a new person. Jack still wanted Don as his assistant, but he thought he might have to use his old position and better salary to attract an experienced person. Two weeks later Townsend announced the hiring of Dr. Herbert Warner. Jack told Don that Warner was an old friend who was technically very good, but that he would need help learning office procedures and the details of the department's business. Jack had, in fact, had to use his old position and higher salary to get Warner to join the office. Townsend commented, "I know you're probably a bit disappointed. What I would like to do is inform my office that you're the number two person and I'll do what I can to get you a raise within the next six months. Can I count on you?"

Questions

1. Evaluate Townsend's approach to filling the vacant position.
2. What factors should Chamberland consider in replying to Townsend?
3. What should Chamberland do?

Alteration of the Basic Work Week

In the autumn of 1973 President Nixon issued his "energy conservation mandate" (i.e., 55 mph, etc.). In keeping with this edict and being a good American citizen and staunch Republican, Jack Armstrong, President of Pinetree Plastics, Inc., initiated a new work schedule. Instead of the 5 day, 40 hour work week, he was going to have a three-day, 13-1/2-hour work day. Industrial engineers and management consultants assured him that it would be 50% more economical and 25% more efficient.

Pinetree employs 2500 nonmanagement people from a town of 8,900, and many were upset with the new schedule. If they quit, they could not find jobs anywhere else—the town's other major employer, the Chrysler Parts Plant, was already furloughing people. Armstrong felt he was being very fair and equitable—anyone and everyone who could not meet the guidelines would be dismissed.

The employees, who were not unionized, selected a group to approach Armstrong with their grievance. He agreed to set up a day-care center for parents whose children had no place or person to stay with them during the time before and after school. Their other requests he rejected. They were:

1. Time-and-a-half for over 8 hours worked in a day. (Armstrong said he could not afford to pay any more, since he would probably have to let people go anyway—also, the employees were free to get second or nighttime jobs now)

2. The establishment of a seniority system, in case workers had to be let go. (Armstrong said it would impair the firm's efficiency—selected cuts in less crucial departments would be more economical to the firm).

3. The employees should be able to help determine which 3 days and which 13 1/2 hours would be worked. (Armstrong felt it was his prerogative)

4. Cost-of-living wage increases. (Armstrong: "too inflationary in these uncertain times!")

The employees were even more upset after this meeting with Armstrong. They brooded over their alternatives:

1. They could ask for a vote to unionize, and let the union air their grievances.

2. They could stage a full or partial "wildcat" strike (but Armstrong hinted that if this happened, he would lock them all out, and then slowly and selectively hire them back later)

3. They could seek a court injunction to enjoin Armstrong from starting and using these "unfair labor practices".

Questions

1. What course of action should the employees take? Why?
2. Would unionization really help the employees in an economic climate such as this?
3. Are there any other viable alternatives?

Education vs. Experience Pay Inequities

Joanne Drew was hired by a medium-sized firm as a sales representative. She was hired for the government sales department, since she had an extensive contracting background. Her draw for her six-month training period was $1,000 per month.

Joanne became very friendly with Jonathan Carter, a commercial sales rep, who had begun work for the company within two weeks of her starting date. Jonathan had a college degree, which Joanne did not, but he had no sales experience. His draw for the training period was $1,500 per month.

When Joanne discovered the discrepancy in their pay, she was sure an error had been made. She went immediately to her supervisor. He promised he would look into it.

Two weeks later, Joanne approached her supervisor again. Her previous government sales experience had stood her in good stead, and she was doing very well. Her supervisor hedged a bit, then attributed the pay discrepancy to Carter's college degree, and to the fact that he was in commercial, not government, sales.

"But that's ridiculous," Joanne exclaimed. "His degree is in biology, and I have had six years of experience in the field. It isn't fair."

"Don't make waves," her supervisor advised. "At the end of your six months training, you will be on straight commission. Then everything will appear more equitable."

Questions

1. Is there discrimination being practiced here?
2. What further recourse does Joanne have?
3. Can Carter's unrelated college degree qualify as the reason for this differential, despite Joanne's extensive direct experience?
4. Can it be properly claimed that commercial sales and government sales for the same company are so substantially different as to justify the pay differential?

Howell Tractor & Equipment Co. vs. the Industrial Commission: A Case of Workers Compensation

Claimant Bower was employed by appellee Howell as a field mechanic for four years. Howell was in the business of selling, renting and servicing various types of heavy equipment like cranes and bulldozers.

Bower and a co-worker were told by their superiors that a road resurfacing machine had broken down in Logansport, Indiana. They were instructed to pick up the repair parts at O'Hare Airport in Chicago and drive to Logansport to repair the machine. Because of the degree of damage to the machine, they were unable to complete the repairs all in one day. At the request of the customer's foreman, they telephoned Howell's field service manager and requested permission to remain overnight at Logansport.

They then went to the Ben Hur Hotel in Logansport and obtained rooms. After washing up, they went out to dinner along with the customer's foreman. After dinner they went to a bar and they had two or three drinks each and remained there until about 11:30 or 11:45 p.m. The customer's foreman then took them to another bar where they remained, again, talking about the machine and other topics, until closing time at about 1:30 in the morning. As the tavern was closing, the customer's foreman and Bower's fellow worker suggested they go out to breakfast. Bower, however, wanted to go back to the motel. He went to the restroom and when he returned to the table, the foreman and his co-worker were gone. The latter testified that they had waited some ten or fifteen minutes in the truck for the claimant Bower, and then drove around the block and returned to the tavern, leaving only when the claimant was not visible.

Although he had never been to Logansport, claimant decided to walk back to the motel. He did not utilize any of the available taxi services, nor did he ask anyone for directions to the motel. After walking a few blocks, he realized that he was lost, and he came upon what was apparently an abandoned railroad station. He thought he had remembered crossing some railroad tracks on the way from the motel, and he started walking alongside the tracks in the direction he thought the motel was located. He testified that a train started to pass him, and that some part of the train made contact with him and dragged him along backwards. He held on for as long as he could with his left arm but finally had to let go. He apparently fell on to the tracks and the train ran over his left leg. He began yelling for help and put his belt around his leg as a tourniquet. A police officer responded to his call and later testified that, in his opinion, Bower was not intoxicated.

Claimant has testified that he has been out of town on several occasions, numbering perhaps more than twenty-five times, to repair equipment for Howell. He also testified that the company never had given him instructions or placed restrictions concerning his conduct after he left the job site on out-of-town business trips. On a number of previous occasions, he had gone out with customers after work for a few drinks. On one occasion, he had sold a customer a piece of equipment and the company paid him a bonus for the sale.

As a result of the injury to his leg, Bower's leg was amputated above the knee. He filed a claim with the Industrial Commission requesting compensation for total temporary disability under worker's compensation.

Questions

1. Should Workers' Compensation be awarded?
2. Should the company continue to employ Bowers? Should they compensate him for his injury?

Resistance to Safety Management

Mr. White has been recently appointed safety director of Atlas Steel, Inc. A union plant, Atlas has approximately 1000 production and maintenance employees at the plant in Detroit, Michigan. As the safety director, Mr. White is very concerned over the high accident rate the company has been experiencing for the past several years. To help solve the problem, a better program of machine guarding and plant maintenance has been initiated. This program did reduce the severity of the accidents; however, work injuries continue to occur just as frequently.

Mr. White decided to analyze all of the work injuries that had occurred over the past year. He found that in a majority of instances, most of the injuries were due to (1) failure to follow safety rules, (2) incorrect use of machines and hand tools, and (3) sloppy cleaning of work areas. Furthermore, Mr. White looked into some literature concerning industrial safety and found some research studies that proved employee attitudes, emotions and knowledge greatly influence accident rates on the job.

Due to the above information, Mr. White concluded that a plant-wide employee education program needs to be initiated. However, the problem of accidents is accentuated by the high rate of employee turnover, due to Atlas' wage level being somewhat lower than the rates paid by other companies in the area. Many quit and take better jobs, especially since Atlas has periodic layoffs.

Mr. White has now obtained the support of top management to try to solve or improve the accident problem. To educate employees in safety, Mr. White decides to have each foreman hold a safety meeting with the workers at least once a month, but finds that the foremen vehemently object to the added burden, claiming the extra time needed for the meeting will slow down production (which will make them look bad).

Questions

1. How should Mr. White handle the foremen who refuse to conduct the safety meetings?

2. How should Mr. White accomplish the objective of teaching the employees about safety, if (a) the foremen do agree to conduct the meetings, and (b) if the foremen do not agree to conduct the meetings, i.e., what methods and channels should be employed in each instance?

OSHA Compliance

XYZ Company is a small manufacturing firm with 820 employees. 430 of these work in the shop and are represented by a small, but strong local union. Although the present union contract has 28 months to run, an issue has arisen which could lead to a union walkout.

Occupational Safety and Health Act (OSHA) standards direct the use of noise-suppressor equipment when decibel readings in the work area exceed a specified level. The purpose of this ruling is to prevent hearing impairment. It is the employer's responsibility to purchase, issue, and enforce wearing of noise suppressors in areas identified as exceeding OSHA safe noise levels.

XYZ Company has been meeting part of the OSHA standards by purchasing and issuing earmuff-type noise suppressors. It has been less than successful insuring that the suppressors are worn by employees. In XYZ's latest attempt to insure compliance, it has announced that employees found not wearing noise suppressors where required, will be suspended for the balance of the workday without pay. Additionally, as an incentive, employees who are not cited for violations will be given a five-dollar bonus each month.

The union's reaction to the company's policy has been negative. Although in favor of the monthly bonus as an incentive for employees' compliance, the union claims the company's action was unilateral and violated a clause in its contract with the union. The clause called for joint agreement between labor and management on changes of company policy. The union also claims that the majority of workers responsible for wearing the devices feel they are cheaply made, uncomfortable, and of no value.

The union has threatened to walk out, unless the company immediately rescinds its noise-protection enforcement policy and agrees to meet with union negotiators to conclude a new joint noise-protection policy.

Questions

1. If the company rescinds its current noise-protection policy, how will it justify *not* meeting OSHA standards?
2. What would be a likely union position, if and when attempts are made to formulate a new policy?
3. Would it be wise for the company to inform OSHA that the OSHA standard is being violated, through no fault of the company?
4. What are alternative incentives that the company might offer, to induce the wearing of noise suppressors?
5. Was the company correct in unilaterally imposing its hearing protection policy?

OSHA Non-compliance and Seniority

TMW Corporation produces 3/4 of the world's micro-synchronizers, an integral part of apartment vacuum systems. This corporation has plants mostly in the midwest, although a few are scattered on both the east and west coasts. The plants in the midwest employ members of the Electronic Workers' Union under a contract that became effective last August and is for three years. This union is very strong and the employees will do anything to preserve and maintain the strong union benefits that have been won.

Last year an OSHA official visited the St. Louis plant and found several discrepancies with the standards established by the act. These included the absence of safety goggles on employees whose job it is to weld tiny wires together, and an automatic shut-off switch on the wire-splicing machine. TMW was issued warnings of the noncompliances, and was told if they were not corrected, the next step would be drastic fines.

The company immediately set about correcting the problems. They had to shut parts of the plants down in the midwest on a rotating basis to take care of the wire-splicing machines. The union members were quite upset, because the employer laid off older employees, not the new trainees on the machines. They threatened a walkout.

Another company problem with the OSHA regulations involved safety goggles. When told of the need to wear their goggles, the welders refused, saying they were not able to see as well. They did not have to wear them before. The welders said they would take the responsibility for not wearing them now. The union backed the welders in their refusal.

Questions

1. Was the TMW Company wrong to lay off the senior employees? Should the trainees be laid off instead?

2. If the union members walked off the job, would they have their jobs when the problem was settled?

3. Can the company force the welders to comply with the wearing of the safety goggles?

4. If an accident occurred to a welder because of the noncompliance with OSHA, would TMW be responsible, even though the welders and union said that they would assume the responsibility?

5. Could the OSHA official fine TMW for their employees not wearing the goggles? The union?

The Limits of OSHA

Mr. Templeton, an employee of ACME Chemical Company, filed a complaint with OSHA. He felt that the air in his working area was both unhealthy and unsafe. After speaking with Mr. Templeton, the OSHA inspector, Mr. Sanyo obtained a warrant to investigate the complaint.

He arrived at ACME, a chemical batching plant that prepared solvent mixtures composed of various organic solvents. Mr. Sanyo, upon entering Mr. Templeton's work area, noticed a very strong odor of organic vapors. He continued his investigation by taking air samples for onsight analysis of vapor concentrations. He determined that the concentrations were quite a bit above OSHA standards. Then Mr. Sanyo spoke to the plant manager and the plant engineer. He asked them what type of ventilation system the plant had, because it seemed to be inadequate for the work they were performing.

Mr. Sanyo called in two more investigators and together they uncovered some severe problems with ACME's ventilation system. First, the batch mixing being conducted was done in open-top containers. This allowed a lot of evaporation. OSHA strongly suggested that ACME close their containers, because of employees' health and safety, and, of course, because of OSHA regulations. There was a major concern about fire, due to the fumes in the air. The second problem dealt mainly with the plant structure. It was found that the floor-level exhaust fans were blocked by solvent drums, which were being stored in the room. OSHA said that they could not keep flammable stock in a room where it might ignite. It would be best for the drums to be stored in another building. Also, the exhaust fans were too small for the room size. (There is a minimum regulation-sized fan, 24 inches, for that particular room size.)

OSHA also discovered that there was no ceiling exhaust system, therefore, fans and ducts needed to be installed. Both the ceiling and floor exhaust fans had to be exhausted directly to the exterior of the building.

In the plant, the air conditioning system that supplied the batching room was just recirculating the "polluted" air, and was not exhausting it. This problem caused inadequate air turnover in the room. The plant manager explained to the OSHA inspectors that the air flow throughout the entire plant was engineered in that particular way, due to the processes that were performed. The room was to maintain an overall positive pressure. Installing exhaust fans the way OSHA suggested would cause difficulties in product runs. OSHA told the plant manager to air lock the room, because there was no way to get around the regulations and standards.

The plant manager said he would investigate the possibilities. OSHA said, "Fine, you have thirty days."

Questions

1. Does Mr. Templeton have the right to go directly to OSHA, before speaking to his immediate superior or the plant manager?
2. Does OSHA have the power to enforce local and state regulations and laws, or are they restricted to enforcing only federal standards?
3. Is there a law which states that the blueprint of such a plant should be checked over by an inspector before the building is erected?

OSHA and Small Business

A small family-owned warehouse firm, the George & Mason Storage Company (George bought out Mason), located in an industrial park with some national and regional firms, was unexpectedly visited by a Department of Labor OSHA inspector. The inspector was officially inspecting the facilities of Company A, going from warehouse to warehouse. As part of this inspection the inspector passed by the warehouse of George & Mason on her way to one of Company A's other warehouses, when she happened to notice that there were no handrails leading up the steps of the G & M loading dock. Since this was her first solo inspection, she took time out to take a quick look at the G & M facility.

The compliance inspector entered the G & M warehouse through the loading dock area where she told two employees who she was, and that she wanted to walk around "just to take a look." The employees, who were about to break for lunch, told her to go ahead. The inspector noted the following conditions:

- loading dock stairway had no handrail.
- one fork lift was leaking oil onto the floor.
- numerous lights in the ceiling were burnt out, making seeing difficult.
- fire extinguishers were blocked by opened cartons and miscellaneous packing materials.

At this time the inspector was approached by the owner's youngest son, who asked if he could be of any help. The inspector told him who she was and what she was doing, at which time the son responded by going to get his father, the owner. About five minutes later the father found the inspector. The inspector informed the father of the hazardous conditions which she had seen and asked to see the safety logs and reports for the firm. The father heatedly responded that the inspector should go inspect the "big guys" in the industrial park, that G & M was too small to be governed by OSHA. The inspector told the father that he would be receiving a report stating the OSHA standards that were being violated and a time table for correction, at which time she left.

The father told the family at dinner about what had happened. His eldest son said that there may be a way out of this, at least for the moment, since the inspector had forgotten to present her credentials, had not asked to meet a company representative upon arrival, had not had that representative present during the walk through the warehouse, and did not give the employer a copy of applicable laws, nor state the scope of the inspection.

Questions

1. Is the eldest son correct in his belief that the conduct of the inspector was improper? Would this technicality relieve G & M from getting into compliance?
2. Did the inspector have the right to inspect the warehouse without filing prior warning? Is it permissable to inspect during the lunch hour?
3. Are there any limits to the applicability of OSHA standards, such as sales volume, number of employees, etc., which could exclude G & M from the OSHA standards?

Implementing Management By Objectives (MBO)

The All-Good Products Corporation was founded by Mr. Donald B. Johnson in 1963. The company was formed to provide a variety of household products that would be sold door-to-door. Products included cleansers of all types, floor wax, furniture polish, mops and brooms, plastic mixing utensils, and shoe polish, just to name a few. The company was organized into six regions throughout the United States, with from six to ten districts in each region. District managers hired salesmen to cover specific areas within their district. Districts, regions, and the company's head office, located in Chicago, had staffs composed of personnel and training, sales, distribution, and comptroller departments. Salesmen reported to the district manager who, in turn, reported to the regional vice president. The regional vice president reported to the president.

The company expanded rapidly after it was initially founded, but by 1971 the volume of sales started to level off. In 1974, the total sales decreased by 2 percent from 1973. Even though the philosophy of the company was to promote a sense of respect for the dignity of each employee and to encourage the spirit of entrepreneurism, the top management came to realize that more and more managers down the line looked to higher headquarters for decisions.

Early in 1975, attitude surveys were given to regional vice presidents, district managers, and salesmen. Results of the survey revealed that subordinate managers down the line and salesmen viewed headquarters as a paternal figure who seemed always to have the right answer. The president, Mr. Johnson, responded by dispatching policy statements and monthly informational newsletters to subordinate managers and salesmen, in an attempt to foster the spirit of entrepreneurism and pride in achievement. These attempts at communicating with the employees had some positive results, as sales during 1975 increased by about 4 percent over the previous year. However, the president still was not satisfied with the situation, at which time he and his staff met with some organization development (OD) experts from the University of Chicago.

In brief, what followed was an intensive effort to diagnose the major problems and select methods which would help the company attain its sales objectives and, at the same time, benefit employees. A management by objectives (MBO) program was devised, stressing that employees establish specific objectives or goals. Even though the company had established a broad goal of increasing sales volume by 8 percent during 1976, top executives wanted to insure that each salesperson established personal objectives which, in turn were to be reported to the district manager. Reports indicated that salespeople responded enthusiastically, in that 87 percent had established objectives exceeding the company goal.

The year-end results for 1976 revealed that sales volume had increased by 6 per cent, short of the company goal for 1976. But more significantly, the results for the first six-month period of 1977 indicated that the year-end sales volume increase might exceed the 10 per cent mark. Top management was pleased with the indicators and felt that after only two years, managers and salesmen were actively participating in attaining realistic, specific, sales objectives. For 1976, the head office followed up by rewarding employees who had exceeded the company goal. Also, assistance in the form of information concerning results and sales techniques, as well as training seminars relating to setting objectives, continued into 1977.

Questions

1. In reviewing this case, could the company have implemented MBO when it was initially founded?

2. Which departments in the company's head office should have been involved in the OD training program? What approach or technique should it have used to implement MBO?

3. How far up the line ("chain of command") should salesmen report objectives they set for themselves? Why?

An Employer's Social Responsibility in Fair Employment Practices

The Variety Store Company operates a chain of retail stores throughout the southwest states. The company has been operating for more than 40 years and has become a well-established firm in the region. The firm has become increasingly aware of the problems facing minorities, and has always hired proportionate numbers of minorities in every locality, in accordance with fair employment regulations. In one store the manager has been asked to answer the local Fair Employment Practice Commission's charges that the store has been discriminating against minorities. The manager is deeply concerned, since he feels the store has done nothing wrong. However, in this case, the charges are that the minorities get only the lowest paying jobs.

The manager recognizes that minority group members do not appear in management positions, but at the same time feels the applicants from the minority groups have not been qualified to assume such positions. He plans to tell the commission that members of minority groups will be hired into management positions as soon as they become qualified. He feels that it is not his responsibility to make sure that minority groups appear in such positions.

Questions

1. Is the manager's reply acceptable and/or reasonable?
2. Should the manager give additional or different arguments?
3. Is there any additional data that the manager should introduce?

Sick Leave and Pregnancy

Jane Doe is a 30-year-old registered nurse who is employed in the Critical Care area of a modern acute-care facility. The hospital is located in the suburbs of a large city on the East Coast. Jane had accepted the position as charge nurse on the evening shift of one of the hospital's Adult Intensive Care Units because she had been impressed with the philosophy of patient care, and she felt the employee benefits were good when compared to other hospitals in the immediate area. Jane quickly adapted to her new position and was respected and well-liked by all her coworkers. She shared her views and suggestions with her Head Nurse and Supervisor without hesitation. During the first six months of her employment she made several positive changes; it was apparent that she had become an influential member of the nursing staff. Jane's former position had been in a large hospital in California where the nurses were highly organized and very involved in changes in nursing service.

Approximately a year after she began employment, Jane was happy to discover that she and her husband were going to begin their family. Jane's first few months of pregnancy were uneventful, and she continued to work as before; her performance was in no way affected. During her fifth month of pregnancy, Jane developed a slight complication and her physician advised her to remain in bed for several days. Not wanting to risk adversely affecting her pregnancy, she complied with the physician's instructions. She called the nursing office, advising the appropriate individual of the situation and informing them that she would be out of work for the next three days.

After contacting her physician and being assured that all was well, Jane returned to duty. Once again her performance was not affected by her pregnancy and she continued to perform all the duties of her position. However, when Jane received her pay check on the following payday, she realized she was missing three day's pay. She knew she had sufficient sick benefits to cover the three days of illness she had experienced, so she inquired in the nursing office as to whether an error had been made in her paycheck. She was informed by the payroll clerk that her three days of illness were the result of her pregnancy, and no sick benefits would be paid. The payroll clerk informed Jane that the hospital policy stated that sick benefits would not be paid for pregnancy or illnesses related to pregnancy. Jane felt that this was a violation of her rights, since she had sufficient sick benefits to cover her illness and pregnancy should not be excluded from these benefits. Jane verbalized this freely and received much support from other staff members.

Jane knew that the hospital had a grievance procedure which would be available to her, but she felt this required stronger action. The following morning she contacted a lawyer and explained her situation. The attorney informed her that he would contact the hospital and make an appointment to see the Personnel Director. Having heard what the attorney wished to discuss at the appointment, the Personnel Director notified the appropriate administrator, who in turn, asked the Personnel Director for advice.

Question

1. As the Personnel Director, what advice would you give?

Promotion Selection

The ABC Corporation is a large merchandise chain with retail stores throughout the country. Headquartered in Minneapolis, ABC has twelve regional offices. Within each region are five districts, each with a sufficient number of subdistricts to control the activities of the approximately eight hundred outlet stores.

The ABC Corporation traditionally promotes from within the organization's structure. Retirement has led to a regional office directorship vacancy in the New England region. The Personnel Department at ABC Corporation headquarters has been tasked with nominating qualified candidates to a special selection board for the purpose of choosing the new New England Regional Director. Through the initial and preselection process, two candidates, Mr. Smith and Mr. Jones, have been recommended to the special selection board. Both candidates have been informed of their nomination.

Seven factors have been identified by the selection board as critical to evaluation for personal advancement decisions by the national headquarters. The factors have been compiled and scored by the Personnel Department. Below are the data pertaining to Mr. Smith and Mr. Jones.

Critical Evaluation
[Weighted 1 (low) – 10 (high)]

Factors	Smith	Jones
1. Years with firm	10	8
2. Sales performance (last 5 years)	10	10
3. Appraisals by superiors	10	10
4. Opinions of subordinates	9	7
5. Personal qualities (Health, personality, social)	7	8
6. Education (beyond high school)	7	8
7. Training with ABC Corporation	10	10
	63	61

Having been notified that he was a candidate for the New England Regional Directorship, Jones wrote to the selection board. He expressed his gratitude for his name being placed in nomination. He further stated that he was black. ABC Corporation has a black work force of 17%, and, since no regional directors are black, Jones added that he believed he should be chosen to head the New England region. If not selected, Jones closed by saying that he would consider lodging racial discrimination complaints with the Equal Employment Opportunity Commission.

Questions

1. What factors listed should be considered as most crucial by the selection board? What other factors, not listed, should also be considered important?
2. How would the board defend the selection of Smith?
3. How would the board defend the selection of Jones?
4. Is there a solution that would be palatable to both Smith and Jones? If so, what is it?

Management Development and Job Rotation

For the last several years the Acme Production Firm has been using job rotation in its management trainee program for young college graduates. This management development program was designed to teach the trainees the managerial policies and practices of the firm. The program was only partially successful, because the trainees were confused by the varied teaching techniques of senior managers, lack of an adequate feedback system, and poor attitudes of some of the senior managers.

You, as the management development officer in the personnel section, realize the need for a better systematic training program for the trainees, as well as for the trainers. You decide to use the "buddy system" to assign a trainee to a senior manager for six months. The manager will be responsible for planning and conducting the training program. The relationship between the two is to be very informal and supportive; a performance evaluation will be conducted after the third and sixth month.

After five months the "buddy system" did not produce satisfactory results. Trainees requested transfers to other sections or quit. Some managers requested reassignment for their trainees and one had even quit.

The standard reasons given by the trainees as well as the managers; for quitting or asking for reassignment were, "we just don't get along with each other," "personality clash," and "mismatch." Currently, the trainees and the managers' morale is low. One trainee stated that he didn't care for the "understudy assignment."

You questioned your supervisor concerning the recruiting methods used from the college campuses and how he selected trainees. He told you the firm used the same method of recruiting and selection as other firms., that is, they picked highly motivated top graduates with a business administration background. He also informed you that the firm didn't have funds available for a formal, centralized training program and the next group of trainees would start in three weeks.

As the management development officer, you have two alternatives:

a. Go back to the job rotation method and avoid using some of the senior managers that gave you the most problems.

b. Stay with the "buddy system," but find another method of assigning trainees to senior managers.

Question

1. What alternative(s) would you select, and why?

Management Appraisal and Human Resource Planning

Jim Nease has had 17 years of experience at American Parcel, 14 at the managerial level. Presently, he is a center manager, with three well-salaried line supervisors reporting to him. These three supervisors have responsibility for a total of 38 delivery personnel, and this number is increasing weekly.

Managers in the company are evaluated quarterly, the main criteria being the output of drivers according to standards developed by the Industrial Engineering Department. The managers are also judged by the number of customer complaints against their drivers. In the ten months since he took over the center, Nease has fared well in the three evaluations.

Nease was well pleased with his progress until recently, when his drivers' outputs declined considerably. This decline came at an inopportune time for the company, since the Personnel Department could not hire and train drivers fast enough to keep up with the increasing volume of packages caused by the recent postal rate hike.

At the same time, complaints also rose rapidly, with no logical explanation. Nease is not only perplexed, he is downright angry that performance has slipped so badly. He has called in the three supervisors to find out what the problem is.

Questions

1. Can anything be done to make the managerial evaluation criteria more accurate during periods of rapid hiring?
2. What can be done to make the standards themselves more realistic?
3. Would human resource planning help this company in the future? What indicators should the company watch to forecast their need for drivers in the future?

Educational Requirements for Promotion

Carla Devon had been employed at the Mercantile Savings and Loan for nine years. For the last four of the nine years she had attempted to obtain promotion to the position of assistant manager at any of Mercantile's 30 branch offices. Due to her inability to obtain this promotion, she felt compelled to lodge a complaint with the state civil rights office. In an interview at this office, it was learned that Carla had made good career progress since joining the company as an assistant teller. Within five years she had been promoted from assistant teller to teller, head teller, loan officer, and senior loan officer. Upon hearing rumors that a number of vacancies existed in other branch offices, Carla sent a letter to management notifying them of her desire to be considered for any such openings. During the next four years, Carla sent numerous communications to Mercantile's management on this same subject, but received no response. During this period of time, numerous assistant branch manager vacancies occurred, but the vacancies were consistently filled by men.

Mercantile's management was shocked and outraged that Carla would feel compelled to file such a complaint. In response to the complaint, the Director of Personnel indicated that, in all instances in which an individual had been promoted into, or hired into, the position of assistant manager of a branch office, the qualifications of that individual were in compliance with the standards set by Mercantile, standards which Carla did not meet. The qualifications were: (1) the attainment of a master's degree in business administration, (2) five years of banking experience, and (3) good job references. It was determined that Carla could meet all except the degree requirement.

Mercantile's personnel manual did not contain promotional procedures or qualifications. The investigation, initiated in response to Carla's complaint, disclosed, however, that every manager and assistant manager did possess an MBA. In attempting to learn the reason for the MBA requirement, the Commission conducting the investigation was told that Mercantile felt that every management person in the organization should possess the MBA because it provided flexibility in handling the banking business. The Personnel Director stated that while he was confident that Carla was familiar with Mercantile's operations, he felt that she did not possess the needed flexibility to hold down the position of assistant branch manager. He stated further that Mercantile did not feel any responsibility to respond to Carla's repeated requests for consideration.

The commission conducted interviews with several assistant branch managers, only to learn that these individuals considered their main function to be assisting in the supervision of the branch, but that any important policy decision was referred to the central office. In addition, a number of those interviewed had, previously in their careers, held jobs identical to those held by Carla – jobs such as teller and loan officer. Lastly, it was learned that only three out of the 30 assistant branch managers were female and that all management positions above that level were filled by men.

Questions

1. Was Carla's complaint of sex discrimination preventing her promotion a valid one?
2. Was the MBA requirement for promotion to assistant branch manager a BFOQ (Bona Fide Occupational Qualification)?
3. Did inclusion of the MBA requirement have an adverse impact on females?

The Availability of
Office Records to Employees

Over the years, salespeople in the ABC Company had developed the habit of perusing office records. Management was anxious to discourage this practice for fear that a salesperson who had become intimately familiar with company costs and customers might go over to a competitor. The problem was intensified when new offices were constructed separating the salepeople's quarters from those occupied by the office staff. The salespeople were now expected to request necessary information from the office staff over a four-foot counter, and were never to enter the new premises. However, it became apparent that the salespeople were determined to preserve the practice of looking at the records.

At first, the salespeople tried to think of every conceivable way to "break the barrier." It became a matter of pride, to see if they could enter the office and walk around. They said they had to speak to the accountant, to consult with the president, to check an order with a clerk, to pick up some supplies—almost any excuse.

Management reacted by making the rules against infiltration even more rigid. All salespeople were absolutely forbidden to enter the office except for exceptional reasons. This time the reaction was even more severe. The salespeople began to complain about every sort of petty detail in the office. The favorite complaint was that the switchboard operator was not giving them all their messages. Next, they began to find fault with their new quarters. The ceiling tile was installed improperly, the phones were on the wrong side of the desk, the lighting was inadequate, the floor was not cleaned regularly. Fights broke out between the salespeople and the sales manager, and the salespeople began to make aggressive remarks about the office force. This further intensified the separation and alienation between the salespeople and the office staff.

Questions

1. The changes management introduced were modest ones that did not basically "hurt" the salespeople. Why were they exhibiting such aggressive behavior?
2. What group factors were affected by the change?
3. To what extent were these reactions predictable, and of what value would such predictions be to the supervisors?

Necessary Personnel Records in
Discrimination Cases

A medium-sized government contractor employing 800 people with sales of $18 million, finds itself in the following situation:

A minority female has filed a charge of discrimination in regard to the company's promotional practices, stating that for various reasons she had been discriminated against and had not been promoted because of her minority status. The company believes the charge to be groundless, however, the new Employee Relations Manager sees potential liability in the event of a detailed audit by the OFCC.

The employee in question has been a nuisance over the past year, often times threatening to file a charge with the government, if she were not allowed to participate in various company programs. She had been with the firm three years, the first year receiving good raises by the company's standards and generally receiving above-average performance ratings. During the past two years, however, her performance has not been rated as highly and she has not been promoted when openings have occurred. Her charge specifically states:

- that she has not been allowed to participate in the company education assistance program
- that she has not been allowed to attend in-house training workshops
- that because of this forced exclusion from these programs, she could not upgrade herself to become promotable
- that because of her protests, she has been "singled out" and harassed by the company

In preparation for the expected visit by government representatives responding to the discrimination charge, the new Employee Relations Manager did some investigating of her own to determine the validity of the case. An examination of the employee's personnel folder revealed the following:

- 6 Month Merit Reviews –

  oldest (1) to most recent (6); (1) and (2) above average, (3), (4), (5) average; (6) below average. A scale of excellent, above average, average, below average and unacceptable was used for 10 different performance criteria. An overall average performance was derived from the 10 answers.

- Increased Tardiness –

  Has been late on numerous occasions within past year. Reprimanded verbally twice, (with memos to the file unsigned by employee), once reprimanded in the form of a written warning that continued tardiness would result in a suspension from work of two days without pay (signed as received by employee).

■ In-House Training –

Since her employment, has attended two in-house seminars that were directly related to her job. (Seminar material was varied and conducted continuously unless demand for a particular seminar was slight).

■ Educational Assistance –

Had applied for assistance to night school to take two college courses. The company will reimburse for "job-related" classes leading to a degree. The employee is a senior computer operator, the courses were in religion and English composition. The company rejected the assistance application, and without the aid, the employee was unable to attend.

■ Promotability –

The next job category would be that of section supervisor which was stipulated in the contract by the government as requiring a minimum of at least two years experience and an AA degree. The employee had seven years overall experience as a computer operator during her career, but lacked a degree.

The company was prepared to defend itself, if necessary by showing that:

■ Its educational assistance plan was applied equally to all employees.

■ That although the employee had not been able to attend as many in-house training seminars as she would have liked, she was not excluded from them.

■ That her tardiness occasioned reasonable doubt as to her ability to become a supervisor.

■ And finally, that the contract with the government specifically required a degree for supervisor positions.

The Employee Relations Manager felt comfortable with the defense of this case, but was worried about the additional statistics which showed that out of 21 supervisors, only 4 were minority, and that of the 150 employees in the educational assistance plan, only 35, or 23%, were minority when the total work force was 49% minority.

Questions

1. Do you feel the company has maintained enough supportive data on the employee? Comment on propriety of data and the company's defense.

2. Is the signed contract with the government stating an educational requirement a valid defense in and of itself?

3. Does the contractor have too few minorities as supervisors and in the educational assistance plan?

Loss of Seniority

Larry Miller has been working as a store decorator for the past six years at the J.T. Penn Co., a large national department-store chain. He has little contact with the public, other than to be seen doing a window display, etc. Larry's job performance has always been above average with little time lost for illness or tardiness. It is widely known among the store employees that Larry is very effeminate. In truth, Larry feels his life would be more meaningful as a woman, and he is planning to have a sex change operation to achieve this end. Larry's plan is also a subject of much gossip throughout the store, among managers and in the regional office. Larry has adequate sick leave and vacation time available to take time off from work to have his operation and return. Larry has requested a transfer to another store, to be effective upon his return as a woman with a new name, etc.

Company management has made it clear to Larry that they would be unwilling to let him return to J.T. Penn after the operation. They have also stated that if he is somehow allowed to return, he would be reassigned to the same store. Management's hope is that the embarrassment of facing his former coworkers will force Larry to quit. J.T. Penn management has also stated that under no circumstances would Larry be allowed to return with his previous seniority and benefits. In effect, he would be treated as a "new hire." This, of course, means less pay, vacation time, etc.

Questions

1. Does the company have a right to prevent Larry from returning to work on the basis of what would be sex?

2. Although a company may have a right to transfer or not transfer its employees, could J.T. Penn use the transfer issue as a way to prevent Larry's return?

3. Does the company have a right to deny Larry his seniority and other benefits, if he is allowed to return?

Employee Appraisal During
Times of Supervisory Turnover

Late one Friday evening, Jason Shell was pondering what to do about his office secretary's request for help. Jessica Savage had just received an annual performance rating. She thought the rating was unfair and would seriously damage her chances for promotion.

Shell worked in a staff position for a large government organization. Day-to-day activities involved highly technical subjects. Due to the formal organizational structure and frequent interagency communications, a large part of the office output consisted of notes, letters, reports and visual aid materials.

For the past year, the office staff consisted of Shell, his boss (Don Jenkins) and two secretaries. Marsha Benson was recognized as Jenkins' secretary. Jessica Savage was assigned to the other staff members—Shell and two other positions which had been vacant for the past year. Because of the vacancies, Savage had acted almost as Shell's personal secretary. Benson was to assist when the workload piled up. However, Benson made it clear that her assistance would not be routine.

Three months ago, Jenkins resigned to take a new position. Ralph Cranston was hired as his replacement. The other two staff positions were also filled at the same time. When interviewing for Jenkins' position, Cranston had been told by various people—including Shell—that Marsha Benson did not measure up and should be removed. The allegations were that Benson was slow, didn't do tasks assigned which she didn't like and had a rather untidy appearance. Savage was described as pleasant, willing to accept most any task, but not the most efficient or accurate secretary. Shell had commented, "You better read what she types very carefully."

Over the past Christmas holidays, Benson took an extended vacation. During that time period, Savage served as Cranston's secretary as well as doing almost all of the office's typing, reproduction and telephone answering. Shell remembered this time period as hectic. But with patience and cooperation, the office had functioned reasonably well. Cranston had been able to get another office to assist with his personal typing.

Three weeks ago, both new staff members indicated plans to leave. As a result, mail and office correspondence was piling up. Shell had asked Savage if she would like to work overtime on Saturday to sort out the critical items requiring office attention and to work on the filing.

Savage approached Shell on Saturday morning with her problem. Company regulations required a yearly performance appraisal covering at least seven areas. Performance is rated for each area as *rarely accomplishes, almost always accomplishes,* and *always accomplishes.* Both the supervisor and the employee sign the appraisal. Cranston had just submitted Savage's appraisal with about one-half in the "almost always" column and one-half in the "always" column. Savage told Shell that she had begun to think about the performance rating. She admitted that she had not taken any exception to the rating when Cranston provided it for signature. However, she said, "I know I did a good job for him when Marsha was on vacation. The appraisal really hurt me. I want to try for a new job with promotion potential. With that rating, Personnel will just toss my application in the trash can. Mr. Shell, what should I do? How can Mr. Cranston rate me when he has been here only three months?"

Questions

1. Does Savage have a valid complaint?
2. What recourse might she have?
3. How should Shell respond to Savage? If he decides to try to help, how might he go about it?

A Question of Security

Mr. X works as a GS-5 civilian guard at Activity A; Dr. Y works as a GS-13 professional at the same office.

Dr. Y's work hours are not standard; they are from 1300 to 2100. Dr. Y's wife usually brings him to work and returns at night to pick him up. Since the activity is secured around 1630, the guard working at the front gate would normally call late-working employees to confirm that a visitor was expected before allowing the visitor on the grounds.

Mr. X has been calling Dr. Y to tell him that his wife has arrived to pick him up, but has grown to feel that it is no longer necessary since it is on a regular basis and Mrs. Y is not a visitor, but a family member. He feels that it is not a security matter, but a courtesy.

Dr. Y has complained to Mr. Z (Mr. X's supervisor) that Mr. X is not properly performing his job. He needs the phone call from Mr. X so that he can go downstairs from his office and unlock the front door to the building and let his wife in to wait with him while he finishes what he is working on. He cannot observe his wife's arrival from his office window.

Mr. X counters that Mrs. Y should call Dr. Y when she leaves home: Dr. Y knows the travel time necessary, and could look out another office window to see when Mrs. Y actually arrives.

Mr. Z supports Mr. X. When he suggested to Dr. Y that Mrs. Y call him when she leaves home, he found out that Mrs. Y used to do this, but too often did not actually leave when she had called. That left Dr. Y standing downstairs waiting for his wife, rather than upstairs finishing his work.

The Security Manager tends to go along with Messrs. X and Z, believing that it has evolved into a courtesy, rather than a true security matter. But he wants everyone to "be happy."

Questions

1. Is this a valid security matter?
2. How would you solve this problem?

The Company Training Program

Widget Manufacturing Company believed in providing every possible aid and encouragement to the development of its management personnel. Among the many extras that it provided was attendance for thirty or forty people each year at the Industrial Management Conference. These conferences were held in a college town and were widely attended, with as many as 1,200 people from various companies present at the annual three-day sessions. The sessions were divided into workshops and discussion groups, with a liberal sprinkling of speakers – experts in various phases of industrial management. The meetings concluded with a major speech and banquet, followed by entertainment.

When John Hamilton joined the staff of the Widget company, he was greatly impressed by the efforts of top management to provide for continuous development of its supervisory staff. He took advantage of the extension courses offered, was present at all foremen's classes, and generally considered himself lucky to be part of such an organization. When one of the supervisors approached him and asked if he would like to attend the conference, he was delighted. It seemed to him that it would be an excellent opportunity to sample some of the best thinking of people who were specialists in their fields.

Customarily the men were sent down in several cars to the conference. John Hamilton found himself in a car with three other men, one of whom was Jim Warner, an old-line supervisor. He noted the holiday atmosphere from the beginning of the trip and felt that the men must indeed get a great deal out of the conferences, because of the enthusiasm with which they greeted the prospect of attending. Several times on the ride to the conference John tried to draw out Jim on the subject matter of the conferences. All he got was remarks such as "You're sure to enjoy yourself John; just relax."

Following the registration, John told Jim that he was going to his room and freshen up. He wanted to be sure and catch the first speaker. Before John could leave, Jim said "Sure, John, just stop in room 325 before you go."

A little while later, John knocked on the door of room 325 and was admitted to the smoke-filled room. Two of the desks had been pushed together and a blanket thrown over them. The supervisors he knew were sitting around in their shirt sleeves, playing poker and drinking. Before John could say anything, someone put a paper cup of lukewarm whisky and ginger ale into his hand. "There's plenty of time before the first speaker," said Jim. "Why don't you play a couple of hands."

Hamilton didn't want to miss the speech: neither did he want to antagonize the other foremen by refusing a few friendly hands of poker with them. "Okay," he said. "But I'm only going to play one deal around: then I'm taking off." Five hands later Jim asked him "How do you like the conference?"

"Look Johnny-boy," said Jim, "this is the conference. That speech-making and all the other stuff is hogwash. The whole purpose of these conferences is to give the boys a three-day vacation for a little drinking and poker playing."

"That doesn't sound right to me," said John. "From the looks of the program, a lot of people have worked hard to line up a very good conference."

"It doesn't make sense to me," said John, "to drive all the way down here to hear these experts speak and stay in our rooms and play poker."

"This is the way the company wants it," said Jim. "The main idea is for the foremen to get together and get to know each other better. It makes for a closer spirit among the foremen."

Hamilton was in a quandary. He wanted to attend the program, but he knew that if he spurned the poker session, more than half of the foremen he knew would think him a "square."

Questions

1. What costs does John incur by going along with the gang?
2. Should John somehow let his supervisor know what went on when he returns and take the chance of being "black-balled" by the rest of the foremen?
3. What would you do in this situation?

Unfair Labor Practices

Tom Jackson has worked on the autoblock assembly line at the Mr. Gilead, Pennsylvania, plant of the American Metal Manufacturing Company for 13 years. During this time he has been quite active in union activity, doing things like helping to organize workers, doing investigative work into health and safety standards, and talking with other workers about problems they are having and urging them to file grievances.

The investigation of health and safety standards by Jackson resulted in charges being brought against the American Metal Manufacturing Company for violation of the 1970 Occupational Safety and Health Act. He testified before members of the agency regarding violations of the standards, some of which included improper ventilation, lighting, operation of equipment, and excessive heat in the welding department. His testimony was largely responsible for American Manufacturing being assessed a stiff penalty and a warning of future consequences, if conditions did not improved.

Shortly after Jackson's testimony, he was told he was being promoted to assistant foreman of the day run. He was promoted, even though there was a person in his department who had greater seniority than he did. His major responsibility was to take over for the foreman during his lunch period and on his days off, and to help distribute work orders and keep track of employee mistakes. He had a few other small duties, but had to confirm everything with the foreman and in all activities was under the foreman's control.

Now that Jackson had become an assistant foreman, he was put on a salary instead of getting an hourly wage, and was also told that he would have to drop his union membership because, according to Taft-Hartley, supervisors and foreman cannot belong to a union.

This action on the part of management thoroughly enraged Jackson, as he felt that while the promotion was a step up in prestige, the job offer was simply a method management had used to get him out of the union. He felt that they had done this because of his recent testimony on safety matters and his continuous union activities over the years. Jackson went to the union and told them of his predicament and asked them to file an unfair labor practice suit with the National Labor Relations Board. The union agreed to file and represent Jackson.

The arguments each side presented before the NLRB were as follows:

Management
1. The position of assistant foreman was created because of the need for someone to take over when the foreman was absent.

2. Tom Jackson was the person with the most seniority.

3. Since Jackson's job is now that of a foreman, according to Taft-Hartley, he must give up his membership in the union.

4. Jackson is now a salaried employee and, under the Fair Labor Standards Act, is no longer entitled to overtime.

The union and Jackson countered these points by stating:

1. That while the job of assistant foreman may be needed, the duties being performed by Jackson do not contain any actual responsibility because he needs to check out everything with his foreman. Since he is not *in actuality* a foreman, he is entitled to overtime.

2. Jackson was promoted over a more-senior employee, for the purpose of getting him out of the union.

3. That the above constitutes an unfair labor practice under the Wagner Act, because the company was discriminating to discourage membership in a labor organization.

The case went to the NLRB and is on the docket to be heard next week.

Questions

1. Is management discriminating because of Jackson's membership in a labor organization?

2. Are the responsibilities of the job sufficient to make Jackson a part of management? If so, does this exclude him from coverage of FLSA?

3. Must he relinquish his membership in the union under Taft-Hartley, as management contends?

Unfair Labor Practices During
Union-Organizing Attempts

John R. Snelt and Sons was a nonunion shoe factory and had had this status since its inception in 1947. Lately, numerous supervisors had been reporting to their managers that talk of joining a union by the employees had been overheard. Needless to say, the owners were upset and a little puzzled as to why the employees would want a union. Mr. Snelt, Sr., felt he had always paid competitive wages, provided good benefits and had been open to employee suggestions. He knew the business had changed dramatically since 1947, but didn't feel these changes warranted the need for a union.

Joe Snelt noted for his father that for the past five years, they had hired new employees and that the few employees left from the inception were now a minority. Perhaps these newer employees were the instigators of the union.

Mr. Snelt decided that not only himself and his managers, but also his supervisors should find out as much information as possible and see if they would be able to change their employees minds about needing union status.

A few of the supervisors decided they would get to the heart of the problem, and did so immediately. They proceeded to ask the employees under them what they thought of all this union talk, and if they were going to join.

As the weeks went on, it seemed to Mr. Snelt that the union discussions were getting very serious. Supervisors were reporting that union literature was being passed out in the parking lot areas and that authorization cards were being distributed.

As the talk became more and more serious and it seemed more of the employees were signing authorization cards, the same group of supervisors decided to visit some of the homes of their friends who were employees to discuss the pros and cons of joining a union.

These employees reported to the other employees that management said many of them would be losing jobs, if the union came in, and that they would have to start from scratch for their fringe benefits. However, they also told them if the union didn't come in, management had made promises of raises, and would try to promote a few more employees.

When the organizers heard what was going on, they claimed unfair labor practices and petitioned the NLRB, claiming that the union should be recognized even without an election.

Mr. Snelt, of course, disagreed and demanded an election.

Questions

1. Does the union have grounds for their unfair labor practices charge? If so, what are they?
2. Could the company claim the union had violated and hampered management rights? If so, how?
3. Is it possible to have a union represent this group without an election?

Distribution of Union Literature on Company Property

John Smith had been warned by his supervisor that if he were late one more time, he would be fired. The day after his last warning, John came to work at 7:45, 45 minutes late. At 7:46, he was fired. He was told that his final pay would be ready around noontime. As a rule, discharged employees were allowed to remain on the premises until receiving their final paycheck.

After staying in the lunchroom for a half hour, Smith left the plant. Shortly afterward, he returned to the lunchroom with an NLRB pamphlet and some union literature. During the morning coffee break, as the former employee was discussing the NLRB pamphlet with other employees, he was interrupted by a supervisor. The supervisor said that it was illegal to have the literature on company property. The supervisor threatened to have Smith arrested, unless he left the plant and took the material with him.

Questions

1. Was the employee within his rights in handing out the NLRB pamphlet? In handing out union literature on company property?
2. What difference, if any, does the fact that Smith is no longer an employee make in the answers to question number 1?

Employee Discharges Preceding
Union Representation Votes

A midwestern department chain store called Plus Value was opening another unit in its chain. A reason for the location choice of the new store was that management knew the unions were not strong in that particular area. Some of Plus Value's stores were union and some were not, and the management strongly wanted the new store to be nonunion.

Management undertook a massive recruitment campaign through advertising in the area newspapers. After testing and interviewing of all the applicants, people were hired as sales clerks, cashiers, and loading dock clerks. As the company grew, the threat of the retail clerks organizing the workers into unions was ever present. Upon opening, Plue Value hired about 40 people to handle the big crowds at the store's grand opening. About 30 of the 40 employees were originally hired as permanent help, while the other ten were temporary.

About two weeks after the store had opened and the ten temporary employees were let go, the union came to the store and started to encourage the employees to organize. Eventually, the union claimed it had at least a 30% quota to call for a union election. The management, having only 30 employees, had a good idea who most of the pro-union employees were, and they also knew there were probably 12–15 employees who were against the union. Overall, the management knew it would be a close vote, in any case.

About a week before the election, a disciplinary incident occurred between the assistant manager of the store and one of the men on the loading dock. They had an agitated verbal exchange, which climaxed in a shoving match. What the fight resulted from was not clearly known, but the dock clerk was known to be very verbal about his pro-union views. In effect, what resulted from this was the dismissal of the dock employee. In protest, two of his friends, who also were dock employees and were on the scene of the fight, quit their jobs also. They said their friend's dismissal was not just, and he did not deserve to be fired. The management took all this at face value and did not discourage the other two from quitting, because they knew they were also pro-union.

The management was faced with 3 loading dock vacancies and 3 less pro-union employees. Immediately, management realized the advantage they had gained in the union vote. Therefore, without hesitation, Plus Value hired three replacements from the pool of the ten temporary employees, who were previously let go. These three happened to be anti-union.

Finally, when the vote for the union did come, the union only came up with 42% of the vote. The union was very upset about the outcome and claimed that

Plus Value had staged the incident with the dock employee, and did not act in good faith in dealing with the union issue.

Questions

1. Does the union have a legal issue in questioning the firing of the pro-union employee?
2. Did Plus Value legally manipulate the vote of the union election?
3. Can the union bring charges against Plus Value for using unfair selection practices for hiring the three new anti-union employees? If so, can the seven other temporary employees not hired, sue Plus Value for discriminatory selection practices?

Favored Employees, Discrimination, and Unfair Labor Practices

About two weeks following the end of a strike of the registered nurses at St. Luke's Hospital, the hospital administrator sent a note of appreciation to the registered nurses who continued to work during the strike and to the extra RN's who were transferred from St. Mary's to help cover the shifts of the striking nurses. In a letter of appreciation, the RN's were praised for their hard work and long working hours and for overcoming hardships and personal sacrifice in a definite gesture of dedication to duty as a professional. The letter indicated that nurses should be concerned with taking care of the sick and walking wounded, rather than striking for higher wages.

For all the nurses who worked more than one shift during the strike, the chief nurse gave compensatory time, or a day off. In addition, the LPN's were given time off with pay for their efforts in assisting in patient treatment during the strike, because, without their services, the hospital would not have been able to fulfill all its goals, according to management.

The union filed an unfair labor practice charge with the National Labor Relations Board, alleging that the hospital had infringed upon their right to strike and shown partial treatment in the working conditions afforded their peer employees. The union also alleged that they should have been consulted, before other nurses were granted time off or a change in work schedules was made.

Questions

1. Under the Wagner Act, has management interfered with a portion of collective bargaining or violated any rights of nonunion members in joining the union?
2. Was management discriminating against the union members?
3. Could the NLRB force the hospital staff to grant days off with pay to all RN's, including the nurses on strike?

Selection of Union Members for Supervisory Positions – A Conflict of Interest?

Wagner Auto Parts is in the business of producing and selling quality automobile parts for American-made cars. It started as a family business over 50 years ago and is still run by the son of the original owner. Its central management and research headquarters is located in St. Louis and its two manufacturing plants are located in Detroit and Newark.

All of the laborers within the plants are unionized. One of the unwritten rules between management and the union concerns seniority. It was well understood that promotions within the plants would be based on seniority. When it came time for a new foreman to be hired, the production worker who had the best combination of merit and seniority was traditionally hired to fill the vacancy.

This method proved to be less and less effective. The foreman invariably remained a member of the union, most often becoming one of the officers, as a result of his new status and position within the management of the company. It usually seemed that their major priority was to work for the goals of the union and the workers, rather than those of the company as a whole.

Two weeks ago, a foreman position in the Newark plant became available. The union members within the plant immediately began to speculate which among them would be chosen and had their candidate pretty well picked out, when management announced their plans to hire someone from outside the plant. By the time the new foreman showed up for work the next day, members of the union had already held a meeting and decided to strike. They demanded that a clause be written into their contract, guaranteeing that all foremen would be chosen from within their membership. Management attempts to compromise with the union failed and three days later the workers in the Detroit plant went on a sympathy strike.

Questions

1. Did the union members have a right to demand that the foremen be chosen from within their membership?

2. Did the management have the right to choose the person whom they feel will best fill the job, regardless of whether or not he is a union member?

3. What are some of the possible implications of the strike?

4. Discuss possible alternatives and solutions to this problem.

Conflict: Low Turnover and EEO Goals

The Greater Odenton Widget Manufacturing Company employs a staff of thirty-five and is involved in interstate commerce. Turnover in the organization has always been very low. The firm's employees are quite content with their relationship with management; consequently, union organizing has never seriously been considered. Workers identify with the firm and display enormous pride in the family-like atmosphere. Respectable profits are reported annually. The company's president attributes the steady growth to the high quality of performance from each individual worker. Their dedication reduces waste and encourages cost effectiveness through important suggestions contributed by the workers. In recognition, management rewards these efforts by liberal yearly bonuses and on-the-spot cash presentations for employee suggestions that are implemented.

Initial hiring when the organization was founded true reflected the demographic composition of the vicinity; however, over the years a greater influx of ethnic minorities appeared. Moreover, the county has some dense pockets of ethnic concentration elsewhere. Consequently, the company's work force eventually did not proportionately represent the community.

The Equal Employment Opportunity Commission was created in 1964 by the enactment of the Civil Rights Act. Congress tasked the EEOC to administer the provisions of Title VII that specifically prohibited discrimination in personnel practices for the reasons of sex, color, race, religion or national origin.

Subsequent interpretations of this law resulted in considerable difficulties for the Greater Odenton Widget Manufacturing Company. The firm was cited for having a disproportionate amount of white males employed, relative to the community profile. The firm was required to place a greater emphasis on the hiring and promotion of minorities. If this were not done, the company would face fines and possible legal sanctions.

This situation was a difficult one. The low turnover rate and high employee satisfaction limited the number of vacancies each year. Moreover, these spaces, even if totally filled by minorities, would not correct the imbalance. Personnel practices soon became numbers-oriented. One could easily suggest discrimination was in progress, while the company attempted to hire a sufficient amount of minority-group members. The end product was that less-than-fully qualified applicants were selected, and that a number of employees who otherwise would not have been considered were advanced in grade or promoted to supervisory positions.

Questions

1. Is the EEO program guilty of forcing employers to put people in jobs for which they may not be qualified?

2. What types of costs (i.e., financial, human, production, etc.) can be expected from emphasizing minority-group hiring and accelerated promotions to compensate for pre-Civil Rights Act personnel practices?

3. Will absenteeism, turnover, and productivity be affected by the sudden hiring and promotion of minority group members?

Seniority and Layoffs:
A Conflict with Affirmative Action

Prior to the Vietnam war, the Eagle Aircraft Co. was a small, family-owned business attempting to stay in the market while competing with other private aviation firms. When the Vietnam war escalated, the company bid on and won the contract to build reconnaissance aircraft for the Army. This helped the company grow to almost 500 employees. During the large boom in business, the union, which was only a token because the management treated all employees fairly, saw a chance to get rich and powerful quickly. The company, attempting not to rock the boat and avoid any strikes with an especially tight time limit, made many large concessions to the union. This included the seniority system for its employees. Since the company had become so large and was a government contractor, it had to follow many government regulations in its hiring practices, including the hiring of minorities.

Post-Vietnam saw an end to the Army contracts, and the company once again returned to the private aviation market. Competition being tough, it had to release approximately half of its employees over a long period of time. The union wanted to make sure that its contract was enforced, so the seniority system was used, and a majority of the employees released were minorities. These people, in turn, stated that the firing practice of the company was not fulfilling government regulations of fair employment practices and went to court to prevent further firings.

Questions

1. The management being in the middle, what would their best course of action be?

2. Who do you think has precedence, the unions or the minorities?

3. Is the union's contract enforceable?

4. Do the minorities have a case?

5. Can the government do something short of sending the company into bankruptcy?

Alcohol: A Disqualifier for Worker's Compensation or Unemployment Compensation

A male applicant, age 47, was hired by a local banking institution as Chief Collection Officer. His wealth of knowledge was vast, and at age 34, he had been the President of the tenth-largest bank in the United States. Alcohol had been his downfall, however, and it was only after extensive medical treatment that he was able to again pursue a career.

The local bank has approximately 180 employees with seven offices throughout the State. It is a State-chartered institution and is not a member of the Federal Deposit Insurance Corporation.

The Chief Collection Officer's principal duty was to offer advice and enter into "sticky" situations. He proved so successful, the Vice President of the bank also made him a member of the Board of Directors.

After approximately fifteen months on the job, he came to work swaying slightly and smelling of alcohol. While walking down the office stairs, he slipped and fell down the remaining stairs. The Vice President, who was walking behind him at the time, rushed up to the employee and immediately had an ambulance summoned.

X-rays revealed three broken ribs and a mild concussion. A blood test was taken and the results showed the employee had a very high concentration of alcohol in his system. At this time the employee was dismissed.

The employee filed for unemployment compensation and also filed suit claiming he had been discriminated against by the firm. The Vice President argued that the employee was hired with the firm understanding that alcohol was not to interfere with his job performance. The Vice President also reiterated that it was a company policy to terminate anyone "whose conduct was unbecoming of a lady or gentleman."

Questions

1. Is the employee eligible for unemployment compensation, given the guidelines set up by federal legislation?
2. Given that alcohol was involved, can the former employee qualify for Worker's Compensation?

The Legal Position on Dismissal for
Personal Appearance

A large northeastern university hired a new law professor, Allan Johnstone, to teach criminal law. He had spent five years as an attorney with the Department of Justice and was considered quite competent. After four months, complaints began to be heard in the dean's office regarding the professor. A petition signed by fifteen senior professors was submitted to the dean, finding fault with Mr. Johnstone's "lax teaching and academic habits and, in general, a demeanor degrading and unworthy of the profession." These professors urged Mr. Johnstone's dismissal and some threatened to resign, if he remained.

The dean consulted most of the professors and then summoned Mr. Johnstone to his office. Upon discussing the situation Mr. Johnstone expressed his opinion that the other professors were not so much against him professionally, but personally. He felt they held a grudge against him, because he sported longish hair and a beard and did not subscribe to a three-piece-suit ritual. Mr. Johnstone argued that the professors had lost touch with the "real world" and that they were "decadent and archaic in nature and thought."

Having heard both sides of the argument, the dean informed Mr. Johnstone that he would be dismissed at the end of the semester, though he still had two-and-a-half years left on his contract. Mr. Johnstone went back to his office to ponder his alternatives.

His first thought was to sue for breach of contract and violation of his Constitutional rights under the Fourteenth Amendment, which guarantees equal protection under the law. He calculated his chances as 50-50, since the university was a State school and the courts usually ruled against plaintiffs unless they were tenured. He also felt the school had weighed these facts beforehand and knew the odds were really more in their favor. He figured the best he could do would be a judgment for a portion of his future salary.

Mr. Johnstone felt he would have a better chance by using a different route. He knew the EEOC under Title VII would not handle the case, because it did not involve discrimination, *per se* because of race, color, sex, religion or national origin. He did know the university held certain federal training contracts and thus, under the OFCC had an affirmative-action program for hiring certain instructors. He felt he could sue for reinstatement, since he was, in effect, a minority of sorts. He was a veteran, he came from a culturally and socially depraved and underrepresented geographical area, and he was one-eighth American Indian.

Being a lawyer, he was not ignorant of the fact that courts very seldom order reinstatement edicts on personal employment contracts. He also recognized the fact that the EEOC and OFCC had been more successful with the courts in having employees reinstated (with back pay) under Title VII.

Questions

1. What approach should Mr. Johnstone pursue?
2. Should the OFCC accept his complaint?
   a. Would it make any difference if he were black or Hispanic, instead of white? Should it make any difference?
   b. Is Mr. Johnstone really a minority? Why or why not?

Just Cause for Separation

Mary Johnson had just graduated from the University of Florida with a Bachelor of Science in Business Administration. She moved to Miami immediately after graduation and looked for a job in retail management. She had worked as an Assistant Manager for a boutique in Gainesville for four years while she attended college and felt she was now qualified to be a manager.

Mary was hired as manager of a fashionable boutique in Miami Beach. The boutique was part of a Florida-based chain and had a reputation for its high fashion merchandise and expensive accessories. Mary had the duties of a regular manager, as well as the responsibility for all hiring and firing of personnel. Although Mary had a degree in Business Administration, she had majored in management and had taken only one basic personnel course. At the time she accepted the position as manager, she felt she would have no trouble handling the personnel responsibilities.

The chain of boutiques that Mary worked for was owned by a husband and wife who visited the stores approximately once a month. On their first visit since the hiring of Mary, they were quite pleased with the shape of the store. Sales figures were good and the store was making good profits under Mary's management. A problem came up, however, when reviewing the new employees that Mary had hired. It seemed that two of the women that were hired did not fit the image of what the owners wanted for their sales personnel. Their merchandise was high fashion and expensive, and the salesgirls had to have "a special look." In other words, the two people in question were just not attractive enough. Mary was called into the back room and was told that she had to fire the two salespeople. Mary was upset over the situation, but had no choice in the matter. Either she fired the two young women or the owners would do it and replace Mary, as well.

Mary made up some story to tell the salespeople about having to cut back the staff and informed them they had to leave. She told them that they had the least seniority and consequently they would have to be the first ones let go. A month later the two girls found out from friends still working at the boutique the real reason they were fired. They considered filing suit against the boutique for wrongful dismissal.

Questions

1. Under what law, if any, could the salespeople have claimed discrimination?
2. Were the two young saleswomen entitled to Unemployment Compensation?

3. If Mary had refused to fire the employees, could she have legally been fired by the owners?

4. If Mary had been fired, could she have received Unemployment Compensation?

Factors to be Considered
During a Reduction in Force

As of July 1, Company X will be changing from a cost reimbursement environment to a grant environment with a resultant budget cut of approximately fifty percent and a fixed source of revenue. As a result of this change, personnel in one division must be reduced from 12 FTE's (Full-Time Equivalent Positions) to 7 FTE's. The question becomes:

1) Who to retain and/or terminate, and

2) What parameters to develop to implement this action.

The positions involved in this personnel action can be divided into two main activities, each requiring specialized knowledge and expertise. One aspect of the job requires medical judgment and background while the remaining job element requires a specialized technical ability. In the original hiring situations, managers preferred employees with medical knowledge and felt that OJT could compensate for the lack of technical ability. At that time, both job elements were performed by a single employee.

As the years progressed, it became apparent that OJT was not sufficient and that hiring practices should recognize this deficiency. Therefore, at the present time, the positions have been filled accordingly, with 9 of the 12 positions having credentialed medical abilities divided into 2 levels of competency, and 3 of the 12 having credentialed technical abilities. With the new grant system, medical personnel will comprise 4.5 FTE's and technical personnel will comprise 2.5 FTE's.

Personnel

Ms. A (Black) has been working for the company for 3 years, has a high-level medical certification and performs her job well. Ms. B (White) has been working for the company for 2 years, has a high level medical certification and her performance is above average. Ms. C (Other) has been working for the company for 6 months, has a language problem, poor work habits and a high-level medical certification. Ms. D (White) has been employed for 11 months, is technically certified, performs well but has some problems in following supervisory directions. She is somewhat outspoken and headstrong. Ms. E (White) has been employed for 7 months, has a high-level medical certification, is an outstanding employee, but has indicated she is only interested in part-time work in the future. Ms. F (Black) has been working for the company for 4 years, has a low-level medical certification, has noticeable deficiencies in certain medical areas, but is well liked and has developed a very good rapport in her work environment that is extremely critical in this position. She performs above average in many areas, but cannot perform adequately in all areas, because of her limited knowledge. Ms. G (Black) has been with the company longer than any other employee. She has a low-level medical certification and it has been noted by a number of people that her medical deficiencies limit the scope of her abilities. She also recognizes her limitations and is attending schooling to eliminate this problem. Ms. H (White), I (Black), and J (Black) all have high level medical certifications, have been with the company approximately the same length of time (2 years), and all perform very well in the work environment. Ms. K (White) has been with the company for 2 months, has certified technical ability, is a quick learner and has proven that she is flexible and an enthusiastic worker. Ms. L (White) has also been with the company 2 months, has certified technical ability, is a good worker, but somewhat less enthusiastic and vivacious than Ms. K. The technical skills of Ms. K and L are equal.

Questions

Management has suggested that high-level medical certification become a requirement for those employees hired to use medical judgment. As the decision maker in this case:

1) Who would you retain and why, and

2) Who would you terminate and why?

Make sure the solution addresses the following issues:

1) Job performance,

2) Race and/or ethnic group, and

3) Longevity.

Implicit Company Policies and Discharge

Alice, Betty and Carol are three of fifteen employees of a private-school cafeteria in a large eastern city. All employees are black. Alice is American-born and has worked at the cafeteria for five years. Betty and Carol were born in the West Indies and have been at the cafeteria one year.

Betty and Carol were observed taking leftover food home one afternoon. Taking leftover food home was not an unusual occurrence in this kitchen, but the pressure to hold down costs has caused management to decide to try to stop it. As a result, Betty and Carol were fired for stealing.

Betty sued for reinstatement, claiming discrimination against her, because she was foreign-born. She did not deny taking the leftover food, but claimed that Alice had been observed doing the same thing, and had not been fired. Management countered that while Alice may have been observed taking food home before the decision to crack down, no discrimination was intended. Betty and Carol were simply the first ones caught after the decision had been made.

Questions

1. How would you expect the local Fair Employment Practices Commission to rule?

2. Should Carol, who did not sue, be entitled to whatever relief, if any, Betty receives?

3. What can management do to avoid being sued again, without assenting to stealing?

Last Hired, First Fired

In 1971, Diane Smith, a former Labor Department administrator, was hired by Gescorp, a large manufacturing firm, to establish and implement the company's court-ordered affirmative-action program. In its decision the court had found Gescorp's hiring policies in violation of Title VII of the Civil Rights Act of 1964, which explicitly prohibits discrimination in hiring on the basis of race, color, religion, sex, or national origin. Furthermore, the court ordered that an affirmative-action program be instituted to insure that blacks would comprise at least ten per cent of the company's work force, and that this ten per cent be distributed evenly through all job levels.

Initially, it was felt that the implementation of this program would be met by stiff resistance from the company's predominantly white work force, but by August 1972 the court goals had been met through the assimilation of the black workers by attrition. No whites had been laid off or fired and the new workers filled positions at all job levels when they became available.

With the success of the affirmative-action program Diane was promoted to Director of Personnel, which expanded her duties to, among other things, the administration of the company's labor-management relations. Although the company had had its share of labor difficulties, the prosperity of the late sixties and early seventies had created a near-amicable labor relationship.

It was not until early in 1974 that problems developed. Gescorp's Board of Directors had decided that due to the perilous and uncertain economic conditions of the entire nation, some twenty per cent of the company's work force had to be laid off for an indefinite period of time. It was the duty of Diane, as Director of Personnel, to determine which employees and jobs must be cut to reduce the work force by this amount.

The union contract, under which labor-management relations operated, contained a seniority clause which specifically said that layoffs would be conducted under the principle of "last in, first out." To comply with the union contract would involve eliminating nearly the entire black portion of the company's work force, since, in compliance with the affirmative-action program, the blacks at Gescorp were, for the most part, the last to be hired. Although a decision could not be put off, Diane did not know what to do.

Questions

1. What do you feel Diane should do?
2. What are the legal and moral consequences, if Diane disavows the union contract and lays off white workers with seniority?

3. What are the legal and moral consequences of laying off the black workers, in violation of the court-ordered affirmative-action program?

4. Is there a compromise, and if so, what is it?

Seniority vs. Ability in
Layoff Determination

Lancor Tool and Maintenance Company has had a history of promotion from within, based on longevity with the company. Employees were hired as apprentice workers and were promoted to better jobs as they learned skills and had more experience with the company.

The more-established workers with the company were eager to get a job driving a company truck of their own and answering trouble calls to surrounding areas when these calls came into the Lancor Company. This traveling repair service was considered more desirable than staying on the premises of the Lancor Company and accepting and repairing equipment from off-the-street customers.

Recently the company became concerned with the fact that the more-senior workers could not repair the new, more-sophisticated equipment as well as the younger, newer workers. Complaints were coming into Lancor concerning problems in the field. The older workers could not repair the equipment on the spot and were forced to bring it back to the inhouse service department of Lancor, so that the younger workers could complete the job.

The company finally negotiated an agreement with the Union permitting it to use ability and skill tests in the selection of new repair crews. The older workers were no longer able to bid on the more desirable jobs. For the first time, Lancor was able to go outside the organization and hire young students just out of trade school. These students learned quickly and had the knowledge and understanding to work on the new equipment. After a while, the older repairmen who had come into their jobs prior to being screened were shifted to less-desirable shop jobs.

The problem that now faces the Lancor Tool and Maintenance Company is one of declining business forcing a cutback in the size of the repair department. Since layoffs are based on seniority, nearly all of the relatively new and more-able younger employees will be laid off, if the present decline continues. Lancor fears the loss of their young, skilled workers will further erode their business, and that eventually, competitors will begin making inroads.

Question

1. What alternative courses of action are available to Lancor? What are the implementation problems and possible implications of each?

Transition and Turnover Problems Caused by Technological Advances

A large firm that manufactures stereophonic equipment and specializes in amplifiers has been a leading regional distributor for over 25 years. Its expansion has been due to continuously increasing profits over the years; however, in the past several years it has incurred a substantial reduction in sales and profits as a result of increased competition from foreign markets.

In an attempt to increase efficiency and sales, the main office called in consultants to advise on updating equipment. Based on their recommendations, new equipment was purchased and subsequently several hundred employees had to be laid off. The new automatic machinery was to increase production and decrease staff by requiring a higher level of skills. Management felt if the new machinery had to remain idle during the training period for the present staff, it would cause further delays in production and that the process of training some employees and gradually reducing the staff would be too costly and too slow.

Since the older employees were unfamiliar with the new machinery, it was advised that an outsider be hired to oversee the training. A supervisor from a competitive company was offered an attractive salary, to which she agreed, and when she came she brought her own staff of operators. The new staff caused a further decrease in older employees and created conflicts between them and the new people. Many departments had a difficult time maintaining morale, in light of the changes that were taking place.

After several months the new staff and new machinery were working smoothly, but expenditures were still higher than the consultants had predicted. Suddenly, one day the main terminal broke down and production had to be halted until the parts arrived. If something were not done immediately, production would fall behind schedule, resulting in financial losses to the company. The only alternative was to return to the old machinery, even though it was slower, and could probably not meet contract deadlines.

A problem developed because the new skilled employees were unfamiliar with the old machinery and there weren't enough of the older employees remaining to do the job. Pressed for time, the remaining older employees were asked to work nights and the following weekend.

Questions

1. Should management have dismissed the old system and staff, before the new machinery had all the bugs out and the new staff proved efficient?
2. How could the old system have been utilized to prevent production slow-down and company loss?

3. How could the impact of the machinery on the employees have been minimized?

Eligibility for Unemployment Compensation

Two years ago, Mike Taylor got married. At that time he had purchased a new car and a home through a finance company. The car payments were $175 a month and the payments on the house were $350 a month. Although this was quite an expense, Taylor was able to make the payments, because he and his wife both worked.

Nine months after their marriage, Mrs. Taylor had twins and could not return to work. In November and December of last year, Mike Taylor did not have the money to make the car payments. In January, the finance company had the car payments deducted from his salary.

Taylor's employer, Mr. Johnson, did not like this, but he was aware of Taylors' situation and did not say anything. However, five months later, the finance company again called, saying Taylor had failed to make the last three payments on his house. Johnson called Taylor into his office and told him he would have to make the payments on his own because he was not going to be troubled with having to deduct the money from his paycheck.

Taylor had exhausted his savings and could not afford to make the payments. When the finance company again asked that the payments be withheld from his pay, Johnson fired Taylor.

Taylor did not have any luck in finding another job. He had been unemployed the amount of time necessary to qualify for unemployment compensation. However, when he went to the State agency, they informed him that he could not collect, because he was ineligible.

Questions

1. Was Johnson justified in firing Taylor? Why or why not?
2. Why wasn't Taylor eligible for unemployment compensation?

Unemployment and Workers' Compensation

A widely recognized car dealership in your area hired what they thought to be a highly competent twenty-year-old mechanic. Along with his favorable references, he had four years of job experience in the field and a strong background in mechanics.

For the first year that he was employed in the company, the mechanic received two evaluations of his work performance. Both performance evaluations were in the form of a Likert scale, with five (5) being an excellent worker and one (1), a poor worker. On each evaluation the mechanic's supervisor rated him as a three (3), which was considered average.

One day on the job the mechanic, while carrying part of an automobile motor, tripped over a bulky extension cord that had various power tools attached to it. The extension cord had been located in that same place for as long as he had worked there. Due to the weight he was carrying, he severely injured his back. He was taken to the hospital for treatment, where he remained under care for two weeks. His employers, fully aware of the occurrence, did not issue a paycheck for him during this span of time.

The doctors released him from the hospital with the stipulation that he would not work for another two weeks. While at home, the mechanic called in to have his paychecks mailed to him. His employers stated they did not give sick pay. The mechanic then realized since he was hurt on the job and his company held a policy for workers' compensation, that he should qualify to receive such benefits. When he inquired about the compensation, his employers explained that he would be unable to collect, due to negligence on his part and also that due to this negligence, his damaging of the motor part, and his being unable to work, he was terminated.

As a last resort the mechanic, who was still unable to work, went to the unemployment commission to file his claim. Having completed the application form for the compensation, he was told to return after two weeks. It was explained to him that during this two-week waiting period, his former employers were to be contacted. When the two-week period had elapsed, the mechanic still had complications with his back and was unable to look for work. The mechanic went back to the commission to complete his interview, and was met with negative news.

His former employers had stated he was fired.

Questions

1. Will the Unemployment Compensation Commission in your area authorize unemployment compensation? If not, can he appeal?

303

2. Can he contact anyone to collect workers' compensation?
3. Can he collect any back pay?

About The Author

Dr. Kenneth A. Kovach is a Full Professor of Personnel and Industrial Relations. He is a specialist and recognized expert in the Personnel Management/Labor Relations areas, and has published four books, over 55 articles, and over 150 cases in these areas. Additionally, he is a consultant to numerous local and national firms including the U.S. Department of Defense, American Red Cross, and the American Council on Education, as well as a senior student negotiator for Anheuser-Busch, Inc.